Looking for *Lost*

# Looking for *Lost*
## *Critical Essays on the Enigmatic Series*

EDITED BY RANDY LAIST

McFarland & Company, Inc., Publishers
*Jefferson, North Carolina, and London*

LIBRARY OF CONGRESS CATALOGUING-IN-PUBLICATION DATA

Looking for Lost : critical essays on the enigmatic series / edited by Randy Laist.
    p.   cm.
Includes bibliographical references and index.

**ISBN 978-0-7864-4716-9**
softcover : 50# alkaline paper

1. Lost (Television program)   I. Laist, Randy, 1974–
PN1992.77.L67L58   2011
791.45'75 — dc22                               2010052801

BRITISH LIBRARY CATALOGUING DATA ARE AVAILABLE

© 2011 Randy Laist. All rights reserved

*No part of this book may be reproduced or transmitted in any form or by any means, electronic or mechanical, including photocopying or recording, or by any information storage and retrieval system, without permission in writing from the publisher.*

On the cover: Matthew Fox as Jack, Evangeline Lilly as Kate, Josh Holloway as Sawyer and Dominic Monaghan as Charlie in *Lost* (ABC/Photofest); background © 2011 Shutterstock

Manufactured in the United States of America

*McFarland & Company, Inc., Publishers*
  *Box 611, Jefferson, North Carolina 28640*
    *www.mcfarlandpub.com*

For Ann,
My Constant

# Table of Contents

*Introduction*
    RANDY LAIST . . . . . . . . . . . . . . . . . . . . . . . . . . . . . . . . . . 1

### PART ONE: LOST IN TIME

"We Have to Go Back": Temporal and Spatial Narrative Strategies
    ERIKA JOHNSON-LEWIS . . . . . . . . . . . . . . . . . . . . . . . . . . 11

Narrative Philosophy in the Series: Fate, Determinism, and the Manipulation of Time
    MICHAEL RENNETT . . . . . . . . . . . . . . . . . . . . . . . . . . . . . 25

"Enslaved by Time and Space": Determinism, Traumatic Temporality, and Global Interconnectedness
    ARIS MOUSOUTZANIS . . . . . . . . . . . . . . . . . . . . . . . . . . . 43

New Space, New Time, and Newly Told Tales: *Lost* and *The Tempest*
    RYAN HOWE . . . . . . . . . . . . . . . . . . . . . . . . . . . . . . . . . . 59

### PART TWO: LOST PHILOSOPHY

*Lost* and Becoming: Reconceptualizing Philosophy
    JASON M. PECK . . . . . . . . . . . . . . . . . . . . . . . . . . . . . . . . 75

*Lost* in Theory: Everything You Always Wanted to Know About *Lost* but Were Afraid to Ask Lacan, Derrida, and Foucault
    GIANCARLO LOMBARDI . . . . . . . . . . . . . . . . . . . . . . . . . 90

"So This Is All in My Mind?" Hugo Crash-Tests the Contemporary Crusoe
    MATTHEW PANGBORN . . . . . . . . . . . . . . . . . . . . . . . . . 105

Primitivizing the Island: The Eclectic Collection of "Non-Western" Imagery
    RENEE MCGARRY . . . . . . . . . . . . . . . . . . . . . . . . . . . . . 120

### PART THREE: LOST MEN AND LOST WOMEN

The *Lost* Boys and Masculinity Found
    DAVID MAGILL . . . . . . . . . . . . . . . . . . . . . . . . . . . . . . . 137

"It Always Ends the Same": Paternal Failures
    HOLLY HASSEL AND NANCY L. CHICK .................... 154

Lost Children: Pregnancy, Parenthood, and Potential
    DEBORAH DAVIDSON AND WAYNE JEBIAN ................. 171

### PART FOUR: LOST IN THE TWENTY-FIRST CENTURY

*Lost* in Capitalism: or, "Down Here Possession's Nine-Tenths"
    ELIZABETH LUNDBERG ............................... 189

"Strangers in a Strange Land": Evading Environmental Apocalypse Through Human Choice
    CARLOS A. TARIN AND STACEY K. SOWARDS ............... 202

Securitizing the Island: The Other Others' Defense of Environmental Management
    J. L. SCHATZ ...................................... 216

We Have to Go Back: *Lost* After 9/11
    JESSE KAVADLO .................................... 230

*About the Contributors* ................................. 243

*Index* ................................................ 247

# Introduction
## Randy Laist

JACK: So, where do we go from here?
SAWYER: I'm working on it.
JACK: Really? Because it looked to me like you were reading a book.
SAWYER: I heard once Winston Churchill read a book every night, even during the blitz. Said it made him think better. That's how I like to run things. I think ["Namaste" 5.9].

It is arguably the case that no show in the history of American network television has been so invested in literary culture as *Lost*. Books appear in almost every episode of *Lost*, not only as props, but as clues. Why is the orientation film in the hatch hidden behind Henry James' *The Turn of the Screw*? Why does Desmond pack a copy of Flann O'Brien's *The Third Policeman* when he is making his escape from that same hatch? Why does Locke give Ben a copy of Philip K. Dick's *Valis* to read while he is in confinement and what is the significance of Ben's already having read it, and of Locke's subsequent advice about the value of double-readings? These literary riddles are satisfying not only for the particular answers they might reveal about the show's many mysteries but also for the playful way in which they open up diverse and textured conceptual connections between the televisual and the print texts. In addition to these explicit literary allusions, the plot of *Lost* is steeped in references to castaway narratives such as *Robinson Crusoe*, *Gulliver's Travels*, and *Lord of the Flies* and parallel-world narratives such as *Alice's Adventures in Wonderland*, *The Wizard of Oz*, and *The Garden of Forking Paths*. Even the names of the characters — John Locke (aka Jeremy Bentham), Sawyer, C. S. Lewis — are blatantly literary. The cumulative effect of this densely allusive atmosphere is insistent enough to suggest that when the Lostaways crashed on that creepy island, they became stranded in a kind of reality that is not altogether real, but one that is eerily continuous with the kind of reality found in fictional literature.

Of course, *Lost* has become famous for the manner in which it encourages cross-over multimedia experiences with the internet, video games, and, indeed, print publishing — the *Lost* franchise has even released a novel, *Bad Twin*, supposedly written by a casualty of the crash of Oceanic flight 815. But whereas most of these multiplatform experiences tend to loop the consumer-audience into self-referring spirals of *Lost* arcana, *Lost*'s literary references escape the gravity of the show itself and present unique invitations to "read" *Lost* rather than simply to watch it. Indeed, *Lost*'s intensely literary atmosphere seems closely related to the textual nature of the show's plot, which is a densely-woven tapestry of interconnecting strands. The cast is made up of a diverse ensemble of characters whose relationships with one another are subtle, shifting, and complex. The elusive network of Dharma hatches, the intimations of a corporate conspiracy invisibly connecting apparently discrete events, the theme of unusual correspondences between different periods of time, and the mutable networks of tribal loyalty and factionalism all work to disperse *Lost*'s patterns of signification into a webiform field of radial associations. This style of narrative has more in common with Pynchon and DeLillo than with *Law and Order* or *Two and a Half Men*. *Lost* is not only a television show that aspires to read like a novel, but one that tries to read like a self-consciously literary novel.

It is no wonder then that *Lost* has enjoyed remarkable popularity among literary critics and has become the focus of numerous conference panels, seminars, and scholarly articles. Critics who have studied the show have discovered much to talk about. In its depiction of an international community, *Lost* is a narrative about globalization. In its treatment of corporate-industrial threats to an unspoiled wilderness, *Lost* is a narrative about ecological awareness. In its dramatization of territorial disputes between aboriginals and settlers, *Lost* is an allegory of postcolonial territoriality. In its technique of revealing obscure patterns buried within streams of data, *Lost* suggests associations with genetic sequencing and hypertextuality. All of these aspects of the show reveal its uniquely contemporary engagement with emerging twenty-first century concerns. But *Lost* does more than merely represent these issues; it enacts them. The watcher, or reader, of *Lost* enters a world that mimics the viral, polysemous, and intricately reticulated quality characteristic of our globalized, ecological, postcolonial, and cybernetic lifeworld. The same qualities that make *Lost* seem so uniquely literary are the same qualities that make it seem so pressingly contemporary. The novelistic Wonderland in which we are stranded once we crash into the peculiar atmosphere of *Lost* is, uncannily, *our* world of post-millennial danger, promise, and overarching strangeness.

To "read" *Lost*, then, is to read ourselves, and the writers in this collection have taken full advantage of this stereoscopic hermeneutic. While the contributors to this volume have much to say about the relevance of the program to the contemporary television industry, our primary objective has been to read the show thematically. Having completed its narrative arc in May of

2010, *Lost* is finally a complete text, making it possible as it has not previously been to discuss the program's treatment of its central concerns. The essays in this collection offer a diverse array of perspectives on *Lost*'s primary preoccupations, including temporality, philosophy, and gender politics. The final section of this volume brings together articles that consider *Lost*'s relevance to particularly contemporary global issues. Collectively, the writers represented in this collection provide a wealth of insight into the fascinating televisual and cultural phenomenon that *Lost* has come to represent.

## *Lost in Time*

From its first season, the most distinguishing narratological feature of *Lost* has been its employment of flashbacks to suggest emotional parallels between its characters' pre-island pasts and their present struggles as castaways. In the third season, this story-telling device was redeployed to present "flash-forwards." In season four, Desmond and Minkowski experienced flashbacks as medical emergencies, lethally pathological symptoms of having become "unstuck in time." In the fifth season, the entire island began skipping around in time, as if the show itself were having flashbacks and flashforwards. A unique style of narrative tension resulted in season six from the depiction of "flash-sideways," an apparently alternate timeline with an ambiguous relation to the events in the island narrative. *Lost* has cleverly adapted the narratological technique of the flashback into a thematic preoccupation with the nature of temporality and its implications for memory, freedom, and identity. Erika Johnson-Lewis provides an ideal overview of *Lost*'s management of narrative temporality. Her examination of the manner in which *Lost* manipulates audience expectations explores what I have referred to above as *Lost*'s "textual" identity while at the same time making a case that this identity is intrinsic to the nature of "post-network" television programming. Starting from the same narratological premises, Michael Rennett examines the implications of *Lost*'s unique narrative structure for the program's thematic concern with fate and free will. While Johnson-Lewis faults the season six sideways flashes for being inconsistent with the spatio-temporal dynamics that ground the rest of the show, Rennett argues that it is precisely this departure from the fatalistic pattern of the rest of *Lost*'s temporalities that allows the sideways world to exist as an arena of free will.

The other two essays in this section focus on the psychohistorical implications of *Lost*'s sense of time. Aris Mousoutzanis reads *Lost* as a narrative of "trauma culture," arguing that the narrative structure of the show represents a sense of being trapped in a deterministic temporality that is held hostage by the compulsive reenactment of a psychic shock. Mousoutzanis compares the claustrophobic mood of this traumatic temporality to the show's parallel concern with globalization and concludes that *Lost* depicts a twenty-first century landscape in which trauma and homelessness are the only meaningful kinds of community available to our castaway culture. Ryan Howe begins by identifying the many parallels between *Lost* and Shakespeare's *The Tempest* and uses this framework to suggest that both texts interrogate the temporality of technological and historical change. As they do so, both island-narratives gesture toward the possibility of transcending mortal, secular, and historical temporalities altogether.

## *Lost Philosophy*

A list of *Lost*'s characters — Locke, Rousseau, Burke, Hume, Bakunin — reads like an Intro to Philosophy syllabus. The precise nature of the relationship between John Locke the British philosopher and John Locke the Lostaway, however, is extremely open to debate. While it is true that the island provides Lostie-Locke with an opportunity to start life over again as what philosopher-Locke famously called a *tabula rasa*, the implication that Lostie-Locke is living out a destiny which precedes his participation in it inscribes the character into a model of psychology that is fundamentally different from Lockean empiricism. The same kind of shifting interpretability characterizes the relationship between all of *Lost*'s characters and the historical figures their names evince. *Lost* is no *Animal Farm*-type allegory of conflicting philosophical positions. As is the case with *Lost*'s literary allusions, the philosophical allusions in *Lost* are not easily collapsible into one-to-one correspondences. The function of these names seems to be primarily to connote philosophical discourse itself and to activate in the *Lost* audience the kinds of attention we associate with philosophical problems. This is one of the many ways that *Lost* non-directively stimulates interpretive behavior on the part of its audience and directs us to contextualize the events of the show within philosophical modes of discourse.

The chapters in the second section of this volume take full advantage of the veritable hermeneutic playground that *Lost* presents to the philosophically-minded critic-viewer. Responding to the fact that the first book-length collection of essays about *Lost* to be published was *Lost and Philosophy*, part of a series on philosophy and popular culture from Blackwell Publishing, Jason M. Peck invites us to consider *Lost* not merely *alongside* philosophical texts, but *as* a philosophical text itself. According to Peck's innovative reading, *Lost* does not simply recapitulate debates from the history of philosophy, but actually constitutes a style of philosophy that "contributes to the reconceptualizing of philosophy itself." Giancarlo Lombardi considers *Lost* within the context of concepts derived from Lacan, Derrida, and Foucault and connects these concepts to the three mythological figures — Jacob, Man in Black, and Christian Shephard — who embody various styles of authority on the island. Matthew Pangborn describes the manner in which *Lost* dramatizes a reenactment of the Crusoe narrative, one of the foremost myths of Enlightenment civilization. While most of the Lostaways seem to play out a conventional version of the Crusoe narrative, Pangborn sees Hurley as a character who personifies a less empirical/imperialist mode of existence that respects otherness, emphasizes intuition over intellect, and values sociability over mastery. Finally, Renee McGarry's essay engages the question of how *Lost*'s cast of European philosophers responds to an environment that is decidedly "Non-Western." While the dynamic of this encounter might initially suggest a classic binary of self and other — orientalizing westerner against primitive innocents — McGarry examines the manner in which the shifting power relationships of *Lost*'s narrative allow characters and viewers "to visually move between existences as colonizers and colonized."

## Lost Men and Lost Women

But *Lost* is not all about philosophical riddles; it is also a soap-operatic melodrama about the various relationships that develop among the population of castaways. In particular, the characterizations of the Losties tend to emphasize their gender roles. Not only do the typical television antics of who's dating whom provide an endless source of speculation and intrigue, but the bare necessities of island existence seem to reduce masculinity and femininity to their biological identities. The men in the show are continually involved in chest-thumping squabbles over leadership, while the women's stories are dominated by reproductive issues. The rarity of LGBT characters on the show has frequently been discussed, and one effect of *Lost*'s heteronormative environment is to amplify the distinction between the male and female characters. Indeed, the island's wrathful commitment to killing women who become pregnant on the island constitutes a brutal type of gender discrimination implicit in the physical landscape of the show. The articles in this section each provide different ways of approaching the representation of gender in *Lost*.

David Magill focuses his attention on the male characters of *Lost* and the manner in which they embody various definitions of masculinity. Although the show's characterizations typically indulge the cultural motif of "wounded white masculinity in crisis," the development of *Lost*'s central characters reveals non-traditional possibilities for the manner in which "ethical manhood" might be conceived and practiced. Holly Hassel and Nancy L. Chick investigate the theme of fatherhood that connects almost all of *Lost*'s characters. Describing the obsessively recurrent pattern of paternal failure that runs throughout the stories of Hurley, Sawyer, Jack, Sun, Ben, Locke, and many other characters (as well as the story of island itself, which is ruled by the fatherless twins, Jacob and the Man in Black), Hassel and Chick suggest that the series examines cultural anxieties about a contemporary crisis of fatherhood. Deborah Davidson and Wayne Jebian approach the status of women in *Lost* by investigating the show's preoccupation with reproductive issues. They argue that, while *Lost* is unique as a television show for the emphasis it places on pregnancy and childbirth, its overall narrative tends to diminish the role of women and co-opt birth imagery as a metaphorical device for telling the stories of adult men.

## *Lost in the Twenty-First Century*

As we look back on the first decade of the twenty-first century, we perceive a trail of wreckage: 9/11, wars in Iraq and Afghanistan, environmental dread, and economic collapse are only the most prominent of many frightening and confusing headlines from this period. In its examination of post-apocalyptic survival, moral ambiguity, and radical skepticism, *Lost* is certainly the television show that most dramatically captures the tone of this strange time. Indeed, the series' final episode, with its plot centered around a well deep underground that uncontrollably spews malevolent energy, seems intentionally to allude to the Deepwater Horizon oil spill that was ongoing when "The End" originally aired. But considering that filming of the final episode ended on April 24, 2010 — only four days after the explosion of the BP rig (April 20) and a full week or so before the cataclysmic consequences of the disaster became common knowledge — one can only conclude that the writers of *Lost* retrieved the imagery of this episode from a flash-forward of their own, compelling us to read the catastrophe at the Source not as a reference or an allusion to real-world events, but as an uncanny precognition. Each of the writers in this final section addresses the manner in which *Lost* captures unique features of the twenty-first century environment shared by the show's characters and audience.

Elizabeth Lundberg's analysis of the importance of objects in the world of *Lost* leads her into a discussion of how the show both critiques and exploits the globalized corporate capitalist system within which *Lost* itself is a commodity. While *Lost*'s narrative encourages reflection on the utopian possibilities of escaping the structures of global capitalism, *Lost* simultaneously draws attention to its own status as a product of that system, most notably through its practice of "reverse product placement," whereby *Lost* markets its own Dharma brand of products, exporting fictional commodities into the real world. Carlos A. Tarin and Stacey K. Sowards read *Lost* as a parable about how we understand environmental issues. They argue that the narrative dynamics of *Lost* privilege an apocalyptic approach to ecological problems that is misleadingly facile and anthropocentric. J. L. Schatz identifies a similar issue in *Lost*'s representation of environmental management. Through an analysis of an interesting parallel between the television show *Lost* and the international Law of the Sea Treaty (LOST), Schatz argues that both the show and the treaty reflect prevailing attitudes, errors, and habits of thinking that characterize our cultural understanding of ecological custodianship. Finally, Jesse Kavadlo investigates the manner in which *Lost* borrows from the imagery of 9/11— the traumatic plane crash, Iraq, torture, and air marshals — to investigate the kind of temporality characteristic of our "post–9/11" mentality.

Collectively, the articles in this volume recreate that most basic feature of *Lost*: the sense of experiencing a single story from a diverse array of perspectives. In the same way that Jack, Locke, and Mr. Eko each arrive at different conclusions about the meaning of the mysterious button that they supposedly must push in order to save the world, these essays have been selected and arranged to provide different points of view on the central themes to which *Lost* directs our attention. Although the six seasons of *Lost* have drawn to a close, the show's ubiquitous availability on DVD and online, its prestige as a watershed program, and its novelistic beginning-middle-and-end cohesiveness assure that it will continue to be viewed and discussed for many years to come. It is hoped that the scholarship in this collection will be useful in inspiring and informing such future discussions.

## Part One
# LOST IN TIME

# "We Have to Go Back": Temporal and Spatial Narrative Strategies

*Erika Johnson-Lewis*

Since its pilot episode — featuring a mysterious mechanical jungle monster, polar bears, and Charlie Pace's exclamation, "Guys, where are we?" — *Lost* has continually played with audience expectations, usually by attempting to confuse or undermine them. Arguably the most successful narrative device the show uses to play with and undermine audience expectation is the narrative's consistent temporal shifting between past, present, and future. These temporal shifts create a rich, if at times frustrating, narrative world that is complicated further by the addition of time travel in season five and the "flash-sideways" in season six.

Time is central not only within the space of the narrative, but also in its consumption through the use and manipulation of spoilers, Easter eggs, and fan interactions with writers and producers that are integrated into the plot, at times expressly to frustrate audience expectations in order to maintain audience attention from week to week and season to season. To this growing discussion of *Lost*'s temporality, I would like to add the importance of spatiality in *Lost*'s narrative structure. The island and its geographical features, landmarks, and various Dharma stations do not merely serve as inert backgrounds against which the narrative takes place, but constitute central components that provide a stabilizing force within the narrative's constantly shifting temporalities. This chapter seeks to analyze the temporal and spatial narrative strategies that provide viewers with tools to navigate *Lost*'s dynamic, intricate, and vast narrative world.

## Post-Network Attention and Lost

*Lost* is a series that has become representative of post-network television; therefore, discussions of *Lost* are enriched when informed by its place within the contemporary "post-network" television landscape. In her book *The Television Will Be Revolutionized*, Amanda Lotz argues that the post-network era represents a shift in the television industry across all of its spheres from production, distribution, advertising and story-telling possibilities. Central to this shift are new digital technologies that have given audiences more control over when, where, and how they consume televisual content. To accommodate this shift, networks sought series that could be successful within this new environment. The transmedia temporality of *Lost*'s narrative world is indicative of post-network changes in content, promotion, and distribution. *Lost*'s experiments with temporality, narratively and thematically, extend beyond the enclosure of individual episodes into other commercial and online texts, and its success has become a model against which successful post-network television programming is judged. Here, I highlight two specific areas of post-network television's changing landscape: the changing relationship between audiences and television texts and innovative narrative strategies.

Describing the emergent relationship between contemporary television audiences and television programs within the context of the post-network condition, Derek Johnson argues that "[a]udiences are not just cultivated as fans, but also invited in, asked to participate in both the world of the television text and the processes of its production" (63, emphasis in original). Johnson further suggests that "multiplatforming" strategies create new sites where audiences can engage with televisual content and have enabled "the increasing collision of diegetic and tangible spaces" (73). He cites *Lost*'s multiplatform content as a primary example of these strategies, describing how fans of the series can draw the narrative into their own everyday experiences by purchasing the *Bad Twin* novel or playing the Lost Experience. "*Lost* has used the connectivity of the digital to allow the textual and the everyday to coalesce" (73). Jason Mittell has argued that many series have become narratively complex, requiring viewers to pay attention not only to narratives but how to how they are constructed. He asserts,

> You cannot simply watch these programs as an unmediated window to a realistic storyworld into which you might escape; rather, narratively complex television demands you pay attention to the window frames, asking you to reflect on how it provides partial access to the diegesis and how the panes of glass distort your vision of the unfolding action ["Narrative Complexity" 38].

Both Johnson and Mittell emphasize the changing level of audience attention required for successful consumption and comprehension of post-network television's narratively complex programming, of which *Lost* has become emblematic. *Lost* is television that cannot be glanced or even gazed at, but must be engaged at various levels.

Prime time television's traditional temporal structure has always provided audiences with narratives that unfolded week to week, at specific times of the evening, and during certain times of the year. The week-to-week episodic nature of even the most serialized narratives, like *Lost*, places a certain claim upon the viewer's time and attention. The increasingly intricate and complex nature of post-network storytelling requires a new level of attention and engagement. *Lost*'s narrative consistently raises questions of causality and its relationship to our ability to create meaning. How do events that happened in the future change in light of events that happened in the past? How is the past changed by events that occur in the future? How is a sense of the present maintained in spite of a constant shift between past, present, and future? Each week, viewers must remember what happened in episodes from the week before, and often from even years before. Understanding the narrative requires the audience to pay careful attention as the story unfolds and is complicated further by its consistent temporal shifting, from island-time to flashbacks in seasons one through three, to the introduction of "game-changing" narrative strategies such as season four's flash-forwards, season five's time travel, and finally the atemporality of season six's flash-sideways.

From a production standpoint, this is brilliant storytelling strategy. Week-to-week audiences are spurred on by the promise of receiving answers to questions that have been left unanswered for years; viewers tune in and wait through commercials to find out why Walt and Aaron are important or why the island heals some people but not others. *Lost* has been such a success in the post-network landscape precisely because of its storytelling strategies. Originally conceived as a *Survivor* knockoff, *Lost*'s creators added the mainstays of cult television — an extended narrative universe and deep mythology — to the reality TV mainstays — personality clashes, romance, survival, and gamesmanship. The success of *Lost* emerged from the intersection of these two kinds of narratives. The series could satisfy its audiences on the macro-level involving mysteries, polar bears, smoke monsters, and a magical island, as well as on a personal level of love, loss, and compelling character portraits.

In addition to *Lost*'s success as a post-network series, two perspectives have driven discussions of its narrative. On the one hand, *Lost* is about the island and its mythology. On the other hand, *Lost* is about its characters and their relationships. These competing assertions, like *Lost*'s narrative strategies, tend to implicitly inform analysis about the series. According to the character-driven view, *Lost* is story about interesting people who happen to have crash-landed on a mysterious island. According to the island-driven view, *Lost* is a story about mysterious island that happens to also have some fairly interesting characters. Of course, the show is about both of these things and a myriad of others (*i.e.*, fate and free will, dysfunctional relationships, existential button pushing, and polar bears). The success of the series is a result of the fact that *Lost* could be many things to many people by providing its audience with many different narrative threads.

Roberta Pearson's essay, "Chain of Events," outlines arguments for and against reading *Lost* as a "character" or "hermeneutic" narrative. She highlights Cuse and Lindleof's assertion that the series is character-driven; that it is "a character show with a mythology frosting over the top" (quoted in Pearson 143). Pearson establishes that although the show runners want to highlight character over plot, in the popular reception of the show, plot has taken precedence over character. When the writers argue "we're going to explain a little more why this guy [Jack] needs to fix things all the time and let the island story support that" (143), they fail to comprehend that when the audience never learns much about Jack beyond his obsessive need to fix things, they may begin to read the continual development of the island narrative as more important over and against the general lack of long term character development.

Episodes featuring Locke provide an excellent example of the lack of long-term development in *Lost*'s characters. We learn repeatedly that Locke is gullible, naive, and desperate for love and attention. In "Walkabout" (1.4), he mistakenly believes that "Helen"—phone sex operator/therapist—will go with him to Australia for his Walkabout. In "Deux et Machina" (1.19), he is conned by his long-absent father into giving up a kidney. In season two, we see more of the same, as he continues to struggle with what his father did to him ("Orientation" 2.3) only to be conned by him again ("Lockdown" 2.17). We learn in "The Man from Tallahassee" (3.13) that his father threw him out an eighth-story window, and in "The Life and Death of Jeremy Bentham" (5.7), Abadon and Ben continue to manipulate him until Ben finally murders him. In each of these examples, the audience learns more about specific events in Locke's past, but his character changes very little. He is easily manipulated into doing what other people wish him to do. The final upshot of Locke's narrative is revealed in the last season, when we learn from the Man in Black/Smoke Monster, who is using Locke's form as a kind of avatar, that Locke was ultimately a sucker whose desperation to believe he was special only led to his sad demise in an old musty hotel room. Other back-stories follow similar trajectories. Kate repeatedly runs away. Jack struggles to fix things. Sayid struggles with his past as a torturer. Sawyer is a reluctant conman. Jin and Sun navigate their rocky relationship. Therefore, while the writers may claim that the island narratives are meant to buttress the character-centered flash narratives, they more often do the opposite. The internal consistency and the continual emphasis on the mystery of the island, as a place rather than merely as an idea or as the empty background on which the narrative plays out, fosters the expectation that the island narrative and the central mystery—

"Where are we?"—take precedence over character development and relationships.

## Flashes in Time

All narratives are essentially temporal, relying on a basic conception of chronology; there is a before, an after, and an aim toward a final end. Narratives are a "temporal arrangement of causally linked events" (Cameron 3) and, as noted by Ivan Askwith, "narratologists often draw a distinction between fabula [story], the actual order in which the narrative's events take place, and sjuzet [plot], the sequence in which those events are related to the reader" (171). *Lost*'s story spans centuries and essentially begins with the arrival of Claudia—Jacob and the Man in Black's mother—to the island and ends with Jack's death among the bamboo reeds. The fact that both of these events take place in the last season demonstrates how *Lost*'s narrative relies on a fundamental disconnect between fabula and sjuzet. The sjuzet deliberately impedes the ability of the audience to follow the fabula. To help explain *Lost*'s temporal shiftiness, we can borrow a description from another popular cult series, *Doctor Who*. The Doctor, a time-traveling alien, explains, "people assume that time is a strict progression of cause to effect, but actually from a non-linear, non-subjective viewpoint, it's more like a big ball of wibbly wobbly, timey wimey stuff" ("Blink"). *Lost*'s plot is a big ball of timey wimey stuff. Yet, there appears to be some kind of internal logic guiding the narrative along, in spite of, or perhaps even because of, this timey wimeyness.

Mittell, writing after the end of season three, suggests that *Lost*'s narrative expresses a "unity of purpose." He argues,

> *Lost*'s aesthetics value a perceived purpose motivating its narrative whole [...] the motivation behind *Lost*'s unity stems more from the assumed sense of purposefulness that seems embedded in the narrative design at the textual level more than in its actual process of creation ["Great Story" 127].

He continues, "The show develops intrinsic norms over time, establishing conventions and rules that viewers internalize as defining the show's storytelling strategies" (132). The narrative structure is itself integral to the plot, such that, being able to understand *how* the narrative is told is integral to understanding *what* it means. The rules and norms apply most obviously to the time shifting strategies: flashbacks, flashfowards, and time travel all feel like natural extensions of the established flashbacks, particularly in light of time jumping Desmond-centric episodes such as "Flashes Before Your Eyes" (3.8) and "The Constant" (4.5).

*Lost*'s narrative structure is introduced and formalized in the first three seasons. "The Pilot" (1.1 and 1.2) initially establishes the flashback/island-time structure as a motif in the short Jack, Kate, and Charlie flashbacks to their time on the plane before the crash. This structure is further established in "Tabula Rasa" (1.3) as the episode alternates between Kate's immediate past of how she came to be on the plane with island-time events. This structure continues as the flashbacks delve further into the castaways' pasts. There are some exceptions; for example, season two's "The Other 48 Days" (2.7) is a flashback to events that take place entirely on the island. The flashbacks generally answer a question about the character's past, but as M. J. Clarke notes, they do not necessarily function as memories that originated within the subjective lifeworld of the character (134–136). Clarke catalogues the transitions between flashes and island-time in an attempt to uncover a consistent relationship between them across the series as a whole. He concludes that "the relationship of the flashes to story present is not consistent with any larger pattern over the course of the series" (133). Instead, Clarke argues that the narrative purpose of the flashbacks and flashforwards in seasons one through four is to gesture towards the presence of a "hypothetical mastermind" who "may be best characterized as the construction of time in the series itself" (139).

The narrative presents the fabula as a puzzle to be solved, adding further evidence that suggests that *Lost* is not primarily a character-driven program. The plot gets increasingly more complicated after season three's game changing "Through the Looking Glass" (3.22 and 3.23). In this episode, Jack Shephard tells Kate, "We have to go back." Up through this point in the series, *Lost*'s narrative was structured by intercutting island-time action with flashbacks that developed points of character and mythology. In this moment, the audience learns (or may have already known, after visiting one of the many spoiler sites on the internet) that the flashback they thought they were viewing was, in fact, a flashfoward to the future in which a few people managed to get off the island. In this scene, Jack's assertion does a few important things. First, at the narrative level, he is trying to convince Kate to return to the island to save their friends they left behind. Second, his assertion functions as an instruction to the audience to "go back" and reevaluate what they thought they knew about the episode they were watching. Third, it comments on the experience of watching the series from the macro-level; we not only have to go back to the beginning of the episode but to the beginning of the entire series to situate events in their full context. Last, it reasserts the central importance of the island to the show's narrative core. They must, literally, return to the space of the island. These four different functions are emblematic of *Lost*'s narrative strategies.

The idea of "going back" implies both a temporal and spatial relationship. Jack's declaration and the revelation that some of the castaways made it off the island sets up part of season four's narrative structure, the addition of the flashforward. The flashback is not abandoned, however, so the two strategies work side-by-side. The flashforwards are (mostly) reserved for those characters who leave the island, the Oceanic Six: Jack, Kate, Aaron, Sun Kwon, Hugo "Hurley" Reyes, and Sayid Jarrah. Other character episodes follow the flashback structure of the previous seasons; for example, the Juliet-centric "The Other Woman" (4.6). "Ji Yeon" (4.7) is the only episode to include both flashbacks and flashforwards. At this point in the season, the identities of all the Oceanic Six are unknown. The narrative plays on this uncertainty; in double flashes, we follow Jin as he purchases a large stuffed panda and rushes to a hospital, presumably to be with Sun who has gone into labor. Sun calls for Jin while in labor, leading the audience to assume that Jin is rushing to meet her. By the end of the sequence, the audience realizes that Jin's flash was a flashback and Sun's flashforward reveals that in the future he is dead.

This structure of this episode mimics the series-long structure. The time shifts frame and call attention to the island, where Jin and Sun quarrel over whether to join Locke's group or to stay with Jack. Sun's flashforwards immediately reveal that she escapes the island and safely gives birth to her daughter, providing the audience with an important development. However, Jin's flashback does not appear to serve any purpose beyond playing upon viewer expectations that he is one of the survivors; nothing new is revealed about his character. Jin's flashback does not expand on the larger island narrative or its mysteries, and, because of this the juxtaposition of the two timelines, it feels gimmicky instead of integral to forwarding the narrative. The island events, overcoming betrayal and deciding to move on together, take precedence over the flash narratives, which lose their intensity once the initial revelations are made. If the flashbacks and forwards were secondary in importance to the overall narrative, the island events should work backwards to enhance them; instead, the island remains central.

If viewers are invited into the text and increasingly asked to follow complex narratives, what strategies of comprehension can viewers use to orient themselves comfortably and consistently within a constantly shifting nonlinear narrative? *Lost*'s time shifts function as a means through which to ground the narrative within the spatial confines of the island to provide narrative stability. The narrative does not unfold in a linear fashion, thus depriving the viewer of the means to quickly orient the narrative within time. In early seasons, the viewer understands that what is happening on the island is happening in the present, while the flashbacks occur in a vaguely defined "past." Once the flashes move forward and jump around in time, viewers become less able to orient themselves temporally, but the viewer can orient herself spatially by dividing the narrative into island and off-island events. The narrative requires the viewer to go back to the island. The narrative structure works in such a way that island-time, the present within the confines of the *Lost* universe, is always privileged within the space of the narrative. So, while the story jumps around in time, the spatial primacy of the island remains consistent. The flashbacks, flashforwards, and sideways flashes are conceived in relationship to what is happening on the island. The time-travel jumps complicate the notion of past and present further and highlight the importance of the island-time events.

The desire to see the series unfold chronologically has manifested in fan culture in a number of places. *Lostpedia*, the fan maintained *Lost* wiki, has a detailed page dedicated to archiving the series chronologically. Mike Maloney uses this information in his "Chronologically Lost" project. He writes,

> *Chronologically LOST* is a project I have undertaken to present the show LOST in its entirety in chronological order. That means taking every flashback, flash forward, and flash sideways, extracting them from the present day storyline, and creating one big timeline, that starts with the earliest flashbacks of the island, and goes through all the way to the end of the series.

Moloney's project captures a desire to contain *Lost*'s vast narrative within the logic of linear causality. While this is an understandable impulse, it can potentially create discontinuities within the show's narrative because events that occur in the chronologically historical past such as the burial of Jughead in 1954 ("Jughead" 5.3) and its detonation in 1977 ("The Incident" 5.16 and 5.17) occur in the characters' future. Organizing the narrative spatially rather than purely chronologically can offer viewers a way to understand the story without compromising the plot.

## *Spatial Narratives*

The previous section describes some of *Lost*'s temporal narrative strategies. The time elements always work to focus audience attention on island-time events. The island is at the heart of *Lost*; "every episode and every character's story can be understood as contributing to a larger understanding of the nature (or artifice) of *Lost*'s island locale" (Mittell, "Great Story" 125). Narratives are also spatial, and spatial relationships exist both within a text and between texts and the viewers who consume them. In Johnson's formulation described above, successful contemporary televisual texts "invite audiences in" to their worlds. To fully appreciate *Lost*'s narrative, we must therefore consider its spatial dimensions as well as its temporal ones.

Moaz Azaryahu and Kenneth E. Foote describe the creation of what they term "spatial narratives" around historical sites such as the Mormon Trail across Iowa or the Gettysburg National Military Park in Pennsylvania. Though Azaryahu and Foote focus on the intersection of geography, history, and narrative, their work on how "spatial narratives" function offers us a way to understand and describe how the island and its landmarks provide the audience with the means to situate themselves within its sprawling narrative. Spatial narratives "involve a complex configuration of geographic elements including buildings, markers, memorials, and inscriptions positioned with great care to provide a spatial story-line or to capture key locational and chronological relations of an historical event" (180).

They discuss three different narrative strategies. Though *Lost* conforms most readily to the third strategy, I want to briefly discuss the other two so as to compare how *Lost*'s spatiality differs from other more conventionally structured programs. The first strategy is "to tell a story from a single point [...] historical sites of this sort are frequently framed by a fence or a wall" (183). In television programs, we often see this kind of spatial organization in sitcoms. The traditional sitcom's narrative space is limited to a few sets on an enclosed soundstage. For example, on *Friends*, each episode is organized around familiar and recurring places: Monica and Rachel's apartment, Joey and Chandler's apartment, and the Central Perk. Though the group occasionally ventures outside of the confines of these sets, those instances are rare, and most of the episodes take place within those familiar settings.

The second strategy is one in which "time and space are sometimes narrated linearly along trails or paths with clear starting and ending points and a chronological progression from point-to-point along the way" (184). HBO's critically acclaimed *The Wire* uses this kind of strategy to tell its intricate and powerful story about the breakdown and failure of institutional systems in Baltimore. Like *Lost*, the episodes are highly serialized, but, unlike *Lost*, there is no disconnection between the story and the plot. The first season establishes key sites within Baltimore such as the pit, the towers, the corners, and the ramshackle office where the wire is monitored. Later seasons add new places such as the docks, the school, and the newsroom. To understand how these new spaces fit within the larger narrative, one must follow along on the predetermined path from season to season, and as the seasons progress, previous locales take on less importance or disappear altogether. The linear flow of time takes precedence in structuring the narrative, though the story is ostensibly about Baltimore as a geographic location.

The third and most relevant set of related strategies are "those involving actions over large areas or long periods of time; a large number of simultaneous events over wide areas; and complex spatial and temporal interactions within the overall event" (187). *Lost* takes place over a period time that by season five stretches into the past and future and spans across the globe from Australia to Iraq. Azaryahu and Foote examine how complex historical narratives are organized within larger geographic locations by reducing their inherent complexity and by privileging geography, chronology, or theme. *Lost*'s narrative can be deconstructed, organized, and understood using all these strategies, and the previous section touched on the chronological strategies of the flashbacks, flashforwards, and time travel elements. It is also fruitful to understand how *Lost*'s narrative is often organized spatially.

At a certain level, the island functions much like the closed set of a sitcom by determining the focus of the narrative action within a circumscribed location; however, on the island, different landmarks, building, geographies, markers, and memorials can be used to manage the temporally complex narrative. Sites such as the hatch, the caves, the wreckage, Dharmaville/Othertown, the *Black Rock*, the beach camp, and the four-toed statue are spaces from which the epic narrative can be organized. Places of narrative significance are found almost exclusively on the island; off-island locations carry no meaningful significance, except perhaps for the mental hospital where Hurley and Libby spend time throughout the series and the Sydney airport to which we periodically return. The absence of important off-island spaces lends further credence to the assertion that the mystery of the island, what and where it is, take precedence over character concerns.

Unlike in *The Wire*, in which certain locations lose their significance as new ones take prominence, *Lost*'s locations grow in significance and accrete meaning and significance as the series progresses. For example, it would be possible to explain *Lost*'s story from the vantage point of the hatch or the beach camp. The hatch, or as we later learn to call it, the Swan station, is first introduced in the season one episode "All the Best Cowboys Have Daddy Issues" (1.11). From that point, the mystery of the hatch — what it is, who built it, and where it goes — drives much of the plot in the rest of the first season, culminating in "Exodus, Part 2" (1.24 and 1.25) with the explosion of the hatch door with dynamite retrieved from the *Black Rock* (another important landmark). Much of season two takes place within the confines of the hatch, in which we see the introduction of Desmond, the imprisonment and torture of Henry Gale/Ben Linus, the murder of Ana Lucia and Libby by Michael, and existential button pushing, culminating with the hatch's destruction when Desmond turns the failsafe key. Throughout the rest of the series, the hatch, or the site where the hatch will eventually be (depending on what year it is), functions as a familiar location where important events occur or originate. Desmond's tardy entry of the numbers turns out to have caused Oceanic flight 815 to crash. In season five, Juliet, Sawyer, Daniel, Miles, and Charlotte travel there in an attempt to make the time jumps stop. The explosion of Jughead at the Swan building site creates "the incident." From these few examples, we can get a sense of how one site serves as an important spatial anchor holding various story elements together. Similar narratives can be culled together around other locations such as Dharmaville or the beach camp. These discrete locations serve as narrative landmarks that link various temporalities and characters together.

## *Season Six: No More Going Back*

The end of *Lost*'s run was determined during the third season, when it was decided that it would run for three more shorter but uninterrupted seasons. The switch from an endlessly deferred narrative to one with an anticipation of closure creates a different set of expectations. Once a definitive endpoint was established, anxiety over how, when, and if the writers were going to answer the myriad of *Lost*'s questions hung over the series. Seasons four and five continued to present viewers with more island mythology and mysteries. The promotional campaign for season six emphasized that "the answers were coming." Aside from revealing answers to the show's mysteries, what other elements make for a satisfying conclusion? Does a program's end necessarily need to conform to the terms established by the narrative itself? In this final section, I want to examine how season six breaks with the previously established narrative strategies and how this break ultimately leads to unsatisfying narrative closure.

Seasons one though five provided the audience with the narrative tools necessary to sustain their interest and engagement by using established temporal and spatial strategies discussed in the previous two sections. Viewers had come to know the island and could situate themselves and the characters in relationship to familiar landmarks and settings such as the hatch, the docks, and Dharmaville, and viewers learned to expect unexpected timey-wimeyness in the form of flashbacks, flashforwards, and time travel that always brought focus back to the island-present regardless of whatever the actual year might be. The flashes in seasons one through four gave the audience insight into characters' pasts and motivations while also explaining important events. In season five's time jumps, viewers encounter young Widmore and Eloise, and "the incident" is brought into the present through the presence of main characters. The ageless Richard becomes more mysterious. The statue is revealed in its original form. Season six breaks with all the previous seasons through the introduction of the flash-sideways, whose relationship to the island-present is not established until the series finale, and by introducing new previously unknown island locations that upset the already well-established island geography.

At the end of season five, Jughead is detonated. This breaks the timeline in two. The characters who were stuck in 1977 appear in the present near the remains of the hatch (again the hatch retains its importance). On the island, we follow them as they try to find Jacob, stop the Man in Black in the guise of Locke, and escape the island. Running alongside this narrative is the flash-sideways, a reality in which the island is sunk deep within the sea and Oceanic flight 815 never crashes over the Pacific Ocean. As we have seen, *Lost* established early on that the flashes (in all directions) served the purpose of complicating, explaining, or refocusing viewer attention on island-time events, which always remained central in the narrative. *Lost* is about what the island is and what happens there and the moments within the flashes act as supplements to the island-action. Therefore, in season six, when the immediate relevance of the flash-sideways remains ambiguous, it frustrates the already established expectations about the purpose the flashes serve. The sideways flashes work as effective character vignettes; for example, in Ben's sideways narrative, we see a redeemed Ben who, unlike his island counterpart, chooses family over power and revenge. As effective as this story is, there is no tangible way to link this narrative to the events on the island. For the majority of the season, the viewer is left wondering what the nature of the sideways world is. Does it exist as a parallel reality within the same temporal dimension as the first five seasons? Is it a series of "what if" scenarios? Is it an epilogue, a kind of flashfoward, of what will happen if Jack can successfully stop the Man in Black? The sideways flashes do not exist in any clear temporal relationship to the island and the characters; therefore, as a "game-changer," they fail by the temporal and spatial logic the series spent five seasons establishing.

In addition to establishing an unclear temporal architecture, season six introduces a number of new and significant geographical locations such as the temple, Jacob's cliff-side cave, and the lighthouse, and re-signifies the importance of the bamboo field in which Jack first appeared in the pilot episode. The appearance of these new sites begs the question: if these places have existed the entire time the castaways have been on the island, why have they not come across them before? Jack even remarks on this phenomenon upon arriving at the Lighthouse; "I don't understand. How is it that we've never seen it before?" ("Lighthouse" 6.5). Hurley's quick reply, "Guess we weren't looking for it," seems to do two things. First, it quickly addresses viewers who would be asking the same question, and second, it indicates that the story they thought they were watching is now something different. What viewers thought they were looking for, it turns out, is not what the series is really about.

What then is the narrative payoff of the series ending in relationship to the rest of the series? The sideways flashes functioned as a set-up for the ultimate reveal in the finale that everyone had died and that the sideways world they inhabited was one they had created collectively so that they could move on together. Jack's father, Christian Shephard explains to his son, "This is the place that you all made together, so that you could find one another. The most, important part of your life was the time that you spent with these people. That's why all of you are here. Nobody does it alone Jack. You needed all of them, and they needed you." ("The End, Part 2" 6.18). This explanation functions as a meta-assertion about the series as much as it provides an explanation of the sideways world. The six years audiences spent with the characters on the island (notice the island remains central) were what mattered. Had the final season more clearly established the spatial and temporal relationships between the newly discovered island locations and the sideways flashes earlier in the season by conforming to the internal logic the series had developed, perhaps these final moments would feel more like a fulfilling closure of the island-time narrative.

In the end, we always have to go back to the island. The notion of island-time woven throughout this analysis has sought to underscore the necessity of situating the narrative temporally and spatially: island(space)-time(temporality). The proposition of "going back," then, implies travel in both time and in space. Jack's imperative offers viewers a simple guide for understanding the narrative. The temporal and spatial elements are woven together to form the fabric of the narrative. *Lost*'s narrative is not a mosaic made from individual pieces, but a tapestry woven together with the multicolored threads of various timelines and locations. The threads can be, and often are, unraveled when new threads are introduced or older ones break. Viewers are required to go back and re-weave the fabric. In one of *Lost*'s many metafictional moments, when Fake-Locke takes Ben to see Jacob, Jacob asks Ben, "You like it? [Jacob indicates his weaving] I did it myself. It takes a very long time when you're making the thread, but, uh…. I suppose that's the point, isn't it?" ("The Incident"). Later in the season six episode, "Across the Sea" (6.15), we see that the Man in Black has destroyed Jacob's tapestry. Like the Man in Black, season six effectively unraveled most of what viewers had come to expect from the series. The temporal logic of the flash-sideways failed to conform to previously established narrative strategies, and the island-time narrative introduced unfamiliar landmarks and buildings, altering the established geography of the island. Despite this misstep, *Lost* created a rich narrative tapestry that will provide viewers with the opportunity to revisit old times and places and spend time with familiar characters. Its ability to sustain audience attention by providing them with the tools to understand and situate themselves within the program's vast narrative world is a testament to the show's success and its place in the history of television.

## WORKS CITED

Askwith, Ian. "'Do You Even Know Where This Is Going?': *Lost*'s Viewers and Narrative Predetermination." *Reading Lost: Perspectives on a Hit Television Show*. Ed. Roberta Pearson. London: I. B. Tauris, 2009. 159–180. Print.

Azaryahu, Maoz, and Kenneth Foote. "Historical space as narrative medium: on the configuration of spatial narratives of time at historical sites." *GeoJournal* 73.3 (2008): 179–194. Web. 29 July 2010.

"Blink." *Doctor Who: The Complete Third Series*. Sci-Fi Channel, 2007. DVD.

Cameron, Allan. *Modular Narratives in Contemporary Cinema*. New York: Palgrave Macmillan, 2008. Print.

"Chronologically LOST: Frequently Asked Questions." Web. 29 July 2010.

Clarke, M.J. "Lost and Mastermind Narration." *Television New Media* 11.2 (2010): 123–142. Web. 29 July 2010.

Johnson, Derek. "Inviting Audiences In." *New Review of Film and Television Studies* 5.1 (2007): 61. Web. 29 July 2010.

Lotz, Amanda. *The Television Will Be Revolutionized*. New York: New York University Press, 2007. Print.

Mittell, Jason. "*Lost* in a Great Story: Evaluation in Narrative Television (and Television Studies)." *Reading Lost: Perspectives on a Hit Television Show*. Ed. Roberta Pearson. London: I. B. Tauris, 2009. 119–138. Print.

\_\_\_\_\_. "Narrative Complexity in Contemporary American Television." *Velvet Light Trap: A Critical Journal of Film & Television* 58 (2006): 29–40. Web. 29 July 2010.

Pearson, Roberta. "Chain of Events: Regimes of Evaluation and *Lost*'s Construction of the Televisual Character." *Reading Lost: Perspectives on a Hit Television Show*. Ed. Roberta Pearson. London: I. B. Tauris, 2009. 139–158. Print.

# Narrative Philosophy in the Series: Fate, Determinism, and the Manipulation of Time
*Michael Rennett*

## Introduction

Storytellers have always relied on a variety of narrative methods in order to alter their audience's expectations. Imagine that you are sitting at a bar and Desmond Hume walks in through the doors and sits down beside you. He turns to you and says, "Let me tell you how I was able to marry the love of my life, Penelope Widmore." As you sit there, enraptured while listening to Desmond's tale of a mysterious island, electromagnetic anomalies, and a button that saves the world, you are fully aware that Desmond's story will eventually return to its main point: Desmond's blissful marriage with the woman he loves. However, if Desmond were to begin by saying, "Let me tell you about this race around the world I once did," then Desmond's romantic conclusion would be surprising to you even though he would be telling the same story. Many narratologists illustrate the critical relationship between the *fabula*, the order of a narrative from beginning to end, and the *sjuzet*, the manner in which that narrative is conveyed. In Desmond's first *sjuzet* (opening with the conclusion), the audience knows the outcome of the story and is consequently aware that Desmond's narrative must reach that ending. In the latter, Desmond's ambiguous beginning means that there is no expectation for the remainder of his story.

The complex narrative structure of the hit television show *Lost* has been placed at the forefront of academic studies dedicated to dissecting the text due to the program's intricately woven mythology and the premeditated approach taken to the entirety of the series by showrunners Carlton Cuse and Damon Lindelof. Television scholar Jason Mittell describes *Lost* as "a unified text, with every episode contributing to a larger whole" (125). He defines *Lost*'s "forensic fandom," a form of audience participation in which viewers are encouraged to sort through various clues scattered throughout *Lost*'s episodes in order to uncover the show's mystery about the enigmatic Island. Mittell argues:

> *Lost*'s narrative design discourages casual consumption. While there are certainly moment-to-moment pleasures of humor, suspense, action and romance, the show's most distinguishing attribute is its central mystery, which demands a hyper-attentive mode of spectatorship. To be a *Lost* fan is to embrace a detective mentality, seeking out clues, charting patterns and assembling evidence into narrative hypotheses and theories [128–129].

Ivan Askwith concurs with Mittell's assessment. Askwith writes, "*Lost*'s narrative teaches us that we must decipher the past in order to understand the present. Yet in doing so, *Lost* offers an implicit promise that the past *will* provide meaning to the present, and as such, that the past was written before the present" (172).

What stands out about *Lost*'s narrative strategy is the manner in which the show's *sjuzet* mirrors the program's philosophical debate between fate and free will. To return to our earlier example about Desmond's storytelling, his first version presents a fatalistic approach. The audience's foreknowledge about Desmond's marriage to Penny will force the listener to anticipate this conclusion and ask, "How does this story lead to your marriage?" instead of, "What happens next?" Meanwhile, Desmond's second method of storytelling presents a philosophy of free will. Since the audience is not cognizant of the conclusion, they can only speculate about what will happen next and where this story will lead. The distinctions between these narrative philosophies can be observed through various television shows and films. The series *How I Met Your Mother* utilizes a flashback framing device to convey its story about Ted Mosby telling his children how he met and married their mother. The show follows a younger Ted's various failed relationships until he finally finds this woman, which will presumably occur in the series finale. *How I Met Your Mother*'s premise is ruled by fate since the audience ultimately knows that Ted must eventually discover and marry this woman, since glimpses of his future children have already been seen. Thus, the suspense surrounds who this woman is as opposed to whether or not she exists. On the other hand, a series like *The Office* can continue *ad infinitum* (or at least until its inevitable cancellation) because of its linear timeline. There are no predetermined events which must occur before the end of the series, meaning that each week is determined only by where the show's writers want to take the story next.

Unlike most television shows, each of *Lost*'s episodes follows two different timelines. The first is the (usually) linear narrative following the survivors of the crash of Oceanic flight 815 on the island up to their eventual defeat of the nefarious Man in Black. Meanwhile, this storyline is punctuated by non-chronological stories such as character flashbacks (used for most of the first three seasons although they appear sporadically in subsequent years), flashforwards (season four), time travel (season five), and flash-sideways visions into the afterlife (season six). Each of these supplementary tales denotes a major manipulation of time within the show's framework. These segments jump to a significant moment in an individual character's life (or afterlife) which either establishes their personality or deepens their connection to the island's mysteries. Writing after the third season finale, Mittell finds that "every episode, every flashback and every character's story can be understood as contributing to a larger understanding of the nature (or artifice) of *Lost*'s island locale" (125). Viewers can find a thrill in witnessing the unintentional off-island encounters between the Oceanic survivors before the crash since it adds to the show's philosophical ambiguity: are these encounters coincidental or is fate bringing them together for a greater purpose? This chapter will address this philosophical debate between fate and free will in *Lost*'s universe by understanding these complexities as they relate to the show's narrative structure.

## *Flashbacks: How the Past Determines the Present and the Future*

The most traditional of *Lost*'s various non-linear narrative techniques is the show's patented use of flashbacks throughout an episode. Since the silent era, filmmakers have employed flashbacks in a variety of methods, with each particular method connoting its own distinct philosophical traits. Perhaps the most discussed example would be the fatalistic flashbacks contained within numerous *films noirs*. Paul Schrader observes in his influential article "Notes on Film Noir" that "in such films as *The Postman Always Rings Twice* [1946], *Laura* [1944], *Double Indemnity* [1944], *The Lady From Shanghai* [1947], *Out of the Past* [1947], and *Sunset Boulevard* [1950], the narration creates a mood of *temps perdu*: an irretrievable past, a predetermined fate and an all-enveloping hopelessness" (57–58). The plot in these films begins with the story's conclusion, after the main character has undergone this ordeal and is about to be arrested or killed (or in the case of *Sunset Boulevard*, is already dead) and is looking back on his experience. As the viewer watches this person's tale, the narrative is unflinchingly bound to return to this point regardless of what the characters or the audience may truly wish to see occur. A different type of subjective flashback can be seen in *The Pawnbroker* (Sidney Lumet, 1964). Throughout this film, the titular Jewish pawnbroker Sol Nazerman continually flashes back to his memories of being imprisoned in a concentration camp during World War II. These flashbacks are not only psychological reflections, but also demonstrate why Nazerman is living this particular life in the Harlem ghetto. Annette Insdorf describes how certain scenes are affected by Nazerman's past:

> When the bitter Jew rejects Jesús' offers of interest and companionship, the offended youth succumbs to his buddies' plans to rob the store. Nazerman also refuses the friendly advances of a social worker, Miss Birchfield (Geraldine Fitzgerald), and spurns Tessie (Marketa Kimbrell), the woman with whom he has been living, especially when her father dies. This cruel indifference is rendered comprehensible only in flashbacks that show Nazerman's earlier brutalization at the hands of the Nazis. Through subliminal flash cuts that gradually lengthen into painful scenes, the linear narrative is thickened with the weight of the past [28].

Unlike the fatalism found in noir films, the flashbacks in *The Pawnbroker* reflect a determinist philosophy by illustrating how these memories of his traumatic experiences in the concentration camp influence Nazerman's contemporaneous decisions. The flashbacks serve as a way to inform the audience about the motivations behind Nazerman's actions by showing the parallels between the present and the past.

Due to the series' longevity and a need to keep episodes fresh and exciting to audiences, *Lost* utilizes three different types of flashbacks to tell its story. The one most frequently used by *Lost* is a determinist decision flashback. Askwith finds that these flashbacks provide "crucial information to contextualize a survivor's otherwise inexplicable actions and motives" (162). On the island, a character has to make a controversial choice which is paralleled in flashback segments that focus on the same character making a similar decision in the past. The episode "The Cost of Living" (3.5) showcases Mr. Eko's lack of regret for doing what he needs to do to survive. In the flashback, a young Eko breaks into a supply shed in order to steal food for his hungry younger brother Yemi. Eko is caught by a nun who orders him to confess his sin. Eko refuses to do so, justifying his crime by saying that Yemi was hungry. Eko later commits various crimes in his flashback such as trafficking drugs and committing murder. On the island, an apparition of Yemi appears to Eko and implores Eko to admit his sins. Instead of confessing, Eko tells his brother:

> I ask for no forgiveness, Father, for I have not sinned. I have only done what I needed to do to survive. A small boy once asked me if I was a bad man. If I could answer him now, I would tell him that when I was a young boy, I killed a man to save my brother's life. I am not sorry for this. I am proud of this. I did not ask for the life that I was given. But it was given, nonetheless. And with it, I did my best.

As in his flashback, Eko is advocating the need to survive over the guilt of committing sins.

Similar determinist decision flashbacks can be found in episodes like "...and Found" (2.5), in which Sun learns to surrender her desperate searches for a husband in her flashback and for her missing wedding ring on the island before she can find them, and "The Whole Truth" (2.16), in which Sun finds it easy to hide her pregnancy from her husband Jin because of her previous lies to him regarding her learning English behind his back and his off-island infertility. Sawyer's predilection to con the rest of the Oceanic survivors in "Confidence Man" (1.8) and "The Long Con" (2.13) is mirrored in his flashback cons of Jessica and Cassidy in those respective episodes. Charles Girard and David Meulemans invoke Aristotle's definition of habit as a "second nature" in order to explain these occurrences on *Lost*:

> Moral virtues, according to [Aristotle], are acquired by habit: it is not by a single choice, but by repeated practice, that we form our moral nature. [...] *Lost*'s flashbacks show us the past moments during which the characters condemned themselves to be what they are by repeatedly acting in the same, often reprehensible, way. They explain why our protagonists, freed from the context that made them act as they did (Kate's abusive father, Sawyer's traumatic witnessing of his parents' death, Sayid's involvement in the Gulf War) and emancipated from the society that saw them as criminals or monsters, seem condemned to repeat again and again the same acts that disgust them [94–95].

However, not all of *Lost*'s flashbacks doom the show's characters to inevitably repeat the same mistakes. Other flashbacks serve to demonstrate character growth as the episode's central character comes to a different decision on the island than he or she did in the past. An example of this pattern is the episode "Outlaws" (1.16). The flashback shows Sawyer tracking down and murdering Frank Duckett, the man whom Sawyer believes had conned his mother and is in turn responsible for his parents' deaths. Unfortunately, Sawyer belatedly discovers that Duckett did not commit the original crime and Sawyer is left with innocent blood on his hands. In the island storyline, Sawyer is terrorized by a boar that ransacks his tent, knocks him down, and destroys his camp at separate times. Sawyer seeks revenge against the boar, as he did against Duckett, but ultimately decides to spare the boar's life instead of shooting it in order to avoid committing the same mistake. The episode "Tricia Tanaka Is Dead" (3.10) features a similar flashback philosophy. In both storylines, Hurley has self-defeating feelings about his continual bad luck. Off the island, he chooses to ignore his father's sound advice about creating his own luck instead of feeling like he is cursed. However, on the island, Hurley decides to risk his own life in an attempt to create his own fate by restarting a decrepit old Dharma van as it is rolling down a steep incline toward a wall of rocks. By confronting his feelings, Hurley overcomes his masochistic notions about luck.

Girard and Meulemans argue that these changes are the result of free will. They reference the episode "Dave" (2.18), in which Hurley's imaginary friend Dave continually encourages Hurley to perform harmful actions such as breaking out of the Santa Rosa Mental Health Institute and stuffing himself with copious amounts of food. On the island, Libby confronts Hurley about his secret stash of food and tells him, "You want to change, then change" after he expresses his desire to eradicate it. Girard and Meulemans find that Libby's faith in free will is contradicted by "the internal determinisms tying *Lost*'s heroes to their past: second nature, subconscious, and bad faith" (100). However, if the characters do not experience these life-altering moments such as Sawyer's murder of an innocent man and Hurley's belief in bad luck, then they would have nothing from which to change in the first place. Hurley's drive to get rid of his secret food is not solely motivated by his internal desire to change, but by his fatigue at hearing other people comment on his weight, whether Dr. Brooks in flashbacks or Sawyer on the island. As such, these decisions still maintain a faith in determinism despite their distinct outcomes.

Another type of flashback featured on *Lost* can be termed a "reversed parallel" flashback. In episodes that employ this device, a character remembers a past event in which they are either doing something or something is being done to them, but their role is reversed in the linear island timeline. Through this experience, the character becomes capable of physically and emotionally understanding the person in the opposing position. The flashback in "Solitary" (1.9) follows Iraqi soldier Sayid Jarrah as he is under orders from his superior officer to torture Nadia, the woman he loves; however, on the island, Sayid is being tortured by the crazed French woman Danielle Rousseau, who believes Sayid to be one of the Others who had stolen her child Alex sixteen years ago. From a psychological perspective, this role reversal allows Sayid to empathize with his numerous victims. He can comprehend the pain and suffering he inflicted on others by now undergoing this ordeal himself. This incident also suggests a fatalistic connection between Sayid and torture, as Scott Parker argues that "the island, as is its way, seems to be forcing or allowing Sayid to face the source of his own psychological torment" (156). Torture becomes an act with which Sayid is inevitably involved, whether as the perpetrator or as the victim. He tortures Sawyer in "Confidence Man," and Ben Linus in "One of Them" (2.14). Additionally he is not only tortured by Rousseau, but by Sami, the husband of one of his victims, in "Enter 77" (3.11) and by Dogen in "What Kate Does" (6.3). Despite his stated desire to refrain from torture ("One of Them" and "Enter 77"), Sayid is inevitably and inextricably linked to this heinous act. Similarly, Sawyer's proclivity for conning people is juxtaposed with an ironic role-reversal in "Every Man for Himself" (3.4). In his flashback, Sawyer has to out-con the prison warden while, on the island, Sawyer is out-conned by his captor Ben. Additionally, John Locke has to persuade Jack Shephard to take a leap of faith after Locke had been convinced to do the same in his flashback by his then-girlfriend Helen in "Orientation" (2.3). In a manner reminiscent of the connection between Sayid and torture, Sawyer and Locke are fatefully linked to conning and faith respectively.

Occasionally, *Lost* presents episodes that fill in important narrative gaps, either completely or partially, in flashback. These flashbacks usually portray the backstory of a character whom the audience has seen on the island, but whose character remains shrouded in mystery. This type of subjective historical flashback is always ruled by fatalism, as the audience is aware of the conclusion before seeing the rest of the story. The first episode to employ this format is "The Other 48 Days" (2.7), which presents the lives of the "Tailies," the tail-section survivors of Oceanic 815, after its crash on the island. Throughout the first few episodes of season two, the audience has been introduced to the Tailies and is aware of certain facts: who is still alive from the group, their discovery of and residence in the Arrow station, and their collective paranoia resulting from their having been infiltrated by a man named Goodwin whom they had discovered to be one of the Others and later killed for this reason. Thus, when their flashback is shown, the audience expects these events to play out on screen, which they eventually do.

Other fatalistic subjective histories can be found in the series' pilot (1.1 and 1.2), which briefly follows Jack, Kate, and Charlie's experiences aboard flight 815 before the crash; in "Exodus" (1.23 and 1.24), which shows various survivors heading to 815 before it takes off; in "Maternity Leave" (2.15), where Claire, who had been suffering from partial amnesia, remembers being kidnapped by Ethan; in "Meet Kevin Johnson" (4.8), when Michael tells Sayid about how he came to be on the freighter; and finally in "316" (5.6), which begins after the Ajira 316 crash with Jack, Kate, and Hurley landing on the island before jumping back forty-six hours earlier to explain how they all embarked on that flight. Episodes like "Ab Aeterno" (6.9) and "Across the Sea" (6.15), which the producers refer to as "mythological download[s]" (Sepinwall), not only answer questions about the island's greater history, but present the motivations for some of the show's more mysterious characters such as the ageless Richard Alpert and the Man in Black. These episodes are certainly fatalistic (for instance, we know Richard will not be killed by an officer aboard the *Black Rock* after that officer murders the rest of the slaves) but they are also determinist in relation to the rest of the series. In "Recon" (6.8), the Man in Black refers to his own "growing pains [...] that [he is] still trying to work [his] way through" as a result of his "crazy mother." By seeing this crazy mother murder the Man in Black's real mother, control his knowledge of the outside world, and ultimately prevent him from leaving the island, the audience can better understand why he resorts to such desperate measures to leave it.

## *The Future's Effect on the Present:* Lost's Flash-Forwards

Askwith claims that during *Lost*'s third season, the showrunners encountered the problems of redundant flashbacks due to an endless middle (162). Since the end date for the series had not been set, *Lost*'s writers were forced to prolong or repeat certain aspects of the narrative in order to fill in this uncontrollable extension. However, after negotiating an end date in May 2007, executive producers Carlton Cuse and Damon Lindelof were able to guide the show toward its conclusion. In an interview with *The Hollywood Reporter* after the announcement, Cuse stated that "by defining the endpoint, we can now map out the rest of the series in confidence" (Andreeva). Due to this newfound freedom, *Lost* swiftly shifted gears by utilizing flash-forwards as its chief narrative device throughout its fourth season, beginning with the season three finale "Through the Looking Glass" (3.22 and 3.23). *Lost* presents its flash-forwards as glimpses ahead to the characters' futures in 2007, after six of the survivors — Jack, Kate, Sayid, Hurley, Sun, and baby Aaron — have been rescued. *Lost*'s implementation of this temporal shift reverses the philosophical structure established by its signature flashbacks. Instead of having the flashbacks build toward the island narrative, the time on the island is conversely building toward this future. It is no longer the linear timeline which has an uncertain future but the off-island flash-forward; the island storyline is instead leading to their eventual rescue and is therefore imbued with the trappings of fatalism.

The narrative ordering of how the flash-forwards appear throughout their season-long tenure presents a fascinating insight into their philosophical implications. The first flash-forward shows a bearded and depressed Jack's erratic behavior as he is now drinking constantly, abusing oxycodone pills, and contemplating suicide. He meets Kate outside of an airport runway imploring her that they "have to go back" to the island. While this moment is the first flash-forward shown to the audience, it is chronologically the final scene from the episodes which implement this narrative device. Consequently, the flash-forwards in season four continually lead toward this event. In fact, the writers include various jokes in "The Beginning of the End" (4.1) that foreshadow this scene. When Jack meets Hurley at the mental health institute,

Jack mentions growing out a beard as a way to deflect public attention. Hurley responds by saying, "You'd look weird with a beard, dude." Within this non-linear structuring, the writers are constantly provoking thoughts about this inevitable future. However, this inexorable future negates *Lost*'s penchant for suspense. The helicopter crash in the season finale, "There's No Place Like Home" (4.12, 4.13 and 4.14), does not force the viewer to ask whether the characters aboard the helicopter survive or not, but *how* they are able to find rescue in such dire circumstances. The narrative slowly builds back to this key meeting between Kate and Jack throughout the fourth season, but never reaches this moment until the season finale. By presenting the flash-forwards in this manner, *Lost* is able to maintain the tenets of fatalism within both of its concurrent storylines.

## *"Whatever Happened, Happened":* Lost's *Fatalistic Rules of Time Travel*

Following season four's flash-forwards, *Lost* restructured its *sjuzet* for its two storylines. The first would progress chronologically in the off-island world seen in the flash-forwards while the other would follow the survivors left behind on the island who are now traveling through time after Ben turns a frozen wheel that is connected to the island's source and which is located underneath the Orchid station ("There's No Place Like Home"). For the first time on the show, both timelines tend to progress linearly throughout the season from the characters' perspectives; there are a couple of moments which divert from this method by utilizing flash-forwards, the opening of "Because You Left" (5.1) and the second scene of "LaFleur" (5.8) in particular. Science fiction writers have frequently used time travel as a device to instigate the debate between fate and free will. If free will exists, then a time traveler would be able to prevent events from happening and consequently change the future. Perhaps the most famous example of this argument is Ray Bradbury's short story "A Sound of Thunder" (1952), in which a time traveling hunter goes to prehistoric times and accidentally steps on a butterfly, thereby changing numerous aspects of the story's present. On the other hand, if fate exists, then various historical events will always occur and it would be impossible for a time traveler to change them. The time traveler would not only be unable to modify these events, but may in fact bring them to fruition, as in *The Terminator* (1984), in which the time traveling Kyle Reese becomes the father of John Connor, the savior of the post-apocalyptic human race and the person who sends Kyle back to 1984 in order to protect his mother.

Daniel Faraday is the character who is most closely associated with time travel on *Lost*. Before arriving on the island, Faraday was a physics professor at Oxford University's Queen's College and performed various experiments centered on time travel, as seen in "The Constant" (4.5). Faraday explains to the time traveling survivors that they have been "dislodged from time," but cannot do anything to change the past:

> Time — it's like a street, all right? We can move forward on that street, we can move in reverse, but we cannot ever create a new street. If we try to do anything different, we will fail every time. Whatever happened, happened ["Because You Left"].

Faraday describes time as being on a single, unchanging timeline — there is nothing that the group can do to change the past. Daniel's statement that "Whatever happened, happened" implies that all of the actions that have occurred on the series have been a result of fate: Oceanic 815 is destined to have crashed on the island, and this group must go back in time to become a part of the Dharma Initiative in order for these time loops to play out correctly. John Locke states to Jack Shepherd in the episode "Exodus,"

> Do you really think all this is an accident — that we, a group of strangers survived, many of us with just superficial injuries? Do you think we crashed on this place by coincidence — especially, this place? We were brought here for a purpose, for a reason, all of us. Each one of us was brought here for a reason.

That reason dictates that these historical loops must be fulfilled in the past in order to avoid a grandfather paradox. If these events had never occurred in the past, then the on-island events shown in the series would have been negated from ever happening. Perhaps this is why Faraday's mother Eloise Hawking tells Desmond that if he does not complete his destiny of going to the island and pressing the button for three years, then "Every single one of us is dead" since this paradox would exist ("Flashes Before Your Eyes" 3.8).

Desmond, however, provides an inexplicable exception to the guidelines of time travel. Faraday asserts that "the rules don't apply to [Desmond]" and that "[Desmond] is uniquely and miraculously special" ("Because You Left"). Desmond's time travels are entirely distinct from his peers'. After turning the failsafe key to the Swan station ("Live Together, Die Alone" 2.23 and 2.24), Desmond's consciousness is transmitted to 1996, when he is about to ask for his girlfriend Penelope's hand in marriage. His experiences crashing on the island and living in the Swan hatch appear to him as flashes that he dismisses as being dreams. He suspects that he may be time traveling after he sees Oceanic 815 survivor Charlie Pace playing guitar on the street in London; however, his theory is supposedly debunked by his friend Donovan, a physics professor who dispels Desmond's visions as a psychological issue. Desmond, inspired by this talk, attempts to purchase an engagement ring from Eloise, only to hear her tell him that he cannot acquire this ring since it would undo his future actions on the island. He convinces her to let him buy the ring, but throws it into the ocean after fully comprehending that he is bound to fulfill his fate. Later in the same episode, Desmond remembers an incident at his local pub in which the bartender is hit in the head with a cricket bat by Jimmy Lennon. As Lennon approaches the bartender, Desmond tells the bartender to duck and Lennon accidentally smashes Desmond's head, causing his consciousness to return to the island timeline.

This particular episode contemplates the existence of free will within time travel, but indicates that taking advantage of it would result in an apocalyptic collapsing of time. Sander Lee interprets this idea as a paradox within the storytelling: "If everything is predetermined and the universe will 'correct' any attempts to alter fate, then how could it be possible for Desmond to derail destiny sufficiently to kill us all?" (75). Lee also cites Desmond's newfound prescience and awareness of this course correction paradox as motivation for Desmond to save Charlie various times throughout the third season. Even within this possibility of free will, Desmond's actions still seem indicative of determinism. Due to Desmond's time-traveling consciousness and subsequent knowledge of this paradox, he is able to save Charlie multiple times until Charlie accomplishes his destiny of turning off the Looking Glass's jamming device, thereby bringing about the rescue of the Oceanic Six and ultimately bringing about the rest of the survivors' time travels, which must occur for the survivors to be brought to the island in the first place. Certain actions in Desmond's travels can therefore be viewed as self-consistent, such as the purchase of Penelope's engagement ring and Desmond's throwing it into the river, or as incorrect memories, such as the exchange between Jimmy Lennon and the bartender. Of course, in the fatalistic timeline that *Lost* suggests, Desmond always would have been struck by Lennon's cricket bat, so his foggy memory of the incident would certainly be explainable.

Film scholar Constance Penley connects time travel to fatalism through Freud's concept of the primal scene by analyzing various science fiction texts. Freud defines the primal scene fantasy as the overhearing or observation of parental intercourse or, in essence, being able to "view" one's own conception. Within time travel stories, this fantasy can become a reality, since the time traveler can witness or even partake in his own conception. Penley argues that in *The Terminator*, "John Connor is the child who orchestrates his own primal scene, one inflected by a family romance, moreover, because he is able to choose his own father, singling out Kyle from the other soldiers" (129). In a fatalistic narrative structure like *The Terminator*, Kyle is destined to travel back in time and impregnate Sarah in order to create the future hero. In fact, it is John's conception that drives the film's fatalism since the characters act with the intention of changing the past. Penley witnesses a metaphorical primal scene fantasy in *La Jetée* (Chris Marker, 1962). While a child, the unnamed protagonist witnesses the death of a man. This event haunts him throughout his life and later inspires him to travel through time. He eventually returns to this moment during his time travels and finds out (unfortunately too late) that he had actually witnessed his own death. Penley finds that the story "insists on the similar paradox at work in the primal scene fantasy by depicting the psychical consequence of attempting to return to a scene from one's childhood: such a compulsion to repeat, and the regression that it implies, leads to the annihilation of the subject" (133). In essence, this moment of the primal scene fantasy begins the hero's original drive to re-watch this scene and effectively seals his fate to be killed.

*Lost* contains two metaphorical primal scenes that, through time travel, fatefully establish Locke and Ben as two deeply important individuals to the island. In the episode "Jughead" (5.3), Locke introduces himself to the Others' leader Richard Alpert when time traveling to 1954. Locke tells Richard that he was sent to this time by Jacob and that he will become the leader of the Others in the future. Since Richard seems unconvinced of Locke's story, Locke implores Richard to visit his upcoming birth in Tustin, California in 1956. Richard witnesses this event (as seen in "Cabin Fever" 4.11) and comprehends that the person he met in 1954 was indeed telling him the truth. Richard thereby realizes that Locke is "special" and predestined to command the Others. In 2004, Ben forces Locke to undergo a test before handing over the leadership to Locke — Locke must murder his father in order to free himself of his past trauma. Richard helps Locke formulate a plan to accomplish this trying ordeal because of the foreknowledge given to him by Locke during their meeting in 1954. Richard has gained this insight due to empirical evidence rather than through prescience or from speaking with the godlike Jacob. This meeting is what inspires Richard to later visit Locke as a child in 1961 ("Cabin Fever"), attempt to recruit Locke to a science camp in 1972 ("Cabin Fever"), and ultimately spread the fact that Locke is special to the rest of the Others. The Others' excitement about Locke joining them ("The Brig" 3.19) is the direct result of Richard's having imparted this legend to them. In effect, Locke has created his own destiny during their meeting in 1954 and that moment can be viewed as Locke's primal scene. It establishes his importance to the island and coerces Richard and the Others to believe in his future role as their leader. Locke's apparent foreknowledge of his own fate inspires Richard's belief, which is passed back to Locke in turn after Oceanic 815 crashes on the island.

Ben also has a preconceived destiny that is established through time travel. When Jack, Kate, Hurley, and Sayid are sent back to 1977 from the

Ajira flight, Sayid shoots a 12-year-old Ben in order to prevent Ben from actualizing his future of terrorizing the Oceanic survivors and employing Sayid as a hit man. Sayid's actions mirror a faith in free will, since he believes that killing Ben as a child would eliminate the future. Similarly, Jack refuses to save young Ben's life because he wants to see the older manipulative Ben die. Jack's refusal to help causes Kate and Sawyer to bring Ben to Richard in order to save Ben's life. Richard explains to them that if he saves Ben's life, then Ben will never be the same:

> RICHARD: And why are you here?
> KATE: Because we need you to save his life. Can you?
> RICHARD: If I take him, he's not ever gonna be the same again.
> KATE: What do you mean by that?
> RICHARD: What I mean is that, he'll forget this ever happened, and that ... his innocence will be gone. He will always be one of us. You still want me to take him?
> KATE: Yes ["Whatever Happened, Happened" 5.11].

Richard is able to successfully fix Ben but, as Richard warns, Ben loses his innocence. The time traveling Sayid and Jack are thereby directly responsible for transforming Ben from a righteous and virtuous child into a cold, calculating and deceitful adult. This sequence of events can be interpreted as Ben's primal scene, since Ben is "reborn" into the man that he will become in the future.

## *Choosing a Second Life: Free Will in the Flash-Sideways*

The sixth and final season of *Lost* introduces the show's most innovative and controversial aspect of its storytelling process: the flash-sideways. The flash-sideways were initially established as an alternative timeline to the linear narrative in which flight 815 had never crashed on the island and the passengers arrived at Los Angeles International Airport safely. This sequence of events was conceived to be a consequence of the Jughead explosion from the season five finale ("The Incident" 5.16 and 5.17) after Faraday's erroneous proposal that the time-traveling Oceanic survivors could negate certain events (like the plane crash) from ever happening by destroying the electromagnetic energy underneath the Swan ("The Variable" 5.14). Through eight of the first eleven episodes of season six, the show re-introduces its main characters as slightly varied versions of them appear in this alternate timeline. In "LA X" (1.1 and 1.2), Jack is the nervous flyer aboard the flight while Rose has to calm him down, in a reversal of what occurred in the show's pilot episode. In addition, Sawyer is now a police officer instead of a con man ("Recon" 6.8), Jin and Sun are no longer married ("The Package" 6.10), Hurley is lucky instead of unlucky ("LA X"), and the island is submerged underwater ("LA X"). Beginning with the episode "Happily Ever After" (6.11), the audience observes that the flash-sideways are connected to the island storyline as Desmond remembers flashes of certain memories from reality, such as Charlie's sacrificial death in the Looking Glass station. From that moment forward, the two narratives are drawn together until the show's finale when it is revealed that the flash-sideways are actually a look into the characters' post-mortem purgatory through which they can eventually ascend into heaven.

*The Catechism of the Catholic Church* describes purgatory as a place after death for "all who die in God's grace and friendship" but are still "imperfectly purified," in order that they may gain this purification and "achieve the holiness necessary to enter the joy of Heaven" (1030). While those who enter purgatory are destined to go to heaven, they must first atone for their past transgressions. Brett Chandler Patterson asserts that purgatory has a direct relationship with redemption, a key theme on *Lost*: "As Christians receive forgiveness from God in the Christian community, they find transformation and new life. Salvation is a journey, where we grow in ways to prevent the same mistakes we made in the past; echoes of (and direct references to) this process appear in several episodes of *Lost*" (205). In order to demonstrate this connection to the past, the flash-sideways are designed to remind viewers of earlier episodes instead of relating to the concurrent storyline within a single episode's structure in the manner typical of the flashbacks and flash-forwards. The first flash-sequences from the first and sixth seasons both occur on board Oceanic 815 when Jack is requesting extra alcohol for his drink from flight attendant Cindy Chandler. The centricity of the flash-sequences is similarly mirrored between the first few episodes of the same seasons. In addition, specific episode titles from season six are explicit references to earlier episodes: "What Kate Does" (6.3) and "Everybody Loves Hugo" (6.12) are the respective opposites of "What Kate Did" (2.9) and "Everybody Hates Hugo" (2.4). Through these blunt throwbacks, the flash-sideways necessitate a focus on island past instead of island present.

*The Catechism* also states that "we cannot be united with God unless we freely choose to love him," thereby identifying purgatory as a place where free will exists (1033). With the characters' respective on-island destinies vanished underwater, the Oceanic 815 passengers can freely choose their own paths in purgatory without Jacob's clandestine manipulation and the constraints of their predetermined fates. For instance, Sawyer decides to become a police officer instead of a conman after his parents' murder-suicide. Perhaps Sawyer would have made this same choice without Jacob's influence in his real life, but Sawyer was not allowed to follow this path since his future had already been determined for him. Likewise, the rest of the characters are enabled to make up for their wrongdoings from their real lives while in purgatory. Jack finally resolves his issues with his father Christian through his relationship with his fictional son David. In the episode "Lighthouse" (6.5), Jack invokes his father's memory in order to repair his familial issues:

> You know when I was your age, my father didn't want to see me fail either. He used to say to me that — he said that I didn't have what it takes. I spent my whole life carrying that around with me. I don't ever want you to feel that way. I will always love you, no matter what you do. In my eyes you can never fail. I just wanna be a part of your life.

Christian's statement about Jack not "hav[ing] what it takes" alludes to their conversation from the flashback in "White Rabbit" (1.5) which spurs Jack to become the leader of the survivors in his real life; of course, Christian's words also disillusioned Jack and contributed to breaking down their relationship. In the flash-sideways, Jack understands Christian's underlying motivations in making this declaration, which allows Jack to build upon his own communicative failures with his own son.

Other characters, such as Ben, change their decisions from real life while in purgatory. In "Dr. Linus" (6.7), Ben — who is now a history teacher — discovers Principal Reynolds' affair with the school nurse and threatens to expose Reynolds' secret unless Reynolds resigns and gives Ben the position of school principal. However, Reynolds shows Ben an e-mail request for a letter of recommendation from Alex Rousseau, one of Ben's prized students and his daughter on the island, and tells Ben that he will ruin Alex's chances at getting into Yale by writing her a scathing letter unless Ben drops his plan for power. On the island, Ben is unwilling to compromise his power and allows mercenary Martin Keamy to murder Alex ("The Shape of Things to Come" 4.9), a decision that haunts Ben and determines his choices to follow the Man in Black ("Dead Is Dead" 5.12) and to stab Jacob to death ("The Incident"). In purgatory, Ben aborts his blackmail of Reynolds in order to preserve Alex's future. By making this choice, Ben is finally able to find redemption.

*Time* magazine writer James Poniewozik questions the purpose of the flash-sideways in relation to *Lost*'s overarching themes. He writes:

> But I, at least, had spent five years thinking of *the Island* as a place where the characters tried to achieve redemption and correct the mistakes of their past. And Jacob re-iterated that this season: They needed the Island as much as it needed them. So then what was the purpose of experiencing a post-life in which they worked through the same redemption issues? If the Island was for redemption, why have a Sideways way station, for, I don't know, *re*-redemption?

Poniewozik's point is certainly valid if we find the island to be a place where free will exists. If the characters are merely re-working their way through issues that have already been resolved, then the alternate timeline would be unnecessary. However, if the island is ruled by fate, then the survivors' real life redemption is not of their own choosing but a predestined outcome designed for them. As such, finding redemption in the flash-sideways represents a choice that is made by each character. They can either change their decisions like Jack and Ben or they can repeat their same mistakes like Ana Lucia, a corrupt cop in purgatory who accepts a bribe and is therefore judged "not ready" to ascend to heaven. Another major instance of free will in the flash-sideways revolves around a character's decision to stay in purgatory if they so desire. Both Ben and Eloise choose to remain in purgatory instead of ascending to heaven because they want to spend more time with their loved ones, Alex and Daniel, in the flash-sideways world because both of their children died far too young in the island's plan ("The End" 6.17 and 6.18).

## *Conclusion: The Philosophical Scope of Lost's Narrative*

One of the most oft-debated questions about *Lost* is whether the survivors of Oceanic 815 were brought to the island by coincidence or by fate. In "White Rabbit," Locke asks Jack, "What if everything that happened here, happened for a reason?" From that moment forward, characters, critics and viewers have been divided into two camps: either the fatalistic faith of Locke or the coincidental scientific leanings of Jack. From a meta-perspective, the same question surrounds the construction of *Lost* itself: whether showrunners Damon Lindelof and Carlton Cuse have created a fatalistic, premeditated, hermeneutically driven gameplan or if the show is constantly being developed in a continuous period of transition (see Askwith 173–176). The show deliberately contradicts itself on this issue. Even after Jack, Kate, Sawyer, and Hurley learn from Jacob that they were indeed brought to the island for the purpose of taking over his position as its protector, Jacob presents the candidates with free will — the choice to accept the position or not. Contrary to Jacob's proposal of free will, Jack invokes destiny when he takes the job stating, "This is what I'm supposed to do" ("What They Died For" 6.16). Girard and Meulemans imply that the series ultimately "leaves it to us to decide if free will is something we can believe in or only a foolish illusion masking the irresistible strength of internal determinism" (101).

While Girard and Meulemans speculate that this question is inconclusive, the show's narrative structure points us toward answers. Both the flashbacks and flash-forwards present the story as determinist and fatalist, each of which contradicts the nature of free will. Similarly, the time travel sequences describe the narrative as a single linear timeline in which whatever happened, happened and, by implication, whatever will happen, will happen. This point is made extensively clear during the group's time-flashes when they jump from 2004 to events that take place in 2007 and/or later. Their second time shift (depicted in "Because You Left") takes the group forward to 2007 when Richard is able to tend Locke's bullet wound and give Locke the compass that is eventually returned to Richard in 1954. Additionally, the jump in "The Little Prince" (5.4) takes Sawyer and his group to an undetermined point in the future when they find a water bottle from Ajira 316 in the outrigger canoes by their old beach camp. From this empirical evidence, we can see that the future, such as the Ajira plane crash, has already been determined even though it had not occurred in the linear timeline yet. Depending on the date to when they time-jump, the events of season six might have even happened, meaning that the island could have already been saved from the Man in Black and Hurley may have been installed as its new protector. Of course, this specific interpretation is fully reliant on the timing of this event which, according to Cuse and Lindelof, will not be answered (Sepinwall); nonetheless, this incident still portrays a predetermined future. Even the flash-sideways discuss the mortality of all of its characters despite ending the series with a small select group leaving the island and Hurley and Ben about to begin their regime running the island.

*Lost*'s various experimental *sjuzets* demonstrate the philosophical relationship between the *sjuzet* and the *fabula* in storytelling. By presenting its storyline in this manner, *Lost* is able to answer its own debates between coincidence and destiny, and fate and free will. Despite the assertions of free will by Jack, Libby, and Juliet, the show's structure ultimately surrenders the main theme to fatalism by creating an illusion of free will. Each "choice" a character faces is instead a moment that leads each to his or her respective destiny within the intricate mosaic of the *fabula* that is designed by some supernatural force, whether God, Jacob, or the island. Juliet may sarcastically state, "Here I am thinking that free will still actually exists" in "A Tale of Two Cities" (3.1), but her remark actually describes *Lost*'s philosophy in its linear timeline: the characters may believe in the existence of free will, but they are instead pawns to the tenets of fate and determinism.

## Works Cited

Andreeva, Nellie. "End in Sight for *Lost*: 48 Episodes, 3 Seasons." *The Hollywood Reporter*. 7 May 2007. Web. 12 June 2010.
Askwith, Ivan. "'Do You Even Know Where This Is Going?': *Lost*'s Viewers and Narrative Premeditation." *Reading Lost: Perspectives on a Hit Television Show*. Ed. Roberta Pearson. London: I.B. Tauris, 2009. 159–180. Print.
*Catechism of the Catholic Church*. 19 June 2010. Web. 12 June 2010.
Girard, Charles, and David Meulemans. "The Island as a Test of Free Will: Freedom of Rein-

vention and Internal Determinism in *Lost.*" *Lost and Philosophy: The Island Has Its Reasons.* Ed. Sharon M. Kaye. Malden, MA: Blackwell, 2008. 89–101. Print.

Jensen, Jeff. "Confused by the *Lost* Premiere? Never Fear! Damon and Carlton Explain a Few Things about the Start of Season 6." *Entertainment Weekly.* 2 February 2010. Web. 18 June 2010.

Mittell, Jason. "*Lost* in a Great Story: Evaluation in Narrative Television (and Television Studies)." *Reading Lost: Perspectives on a Hit Television Show.* Ed. Roberta Pearson. London: I.B. Tauris, 2009. 119–138. Print.

Parker, Scott. "Tortured Souls." *Lost and Philosophy: The Island Has Its Reasons.* Ed. Sharon M. Kaye. Malden, MA: Blackwell, 2008. 148–158. Print.

Patterson, Brett Chandler. "Of Moths and Men: Paths of Redemption on the Island of Second Chances." *Lost and Philosophy: The Island Has Its Reasons.* Ed. Sharon M. Kaye. Malden, MA: Blackwell, 2008. 204–220. Print.

Penley, Constance. "Time Travel, Primal Scene and the Critical Dystopia." *Liquid Metal: The Science Fiction Film Reader.* Ed. Sean Redmond. London: Wallflower, 2004. 126–135. Print.

Poniewozik, James. "The *Lost* Finale and Season 6, Reconsidered." *Time.* 27 May 2010. Web. 20 June 2010.

Schrader, Paul. "Notes on Film Noir." *Film Comment* (Spring 1972). Rpt. in *Film Noir Reader.* Eds. Alain Silver and James Ursini. New York: Limelight Editions, 1996. 53–63. Print.

Sepinwall, Alan. "Exclusive Interview: *Lost* Producers Damon Lindelof and Carlton Cuse Talk "Across the Sea.'" *HitFix.* 12 May 2010. Web. 11 June 2010.

# "Enslaved by Time and Space": Determinism, Traumatic Temporality, and Global Interconnectedness

*Aris Mousoutzanis*

There is a scene in an episode from season three of *Lost*, "Not in Portland" (3.7), where, while trying to escape from the Hydra Island, Jack and Kate are led by Alex to a room inside a compound of the Dharma Initiative where they are confronted with a scene reminiscent of Stanley Kubrick's *Clockwork Orange* (1971): Alex's boyfriend, Karl, is strapped to a chair, wearing LED goggles and forced to watch a brainwashing video that displays flashing images and phrases with drum'n'bass music and indecipherable sounds in the background. This is one of the numerous scenes of the show to contain "Easter eggs" for the fans to identify. If the video is played in reverse, the background sounds turn out to be a voice repeating, "Only fools are enslaved by time and space." The phrase directly relates to the show's appropriations of Buddhism, but I see this hidden reference as symbolic of an important aspect of *Lost* that I will be discussing in this paper. The allusion to "slavery" points toward a strong sense of entrapment that the show conveys at many different levels of its narrative. The survivors of Oceanic 815 are not just stranded on an island, they also come to realize they have been bound together in different times and places before or after their time on the island, in accordance with one of the show's major themes: the conflict between choice and fate, accident and destiny, free will and determinism. These are just instances of the strong determinist orientation that permeates *Lost*, one that I will be discussing with regard to the show's treatment of time and space. *Lost* must be seen as a show symptomatic of its cultural moment in its ability to reflect a convergence of a number of diverse discourses of determinism and interconnectedness that has been taking place during the last few decades to form what I describe as a "determinist paradigm." The temporal structure of the show, for instance, relies on a strictly deterministic model of time: even traveling in time would not change history — whatever happened, happened. Temporal determinism in *Lost*, however, may be interpreted with regard to the show's major preoccupation with themes of loss and trauma. As a psychopathology that constantly returns patients to the traumatic event, which they relive in nightmares or flashback memories, trauma affects their consciousness and experience of time, even as it is indebted to what Sigmund Freud termed "psychic determinism," the assumption that one's past actions affect one's present mental processes. Furthermore, this sense of entrapment in time is accompanied by a sense of interconnectedness in space, as different individuals from diverse backgrounds around the globe find themselves entangled in an intricate plot of loss and displacement extending across different countries, continents, and cultures. In its attempt to explore the repercussions of personal tragedy and collective trauma in an increasingly globalized world, *Lost* must be seen as a cultural text symptomatic of an emerging dialectic between trauma and globalization, one that operates within the wider framework provided by the determinist paradigm.

Around the last two decades of the twentieth century, critics in the humanities became increasingly fascinated with a body of "theory" often associated with the theoretical movements of poststructuralism and postmodernism that, heavily influenced by the writings of Jacques Derrida, Michel Foucault, Jacques Lacan, and Roland Barthes, among others, was invested with terms such as "fragmentation," "heterogeneity," "disruption," and "subversion." And yet, it is striking how little attention has been paid to the ways in which processes and discourses discussed within this theoretical orientation are neither necessarily nor exclusively founded on indeterminacy and heterogeneity, but mostly permeated by a determinist orientation. A prominent example would be the scientific discipline of nonlinear dynamics, commonly called "chaos theory," that was often hailed as a postmodern science "theorizing its own evolution as discontinuous, catastrophic, nonrectifiable, and paradoxical" (5, 7, 60). Scholars such as N. Katherine Hayles, however, have demonstrated the extent to which nonlinear dynamics is a very deterministic discourse invested in canonizing and "taming" chaos rather than privileging it.[1] Chaos theory, in fact, turned out to be less a "postmodern science" than the science of globalization, which, also originally included in discussions of postmodernism, is now constantly theorized in terms of "connexity," interconnectedness, and networking.[2] Accordingly, the same period witnessed the emergence of a number of fictional "narratives of interconnectedness" whose plots weave together different characters and storylines from diverse times and places, such as the novels of David Mitchell and David Cunningham, as well as popular TV shows such as *Heroes*— and *Lost*. The indebtedness of *Lost* to this paradigm is evident, beyond its preoccupation with themes of destiny and fate, in its use of flashbacks and flashforwards to weave a sense of interconnectedness among its major characters. This latter sense must be seen as related to the status of *Lost* as a text symptomatic of the cultures of globalization, which I discuss in the second half of this discussion. That *Lost* chose to convey this sense through these specific narrative techniques is only indicative of the show's embeddedness in other contemporary determinist discourses, such as those of trauma theory and trauma culture, which is the first focus of my discussion.

## *"A Tale of Survival":* Lost *and Trauma Culture*

> JACK: Rose, you shouldn't be out here alone. You're suffering from post-traumatic shock.
> ROSE: Aren't we all? ["Walkabout" 1.4].

During the last fifty years, the concept of psychological trauma became the focus of a number of debates and representations across diverse disciplines and discourses to such an extent that critics have argued for the emergence of a "trauma culture," a "wound culture," or a "post-traumatic culture."[3] Originally theorized during a period ranging roughly from the 1860s to the 1930s, psychopathology began receiving renewed attention within the climate of the identity politics of the 1960s and the 1970s. Bringing the topic of trauma to the foreground of public debate, for instance, became part of the efforts of the feminist movement to expose secrets and abuses of patriarchy such as sexual assault, harassment, and rape. Around the same period, the contemporary antiwar movement was seeking to turn public attention to issues such as the combat neuroses suffered by Vietnam veterans. Research on veterans finally led to the inclusion of the term "post-traumatic stress disorder" (PTSD) in the American Psychiatric Association Diagnostic Manual in 1980, which is generally considered to be a turning point in the genealogy of the disease. This was followed by a series of intense debates among members of psychiatric communities on the nature and function of traumatic memory during the 1990s. Alongside these debates was a growing preoccupation in the Humanities with the question of representation of atrocious historical events such as the Holocaust, which eventually led to the emergence of "trauma theory"—a body of work which has engaged in deconstructive readings of Freud in order to investigate the philosophical implications of trauma for ideas of representation and referentiality, narrative and epistemology, and memory and history.

Theoretical speculations such as these were taking place at the same time as the emergence of a media culture of testimony and confession, represented by the increasing popularity of the talk show, the "real-life police show," and "court television," the rise of interest in Holocaust writing and the autobiographical memoir in fiction, and even the increasing appeal of documentaries and dramas on "near-death experiences" and alien abductions. Accompanying this trend was another emerging fascination with images of violence and destruction in genres such as the horror movie, the sci-fi blockbuster, and the serial killer film, followed by recurrent debates on internet pornography, pedophilia, and "violence in the media." By the late 90s, trauma seemed to be, according to Kirby Farrell, "both a clinical syndrome and a trope [...] a strategic fiction that a complex, stressful society is using to account for a world that seems threateningly out of control" (2). These diverse debates and discourses served as conditions for the emergence of "a culture centered on trauma," in Mark Seltzer's words: "a culture of the atrocity exhibition, in which people wear their damage like badges of identity" (2). In trauma culture, individuals and communities form their identities in terms of their shared experiences of suffering and victimhood, whether inflicted by colonialism and war or patriarchy and exploitation, in a cultural context where "extremity and survival are privileged markers of identity" (Luckhurst 2). "Survival" indeed is one of the defining experiences of post-traumatic culture, insofar as trauma has been described by Cathy Caruth as "an enigma of survival" (58). For Caruth, the incomprehensibility of trauma lies in its liminal positioning between destruction and survival, in its status as "a historical experience of a survival exceeding the grasp of the one who survives" (66). It is hardly a coincidence, then, that several of the features of trauma culture identified above have been seen by James Berger as part of a wider "fascination with and authority vested in the figure of the survivor" that he identifies in American culture from the late 1970s onwards (47). One specific example to demonstrate this fascination would be the Reality TV show *Survivor*, which was what the head of ABC, Lloyd Braun, had in mind when, in January 2004, he ordered an initial script for a show based on a crossover between *Survivor* and *Cast Away* (2000), a script that led to the pilot of *Lost*. The fact that *Lost* was originally promoted as "a tale of survival" only underscores the show's firm positioning within trauma culture.

In its early stages, *Lost* included trauma among its major themes, often referred to directly in dialogue. Within the first few episodes, we see Boone and Shannon arguing about how her constant denial of their situation results from the fact that she's "just been through a trauma," Rose is in a state of post-traumatic dissociation, and Jack interprets his visions of his father as a symptom of post-traumatic stress and considers Claire's claims to have been assaulted in her sleep to be stress-related hallucinations. Later, in "Outlaws" (1.16), after Charlie kills Ethan, Hurley is worried that he may be suffering from PTSD, which he discusses with Sayid, who is the character that *Lost* focuses on the most in order to deal with themes of trauma and guilt. In several episodes, Sayid mentions having nightmares about the people he tortured, some of whose voices he can still hear in his head — the flashback of the season three episode "Enter 77" (3.11) directly addresses this issue, as Sayid is captured by the husband of a woman he had tortured when still a member of the Republican Guard, and held captive until he admits that he remembers her and acknowledge his crimes. Trauma is therefore a theme permeating many different storylines, on and off the island. "One of the key preoccupations of *Lost*," Celeste-Marie Bernier confirms, concerns "the ways in which characters simultaneously deny and confront their sense of psychological, moral or emotional enslavement in traumatic acts of remembering and forgetting" (249).

*Lost* diverged from its interest in the subject of trauma in later seasons, when the plot came to concentrate more on the mythological, religious, and philosophical orientations of the show. But at the same time, paradoxically, the show embedded itself deeper within trauma culture in more sophisticated ways that affected the organization of its narrative structure and temporality. As I discuss below, there has been a lot of criticism on the peculiar, nonlinear temporality of trauma and the way in which it affects the production of narrative. Fictions of trauma attempt to convey that aspect of the disease by going "beyond presenting trauma as a subject matter or in characterization; they also incorporate the rhythms, processes, and uncertainties of trauma within the consciousness and structures of these works" (Vickroy xiv). The experimentation with temporality in *Lost*, in its use of flashbacks, flashforwards, and the motif of time travel itself, is tightly connected to its preoccupation with trauma and places the show even deeper within trauma culture.

## *"Nothing Is Irreversible":* Lost, *Temporality, and Trauma*

> MICHAEL: I found this in the wreckage and, hey, I figured why let a twenty-thousand-dollar watch go to waste, which is ridiculous, since time doesn't matter on a damn island! ["House of the Rising Sun" 1.6].

The most pervasive way in which *Lost* engages with the theme of trauma is its persistent return to "the scene of the accident," which the show almost obsessively restages in different ways throughout its six seasons. *Lost* opened with a spectacular scene of the plane crash, which the show returned to several times afterwards — for instance, we see the crash again from the perspective of the survivors of the tail section in "The Other 48 Days" (2.7) or of the Others in "A Tale of Two Cities" (3.1). The plane crash was soon restaged, albeit on a smaller scale, when the crashed plane from Nigeria collapses from the trees and causes Boone's death, whereas, in the outside world, Charles Widmore went as far as to restage an entire fake plane crash to prevent anyone from looking for the island. After leaving the island, a guilt-ridden Jack is obsessively traveling by plane in the hope of another crash, whereas all members of the Oceanic Six finally realize that they need to reproduce the conditions of the original crash, by boarding Ajira Flight 316, in order to go back. More generally, individual flashbacks and flashforwards also reveal several characters to have been victims or survivors of accidents: Jack, Claire, Locke's mother, Juliet's ex-husband, Locke himself, Michael — even Jacob's mother Claudia and the old woman before her arrived at the island two millennia ago "by accident." The accident, "the exemplary scene of trauma *par excellence*" (Caruth 6), was at the heart of the very origins of the mythology of *Lost*.

Someone might read these examples of narrative repetition as part of the general cyclical structure of *Lost* and link them to central themes such as those of rebirth, reconciliation and closure.[4] That *Lost* was progressing in cycles was only confirmed by its final images, which return to the Pilot's opening shots of Jack's eye and of Jack himself on the ground staring at the tops of trees before a blue sky. However, the show's persistent association of repetition with themes of loss and mourning seems to encourage an approach from the perspective of trauma theory. This is because one common post-traumatic symptom is the constant re-enactment of the traumatic incident in the patient's nightmares or hallucinations. Sayid's account of his experience of shooting a man while in the Republican Guard is representative: "I volunteered to be on the firing squad, and I did my duty without a single ounce of remorse. Then, for no reason, I found myself waking up at night, replaying what I did in my head" ("Outlaws" 1.16). What Freud termed the "repetition compulsion" was "a clear indication that a fixation to the moment of the traumatic accident lies at their root" whereby the patients "have not finished with the traumatic situation" but "were still faced by it as an immediate task which had not been dealt with" (274–5). It is for the sake of assimilating and mastering an experience originally too overwhelming to register in the psyche that traumatized subjects constantly revisit the scene of the incident: they have to go back.

The significance of trauma for *Lost* and its indebtedness to the determinist paradigm become obvious when focusing on the ways in which its overarching narrative constantly revolves around a series of major accidents, each of them interlinked to one another. After the crash, there is a growing suspicion that the island is in the aftermath of some disaster: the castaways find a distress call by Rousseau endlessly repeating itself for sixteen years, after her group arrived to the island in response to another recurrent transmission of the Numbers in endless loops. Repetition thus serves as a marker of some disaster, later referred to as "the incident," an industrial accident of a Dharma facility after which the Numbers have to be inputted into the computer of the hatch every 108 minutes, a loop the survivors find themselves caught up in during season two, only to bring about another incident in the season finale, after Locke's refusal to press the button. We also realize, in "Live Together, Die Alone" (2.23 and 2.24), that the plane crash itself was the result of a "system failure" in the hatch after Desmond delayed inputting the numbers. The megatext of *Lost* was therefore constantly revolving around these major incidents, each of them interconnected to one another through narrative repetition.

The "incident," in particular, is mentioned just briefly in the Dharma video shown in "Orientation" (2.3), only to lurk in the background as an absent presence before it is finally represented at the finale of season five. The repressed returns not from the past but from the future, as if in accordance with the second feature of traumatic temporality often discussed in terms of its implications for narrative and which has been termed by Freud as *Nachträglichkeit* (translated as "belatedness" or "deferred action"): individuals exposed to a trauma appear originally unaffected, only to develop symptoms — such as nightmares, amnesia, anxiety, or dissociation — after a period of "latency," usually lasting a few weeks. Trauma is therefore constituted by the relationship between two events, an earlier one that was not experienced as traumatic at its occurrence and a later one, again not inherently traumatic in itself, but responsible for triggering a memory of the earlier event that ascribes it with traumatic meaning. For Freud, "trauma was thus constituted by a dialectic between two events, neither of which was intrinsically traumatic, and a temporal delay or latency through which the past was available only by a deferred act of understanding and interpretation" (Leys 20). Narratives of trauma have conveyed that aspect of traumatic temporality by recourse to the technique of the "intrusive flashback trope" which, Maureen Turim confirms, is often used as "a way of signaling and exploring the return of trauma" (207). That the flashbacks of *Lost* served this function was easily recognizable during the first three seasons, as most of the backstories involved stories of loss, mourning, and death, played out against similar or reminiscent situations on the island, which the characters had to deal with in order to atone for their sense of guilt. *Lost*, however, conveyed traumatic belatedness in even more sophisticated ways later on, in its introduction of "flash-forwards." A major implication of the concept of belatedness is the reversal of ordinary causality, of the relationship between cause and effect: the trauma is experienced only when it is remembered, in the future. Trauma therefore, Thomas Elsaesser suggests, "not only names the delay between an event and its (persistent, obsessive) return, but also a reversal of affect and meaning across this gap in time" (197). In this respect, the "future memory" introduced in the narrative by the technique of the flashforward may be seen as nothing other than a literalization of this aspect of traumatic belatedness. *Lost* almost begs for such a reading, as it introduced the concept of the flashfoward precisely at the level of character psychology, by focusing on Desmond, whose ability to "remember" scenes from the future was presented as a *symptom*, a result of his exposure to electromagnetism at the implosion of the hatch.

It was precisely through this focus on trauma and the accompanying determinist orientation that the show introduced the theme of time travel in season five — it is hardly coincidence, for instance, that Locke's very first "time travel" in "Because You Left" (5.1) takes him back to the scene of Boone's death, the Nigerian plane crash. *Lost* directly establishes parallelisms between time travel and trauma, as may be seen in the dialogue between Sawyer and Daniel in the same episode: as the two are arguing, Daniel is trying to convince him that, from the perspective of physics, he cannot change the past. Sawyer replies: "Everyone I care about just blew up on your damn boat. I know what I can't change," in a exchange that raises a parallelism between the former's understanding of the inability to alter the past in theoretical terms and the latter's reference to death and loss. Accordingly, the temporal anomaly between the island and the outside world in "The Shape of Things to Come" (4.9) follows the rhythms of traumatic belatedness: the survivors find the dead body of the doctor of the freighter washed on the beach before the doctor is actually killed by Keamy on the freighter. From this perspective, even if many felt that *Lost* "jumped the shark" after it introduced time travel, this direction was very much in line both with its own previous engagement with trauma and with an existing tradition of fictional narratives of time travel. As a "disease of time," trauma may be seen as a form of perpetual repetitive "time travel" back to the moment of the traumatic event.[5] It is for this reason that time-travel narratives often revolve around a major event which structures their temporal pattern: recent examples would include films like *Déjà Vu* (2006), *The Butterfly Effect* (2006), or *Twelve Monkeys* (1995), whereas even the archetypal story of time travel, H.G. Wells's *The Time Machine*, may be read as a fragmented, disjointed, non-linear narrative whereby the Time Traveler tries to narrate his experience: "This room and you and the atmosphere of every day is too much for my memory. Did I ever make a Time Machine, or a model of a Time Machine? Or is it all only a dream?" (68).

The indebtedness of the show to the determinist paradigm in its treatment of temporality and trauma is obvious in the episode "Flashes Before Your Eyes" (3.8): In one of his "mind travels," Desmond is with Ms. Hawking when they witness — again — an accident involving a man wearing red shoes. When Desmond asks her why she did not prevent it when she knew it would happen, Ms. Hawking informs him that it is impossible to change the past: "The universe has a way of course correcting." One cannot "undo" past trauma; the only way for someone to deal with it is to learn to live with it. The strong determinism of the show's treatment of temporality and trauma, however, is parallel to its engagement with ideas of interconnectedness in space, an aspect that I discuss in the following section of this article.

## *"No Place Like Home": Mobility, Displacement, and the Global Unhomely*

> MELISSA COLE: Always moving. There's always two reasons why a man would do that, Sayid. Either he's running away from something. Or he's looking for something ["The Greater Good" 1.21].

"When, days after September 2001, our gaze was transfixed by the images of the plane hitting one of the WTC towers, we were all forced to experience [...] the compulsion to repeat [...]: we wanted to see it again and again; the same shots were repeated *ad nauseam*" (Žižek 11–12). Slavoj Žižek's discussion of 9/11 offers a pertinent example of traumatic repetition which may be read against the politics of trauma in *Lost*. The terrorist attacks on the World Trade Center gave the concept of trauma further currency on a global scale. Shortly after the attacks, Susannah Radstone was claiming that "as the events of September 11 emerge as auguries that diminish hopes for a 'new' millennium, the 'turn to trauma' appears to be deepening" (118). More recently, Allen Meek has confirmed that "the events of September 11, 2001, brought the representation of traumatic experience right to the centre of contemporary media culture in new and dramatic ways" (4). More relevant, however, is Walter Kalaidjian's description of 9/11 as "the inaugural trauma of the twenty-first century" that "decisively sutured globalization and disaster into the defining symptom of our times" (829). Originally accompanied by a utopian rhetoric promising the mutual interaction of diverse cultures, the improvement of living standards in Third World countries, and the expansion of human rights and liberal democracy around the globe, globalization has, during the last three decades, been increasingly associated with imperialism, exploitation, disaster and catastrophe: "Not simply an effect or cause of globalization, disaster happens more as the former's internal limit: one that demystifies globalization as itself being the disastrous object rather than the idealized subject of its encompassing historicity."[6] The 9/11 attack was only one of a series of events that strengthened the associations between global interconnectedness and destruction:

> Financed by a network of global fundraising organizations, facilitated by international wire transfers of capital, coordinated in real time through sophisti-

cated telecommunications networks involving cell phones and the Internet, not to mention aviation as such — all in the service of orchestrating a media spectacle surpassing even the wildest imaginings of Hollywood cinema — 9/11 was in every sense a product of advanced globalization itself, homegrown on American soil [831].

From the beginning, *Lost* consciously presented itself as a post–9/11 text. Imagery of plane crashes was bound to bring associations with the Twin Towers attacks to audiences only three years after the event, a reading encouraged by the writers, who chose to set the date of the crash on September 22. Furthermore, the networks of financial institutions, transnational corporations, and the technologies of surveillance and global transportation that Kalaidjian mentions above are hardly absent from the universe of *Lost*. The Others turn out to operate in the outside world as the privately funded Mittelos Bioscience corporation, whereas when the Oceanic Six leave the island, they find themselves enmeshed in networks of surveillance set up by Ben and Widmore: the "real world" of season five turned out to be one of paranoia and conspiracy. In its invocation of conspiracy culture, *Lost* establishes further connections with discourses of globalization, insofar as conspiracy has been diagnosed by Fredric Jameson as "a degraded attempt ... to think of the impossible totality of the contemporary world system" (38). The figure to best represent the forces of global corporate power would be Charles Widmore, who, as part of his intricate plan to find the island—which, it is hinted, may be motivated by plans to exploit it—he sponsors Faraday's research and Desmond's race around the world. Desmond is only one of a number of characters who, before or after their time on the island, are seen as being in a state of constant mobility: Sayid is in search of Nadia, Kate is "born to run" as the object of pursuit by Edward Mars across countries and continents, and so on. It is perhaps more accurate to suggest that the universe of *Lost* is one oscillating between a sense of entrapment and a sense of constant mobility and flux; a world where, with enough money and enough determination, you can find anyone.

Furthermore, from the beginning, the show tried to deal with issues directly relevant to the post–9/11 global political landscape. In fact, *Lost* was set up in such a way during its first season that it seemed as if it were going to address issues of cultural difference and conflict within the multicultural group of survivors more than it actually did in later seasons. In the pilot, we see African American Michael confronted with the strict patriarchal culture of the Korean couple, Jin getting offended when Hurley will not eat his food, Charlie making jokes about the French, and Sawyer fighting with Sayid because he thinks he may be a terrorist. Sayid was the character that *Lost* focused on the most in order to deal with issues of cultural difference, Islamophobia, and terrorism, issues which, importantly, the show chose to address through references to practices of burial and mourning: in several episodes Sayid is shown to insist that the dead are buried according to their wishes and religious beliefs, whether it is the bodies of the dead of the plane crash (in "Walkabout" 1.4), his friend Essam (in the flashback of "The Greater Good"), or the body of Naomi (in "The Economist" 4.3). This focus on mourning as a practice signifying cultural difference further underscores the status of *Lost* as a text symptomatic of the emerging dialectic between trauma and globalization.

The relation of *Lost* to this dialectic, however, extends further, in its references to discourses of imperial and global power. In her reading of the colonial subtext of *Lost*, Berrnier reads the presence of the slave ship *Black Rock* and the crashed Nigerian plane loaded with heroin as "visceral reminders of African and African American histories of European colonization and slavery" (242) and the island itself as "fraught with issues of colonialism, nationhood, race, difference and military conflicts for power" (245). These references may be seen as relevant to the indebtedness of *Lost* to discourses of globalization, especially when bearing in mind the theoretical view of the latter as a renewed form of neo-colonialism, "cultural imperialism," or "recolonization of subject peoples" by the imperial North that extends its economic, political, and cultural sources of control over subordinated peoples of the South (Tandon 173). More important, however, is Bernier's association of the show's colonial subtext with its engagement with trauma culture: these "physical artifacts of slavery and colonialism" are compared to the intrusive flashbacks, which "reveal the internal lives of individuals to establish their needs to exorcise repressed memories and come to terms with their respective pasts" (248). Personal memories of death, loss, and trauma are thus interwoven with collective histories of oppression, destruction, and subordination through the juxtaposition of different timelines:

> By relying on a fragmented, cyclical, and elliptical narrative framework, this series dramatizes the ways in which hidden histories of racial difference and legacies of amnesia, as perpetuated by dominant groups, can impact upon the personal psychological journeys of individuals, regardless of historical period or national origins [245].

Indeed, a closer examination of the island's past reveals its history to be nothing but a series of arrivals, invasions, and settlements. *Lost* persistently tries to represent conflicts between different groups on the island in geopolitical terms, relying on binary oppositions of "us" and "them," self and "Other," specifically within a Cold War context. Apart from serving as a site for U.S. military testings of H-bombs in the fifties, the arrival of the Dharma initiative on the island in the seventies is presented as an occupation of territory that creates friction and conflict with the existing inhabitants of the island, the Hostiles, which actually leads to the genocide of the Dharma Initiative during the so-called "purge." After the purge, the former Soviet soldier Mikhail reveals in "Enter 77" that four men arrived to his station to set a "line extending through the valley" that he is not supposed to cross, something that the Others also demand of the survivors of flight 815 in "The Hunting Party" (2.11). The significance of borders, "lines," limits, and boundaries seems to betray an affiliation more with earlier political formations associated with classic forms of imperialism, such as the nation-state, which has been described by Benedict Anderson as "*limited* because even the largest of them, encompassing perhaps a billion living human beings, has finite, if elastic, boundaries, beyond which lie other nations" (7), than with contemporary networks of power and sovereignty associated with globalization, which is often seen as "a *decentered* and *deterritorializing* apparatus of rule that progressively incorporates the entire global realm within its open, expanding frontiers" (Hardt and Negri xii). It is therefore tempting to see the politics of *Lost* as reactionary, regressive, and nostalgic of the "safety" of Cold War dialectics, a reading offered by Michael Newbury who has seen the Others as a group that lives in "cozy 1950s subdivisions complete with lawn furniture" and works in hatches that look like "bomb shelters frozen in the styles of the 1970s" and, as such, functions "more fully through images and practices aligned with the nation-state than they do through familiar representations of the terrorist, insurgent or even dissident" (204). The intrusive flashbacks serve to repress individual narratives of global mobility and cultural difference in order to keep the group of survivors united in terms of their shared "hostility to the sterile, white and bipolar past" (205). *Lost* turns out to be "more a narrative of assimilation than a narrative of multinationalism or transnational affiliation" (206).

Newbury is right to identify the strong Cold War context of the show, but perhaps not enough attention is paid to the extent to which *Lost* is constantly "othering" the Cold War past, as both the Dharma Initiative and the Others were exposed for being more corrupt than their utopian pretensions would suggest. Furthermore, *Lost* was increasingly characterized by a tendency to destabilize distinctions between self and other: often the castaways are seen as or are accused of being worse than the Others as they capture, torture, and even kill members of their group. Each group also ends up becoming joined, even if fleetingly at times, by members of the opposite camp — such as Jack, Juliet, Ben, and Locke — in storylines that consistently foreground their status as the "other" of the group. The boundaries between self and other are challenged even further when some of the survivors end up occupying and living in the Barracks of the Others, whereas in season five, some of them end up becoming members of the Dharma Initiative in the seventies. During season four, both groups join forces against Widmore and the multicultural group he sent to the island to find Ben. If anything, *Lost* demonstrates the difficulty of sustaining clear-cut distinctions between "us" and "them" under the global order of things.

Widmore's motives, however, turn out to go beyond the potential exploitation of the island: he just wants to return back "home," from where he had been exiled by Ben. Like many other major characters on *Lost*, his entire behavior is triggered by a sense of displacement, rootlessness, and "unhomeliness" that permeates *Lost* at many different levels. Jack, Locke, Juliet, Ben, Widmore, and even minor characters like Miles and Charlotte are driven by a quest to locate and arrive at what they understand to be "home." During its six years, *Lost* set out to demonstrate that, under a global order often theorized in terms of constant flow, flux, mobility, and travel, the unhomely has become a constant state of being and "going home" is not as simple as it used to be. It is within this focus on ideas of displacement and unhomeliness that we may approach the treatment of the theme of abduction in *Lost*. Roger Luckhurst has demonstrated the ways in which the proliferation of abduction scenarios in American culture of the 1990s served as fantasy spaces for the "science-fictionalization of traumas" of imperial states such as the United States and allegorize "post-national anxiety perversely reiterating the foundation of America — an economy based, after all, on the abduction of Africans into slavery" (44). *Lost* follows the tradition of shows such as *The X-Files* that represent abduction in terms and images from trauma culture, even if it moves away from Chris Carter's show by domesticating the theme: it is not little green men, but people, the Others, that abduct "fit" men and subject women to medical tests on birth control and surveillance. After being abducted and returned, Claire suffers from traumatic amnesia, only to get intrusive flashbacks in "Maternity Leave" (2.15) and agree to get hypnotized by Libby in order to access her repressed memories. Claire, however, is hardly the only one to be abducted on the show: so is Charlie, who in "Fire + Water" (2.12) also tries to abduct Aaron while sleepwalking, something that Rousseau, whose own daughter Alex was taken by the Others, also tries to do in "Exodus" (1.23, 1.24, and 1.25). In fact, the entire mythology of *Lost* is founded on abduction, as, in "Across the Sea" (6.15), we find out that Jacob and his brother are taken away from their mother Claudia after she was murdered by the unnamed old woman. The "loss" of *Lost* thus consists precisely at the eruption of the uncanny, at an individual, familial, communal, or global level. The unhomely, "the paradigmatic colonial and post-colonial condition" (9), turns out to be at the very origins of the mythology of *Lost*: when the old woman asks the Man in Black, later to turn into the Black Smoke, why he is so desperate to leave the island, he replies: "I don't belong here!"

It is for this reason that *Lost* responds to the sense of temporal entrapment and spatial displacement with a constant effort to "erase" the uncanny through its persistent focus on the significance of "home," community, and utopia, an aspect of the show that leads to its final closure. From as early as the episode "White Rabbit" (1.5), Jack urges the group to stay together and collaborate if they want to survive on the island: "Every man for himself is not gonna work." The importance of community is also underlined often by scenes, usually at the end of an episode, where the camera pans around the group in scenes of everyday life activities. A second set of scenes focusing on communal existence, however, complementary to the previous ones, are those featuring moments of burial and mourning. In the universe of *Lost,* mourning is one of the practices that safeguards a sense of community and its boundaries: it is for this reason that, in his attempt to recruit Jack to join the Others, Ben asks him, in "The Cost of Living" (3.5), to attend the funeral ritual of one of their members. It is for this same reason that, in "LaFleur" (5.8), at the event of a conflict with the Hostiles, the Dharma Initiative have to bury any Hostiles they may kill and take any dead bodies of their own back to their own territory. By the end of the show, Jacob directly reveals to the major characters that he chose to bring them together because they were all "flawed" and "lonely." In this respect, *Lost* exemplifies a common argument often made in trauma studies, that trauma creates new identities based on shared experiences of victimhood and suffering. In a world that has witnessed what Charles Turner has described as a "rejection of the claims of collective belonging and obligation which a state or political community might make on individuals" (47), the discourse of grief, suffering, and trauma has become the best model in which to conceptualize social collectives since, in Judith Butler's words, it "furnishes a sense of political community of a complex order" (22). In this respect, the finale of *Lost* provides a closure to its narrative that is entirely consistent to its relation to the dialectic between trauma and globalization outlined above: all the major characters are driven, despite themselves, to a church at an unidentified time and place, in order to reunite, remember, and let go.

This discussion has far from exhausted the subject. More issues might need to be addressed relating either to the gender politics of the psychoanalytic orientation of *Lost* and its persistent staging of Oedipal conflicts with "bad fathers," its politics of traumatic representation (who defines an event as traumatic? for whom?), or its Orientalist representations of South East Asian cultures. Regardless of its arguable shortcomings, however, *Lost* proves itself to be a text that successfully manages to convey the ways in which individual tragedy and collective trauma reverberate in an increasingly interconnected world.

## NOTES

1. See Hayles.
2. See Mulgan.
3. See Seltzer, Farrell, and Kaplan.
4. For a reading that interprets the function of memory and temporality from a philosophical perspective, see J. M. Berger.
5. See Young.

## WORKS CITED

Anderson, Benedict. *Imagined Communities*. London: Verso, 1991. Print.
Berger, James. *After the End: Representations of Post-Apocalypse*. Minneapolis: University of Minnesota Press, 1999. Print.
Berger, J. M. "Flashbacks, Memory and Non-Linear Time." *Lost Online Studies*, 1.2 (2006). Web. 31 June 2010.
Bernier, Celeste-Marie. "'A Fabricated Africanist Persona': Race, Representation and Narrative Experimentation in *Lost*." *Reading Lost: Perspectives on a Hit Television Show*. Ed. Roberta Pearson. London: I.B. Tauris, 2009. 241–260. Print.
Bhabha, Homi K. *The Location of Culture*. London: Routledge, 1994. Print.
Butler, Judith. *Precarious Life: The Powers of Mourning and Violence*. London: Verso, 2004. Print.
Caruth, Cathy. *Unclaimed Experience: Trauma, Narrative, and History*. Baltimore and London: John Hopkins University Press, 1996. Print.
Elsaesser, Thomas. "Postmodernism as Mourning Work." *Screen* 42:2 (2001). 193–201. Print.
Farrell, Kirby. *Post-Traumatic Culture: Injury and Interpretation in the Nineties*. Baltimore and London: John Hopkins University Press, 1998. Print.
Freud, Sigmund. "Fixation to Traumas—The Unconscious." *The Standard Edition of the Complete Psychological Works of Sigmund Freud*, vol. 16. Trans. James Strachey, Eds. James Strachey et al. London: Hogarth Press, 1963. 274–5. Print.
Hardt, Michael and Antonio Negri. *Empire*. London and Cambridge, Mass.: Harvard University Press, 2000. Print.
Hayles, Katherine N. *Chaos Bound: Orderly Disorder in Contemporary Literature and Science*. Ithaca and London: Cornell University Press, 1990. Print.
Jameson, Frederic. *Postmodernism or, the Cultural Logic of Late Capitalism*. London: Verso, 1991. Print.
Kalaidjian, Walter. "Incoming: Globalisation, Disaster, Poetics." *South Atlantic Quarterly* 106:4 (2007), 825–48. Print.
Kaplan, E. Ann. *Trauma Culture: The Politics of Terror and Loss in Media and Literature*. New Brunswick, NJ: Rutgers University Press, 2005. Print.
Leys, Ruth. *Trauma: A Genealogy*. Chicago and London: The University of Chicago Press, 2000. Print.
Luckhurst, Roger. "The Science-Fictionalization of Trauma: Remarks on Narratives of Alien Abduction." *Science-Fiction Studies* 25:1 (1998). 29–52. Print.
_____. *The Trauma Question*. London: Routledge, 2008. Print.
Lyotard, Jean-Francois. *The Postmodern Condition: A Report on Knowledge*. Trans. Geoff Bennington and Brian Massumi. Minneapolis: University of Minnesota Press, 1984. Print.
Meek, Allen. *Trauma and Media: Theories, Histories, and Images*. London: Routledge, 2010. Print.
Mulgan, Geoff. *Connexity: Responsibility, Freedom, Business and Poser in the New Century*. London: Vintage, 1998. Print.
Newbury, Michael. "Lost in the Orient: Transnationalism Interrupted." *Reading Lost: Perspectives*

*on a Hit Television Show.* Ed. Roberta Pearson. London: I.B. Tauris, 2009. 201–220. Print.

Radstone, Susannah. "The War of the Fathers: Trauma, Fantasy, and September 11." *Trauma at Home: After 9/11.* Ed. Judith Greenberg. Lincoln and London: The University of Nebraska Press, 2003. 117–23. Print.

Seltzer, Mark. *Serial Killers: Death and Life in America's Wound Culture.* New York: Routledge, 1998. Print.

Tandon, Yash. "Recolonization of Subject Peoples." *Alternatives* 19:2 (1994), 173–83. Print.

Turim, Maureen. "The Trauma of History: Flashbacks upon Flashbacks." *Screen* 42:2 (2001). 205–210. Print.

Turner, Charles. "Holocaust Memories and History." *History of the Human Sciences* 9:4 (1996). 45–63. Print.

Wells, H.G. *The Time Machine*, in *The Science Fiction: Volume I*. London: Phoenix, 1995. Print.

Vickroy, Laurie. *Trauma and Survival in Contemporary Fiction.* Charlottesville, VA: University of Virginia Press, 2002. Print.

Young, Allan. *The Harmony of Illusions: The Invention of Post-Traumatic Stress Disorder.* Princeton: Princeton University Press, 1995. Print.

Žižek, Slavoj. *Welcome to the Desert of the Real.* London and New York: Verso, 2002. Print.

# New Space, New Time, and Newly Told Tales: *Lost* and *The Tempest*

*Ryan Howe*

There is a famous romantic adventure story about survivors of a crash who are stranded on an island thought to be uninhabited. As the story unfolds, the island's magical properties appear. There is a mysterious and dangerous monster plotting mischief. Intersecting groups battle to control the island. Past relationships between parents and children and between siblings prompt significant dramatic action. Of course I am describing *Lost*, but William Shakespeare's play *The Tempest* also fits that description, despite being written nearly four centuries before the six-season run of the television show that is the subject of this book.

The similarities between these two dramatic narratives stretch well beyond the surface level. The television series echoes the play in setting, form, and theme. The show's writers most overtly reference Shakespeare's island drama by naming a Dharma station — the poison delivery system — after the play, but the play echoes throughout the series in many ways. Of course, with *Lost*, it is not terribly surprising to find such connections with another work of literature.

From the Bible to Stephen King, *Lost* revels in its hypertextuality. Some references might easily be dismissed as comical or whimsical, but their pervasiveness compels contemplation from the dedicated audience member. Indeed, throughout the series, fans of the television series "theorized" about the plot and meaning of the story based on its usage of recognizable references to countless literary and popular works. In the case of *The Tempest*, the deep connections between the works reveal more than the admittedly fun hypertextual wit of television writers. *Lost* and *The Tempest* share elements of form and content that derive from the way they address advancing technology and accelerating cultural change in the worlds of their creations. These two dramatic narratives, separated by four centuries, experiment with space, time, and ideas about the afterlife that derive from and feed off the cultural anxieties of their respective worlds.

William Shakespeare probably wrote *The Tempest* late in his career. Most scholars consider it to be the final play he wrote without significant collaboration. Because of this, many view the play as Shakespeare's farewell to the theatre. It opens with the titular terrible storm that leaves a royal entourage from Milan shipwrecked on a seemingly deserted island far away from civilization. The royal party includes the King of Naples (Alonso), his younger brother (Sebastian), his son (Ferdinand), and the duke of Milan (Antonio), as well as other characters such as the old councilor Gonzalo, the drunken butler (Stefano), and the jester (Trinculo). After the shipwreck, Ferdinand is mistakenly thought to be dead. Instead, he has washed ashore on a part of the island inhabited by the magician Prospero, his daughter Miranda, and Ariel, a magical spirit under Prospero's control. During a long second scene, Prospero reveals to his daughter (and the audience) that he is actually the rightful duke of Milan. Twelve years prior, his brother Antonio usurped the dukedom and abandoned Prospero and his young daughter on a raft at sea. With the help of the old councilor Gonzalo, who secretly provided Prospero with supplies and a collection of books, Prospero manages to land and survive on the island, where he uses his books to develop his magical capabilities. Prospero then recounts how the island was previously controlled by the witch Sycorax, who imprisoned Ariel and left her monster-son Caliban on the island. Lost and alone, the king's son Ferdinand stumbles upon Prospero's daughter Miranda, who remembers seeing no man heretofore except for her father and Caliban. Miranda and Ferdinand fall in love and plan a wedding. Meanwhile, Antonio and Sebastian plot to kill the grieving Alonso so that Sebastian can become king, and Stefano and Trinculo conspire with Caliban to overthrow Prospero as ruler of the island. Following the wedding ceremony, Prospero uncovers both nefarious plots and announces his identity and his intention to return to Milan as the rightful Duke. Following a night of storytelling, they will return to Milan and the spirit Ariel will be set free.

As many scholars have noted, the play is heavily influenced by popular accounts of new world exploration, such as references to the wreck of the *Sea Adventure* in 1609 (Shakespeare, 218). For Shakespeare's England of the early seventeenth century, recent technology — especially in transportation — must have simultaneously seemed to shrink and expand the world. Europeans traveled back and forth across vast oceans once considered too large to traverse. At the same time, colonial interactions with new peoples (unfortunately often destructive) sparked imagination and anxiety inherent in the collisions of previously disconnected cultures.

Starting with a passenger jet crash, *Lost* premiered merely three years following a terrorist attack in which the violent exploitation of such jets alerted people around the world to just how small their planet had become. The terrorist attacks of September 11, 2001 shocked America. At the start of the twenty-first century, geography no longer isolated such a powerful nation and culture from its global neighbors — for better or worse. Communication technology also successfully minimized geographic distance between individual people. Just about a century earlier than *Lost*'s premiere, communication between people in Sydney and Los Angeles would have meant a written letter or a still photograph delivered by ocean vessel over the course of weeks. By 2004, technology allowed for immediate audio and video communication. In such ways, technology has changed previous limits imposed by geographic space — both in terms of the security isolation provides and the temporal distance it demands.

Similarly, communication technologies have broken down traditional understandings of time. Recording technology allows for the screening of events long past and people long dead, and instantaneous communication has forced a new understanding of time differences around the world. No doubt, these changes precipitate reactionary anxieties in cultures around the world. All of this is not to say, of course, that the early seventeenth and twenty-first centuries are entirely unique as times of particular global anxiety. Every era, relative to the perspective of its inhabitants, balances imagination and anxiety over the changes accumulated knowledge brings. Nevertheless, there can be little doubt that technological innovation characterizes the cultural context of both *The Tempest* and *Lost*.

In examining the origin of these stories, I do not suggest that the culture at large or its circumstances fully spurred their creations. Surely, the individual authors tell imaginative tales that are not solely derivations of community anxieties. Still, both works draw from the predilection of popular audiences. Like contemporary broadcast television, the theatres of Shakespeare's London had every financial imperative to appeal to the broadest possible audience. There are many ways to reconcile the complicated origins of popular stories. In this case, I find Brian Boyd's "evocritical" approach particularly useful in my continued discussion of these works. In *On the Origin of Stories*, Boyd makes use of the natural science of evolution to explain the human capacity for and attraction to narrative and storytelling. In short, Boyd proposes that narrative storytelling derives from its usefulness in promoting human adaptation to the unknown. This is similar to the evolutionary purpose of play: to practice for unknown and emergent dangers. Boyd points out that many animals, including humans, find great joy in play that, at its evolutionary core, serves as a rehearsal for survival situations. Running and wrestling, for example, provide practice for flight and fight situations. Adding an advantage to mere instinct, play provides complex species like humans the opportunity to prepare for unknown — or rapidly changing — circumstances. Because humans are primarily social creatures, positive social positioning prompts protection from an individual's community, diminishes the likelihood of demise, and increases the likelihood of sexual success. According to Boyd, creative, fictional narratives can prepare individuals to cope with unknown circumstances in the future — especially those of a social nature. Thus, Boyd argues, there is a distinct evolutionary advantage to the social agility and understanding gained through storytelling. In this essay, I approach these two dramas while keeping Boyd's ideas in mind.

If Boyd is correct, then our brains have evolved with genetic tendencies to find ways of adapting to broad changes in circumstance. Storytelling has the capacity to provide aid in accommodating and adapting to changes that are continual and unpredictable. In the context of the accelerated technological innovation that I have suggested alter human conceptions of space and time, both audience attention and the storytellers themselves look to fictional narratives for how to best deal with these changes. At the risk of oversimplification, one might consider whether or not the dramas ask: "How might our stories fit our *new* and changing world?" That question itself reveals a preoccupation about a particular kind of passage of time: from one era to another. Both *Lost* and *The Tempest* investigate the rapidly changing perceptions of the world in a peculiarly similar way: by deviating from conventional dramatic forms. These deviations specifically address conventions of time and space within the stories' respective genres.

Late in his career, William Shakespeare wrote a series of plays not easily sorted into one of the three conventional categories of drama: tragedy, comedy, and history. *Cymbeline*, *Pericles*, and *The Winter's Tale*, along with *The Tempest*, are usually considered to be *romances*. Each of these plays contains expanses of time and space — well beyond the narrative limitations of one day and one place. In *The Winter's Tale*, for example, Time himself walks on stage, and, functioning as chorus, declares that sixteen years have passed since the previous act. Pericles' odyssey takes him from one side of the Mediterranean to the other. This distinctive expansion of time and space, along with life-and-death stakes, tragicomic swings of action, dramatic focus on personal redemption, and discovery of long lost family members, characterize the plays' collective grouping as romances. Yet *The Tempest* takes the inverse approach to time and place when compared to the other three. Instead of literally setting the dramatic action across time and space — a narrative technique that allows for genre-defying stories on a grand, sweeping scale — *The Tempest* takes place over no more than a few hours in a small island setting.

In some ways similar to the generic classification of Elizabethan and

Jacobean England, contemporary television relies on attention to genre and form. Even when that consideration functions to allow producers to defy audience expectation, most every television drama is categorized as either an hour-long "drama" or a half-hour "comedy." Also like Shakespeare's England, these forms are malleable, and the most interesting of storytellers twist them into captivating shapes. In his essay, "Narrative Complexity in Contemporary American Television," Jason Mittel refers to the ways in which contemporary American television writers manipulate narrative expectations as "narrative complexity" (Mittel 29). Among the television series Mittel identifies, *Lost* uses time and space in the most complex ways. Over the course of six seasons, *Lost* compresses and expands both time and space in complicated and entertaining patterns. But rather than experimenting with such forms on an episode-by-episode basis, *Lost* shifts from season to season. In the remainder of this essay, I examine both *The Tempest* and *Lost* by identifying both *how* they approach physical and metaphysical space and time and the *possible* reasons *why* they do so in the context of new cultural perceptions of space and time.

## Space

Adventure stories, or romances, usually include great expanses of space. Whether it is Odysseus' eventful travels around the Mediterranean or Indiana Jones's plane trips (helpfully represented with a red line moving across a map), geographic distance excites an audience's imagination. Taking narrative as an evolutionary advantage, why might we be drawn to such stories? First, it is surely to our advantage to learn of exotic locales prior to encountering them ("What if I'm kidnapped by pirates and taken to a land far away?"). As Boyd argues, our interest in telling and following fictional narratives provides us a chance to understand the vast potentials of the unknown. There is an evolutionary advantage in adapting to exotic terrain, climate, and culture. These kinds of stories have the potential to prepare us for such adaptation. In the context of technological innovation that allows people to travel across great distances, we need to adapt to the possibility of such travel as well as to adapt to the people who travel to our location and culture.

Scholars have argued over whether the *Tempest* island is in the Mediterranean or somewhere in the western hemisphere. John Gillies, for example, makes a strong case for the connections between the play and contemporary ideas of the British colony in Virginia (Shakespeare 215). Others, such as Barbara Fuchs, have argued that the island in the play pertains to England's colonization of Ireland and islands in the Mediterranean. At the literal level, of course, most agree that the geography of the island is ambiguous. This ambiguity has prompted centuries of discourse over how to identify the monstrous Caliban and his mother Sycorax in terms of their cultures. I have no interest here in engaging in the debate about the play's relevance regarding colonialization, but the debate's prominence suggests, at the minimum, that the play engages the fantasies and anxieties regarding a more connected globe. At the risk of oversimplifying complicated notions, it is easily possible to see how the island drama inspires such fantasies and excites such anxieties. If Ariel and Caliban are "others" with magical capabilities and dangerous instincts, it doesn't take much to understand that Miranda's "brave new world" is surely the audience's own, too. Yet at first glance, the spatial limitations of the play's setting seem to undermine its expansive themes. Unlike Shakespeare's other romances, the dramatic action of the play only occurs on one small island. This limitation, however, might be considered a way of "zooming in" on a particular geography. From that perspective, the discrete setting effectively magnifies the space in which the collision of creatures of exotic origins occurs. In a way then, the *Tempest* island reflects the perspective of the shrunken world at the same time as its characters mark the diversity of an expansive globe.

*Lost*'s geography functions similarly. The main thrust of the story occurs on a similarly isolated island. Like the *Tempest* island, the *Lost* island serves as the setting for the collision of cultures — some of which are profoundly mysterious and perhaps even magical. The close proximity of the survivors of flight 815 to the "Others," the Dharma Initiative, the "freighter folk," and the Ajira passengers parallels the tensions present between cultural collisions prompted by a shrinking world. *Lost*'s cast of characters similarly reflects the significance of contemporary globalization. The Oceanic survivors not only include principal characters from America, Australia, Great Britain, Iraq, Korea, and Nigeria, but are also played by actors from around the world. As each season of the series progresses, characters from all over the world join the story.

The drawing from peoples around the world to a discrete geographic space serves more than allegorical purposes. After all, this particular collision of cultures occurs outside of regular concepts of geography. As Desmond's frustrated attempts to sail away from the island prove, leaving the island is not as simple as leaving other places. Frank's successful attempts to fly from the island require a complex approach to conventional geography. The end of season four climaxes with the island "moving," an act prompted by the turning of a large wheel. *Lost* occurs on an island that is both discrete and limited, but not ordinary. The island is easily comprehensible at first glance, but extraordinary as the story progresses. Its extraordinary nature holds great value even within the story as Charles Widmore and his daughter Penny, for example, spend millions of dollars in a competitive search to locate the island. During the final episodes of the television series, the narrative answers some questions about the extraordinary power of the island. The plugged light source at the center of the cave definitely appears to mark a battleground between right and wrong, light and dark, and Jacob and the Man in Black. People from all over the globe are drawn to this discrete and elusive location for an enactment of the oldest of conflicts — the one between good and evil. Regardless of their complicated and exotic origins, the final dramatic conflicts are reduced to a simple, foundational one. On the *Tempest* island, Prospero has ruled for twelve years — as he should have been doing in Milan. In order to regain his usurped dukedom, Prospero must bring his brother to his magical island. Once on the island, the good can prevail.

Both stories entertain with exotic settings. The characters that populate the stories come from distant lands. Both stories take place in isolated, small places of universal importance. Jacob, then Jack, then Hurley, protects the universal good by ruling over the *Lost* island. Prospero justly rules the *Tempest* island in proxy for Milan, before regaining his rightful place by harnessing the power of the island. The anxieties of a vast world shrunken by technology reverberate through both of these stories. By shrinking the globe to geographically ambiguous and isolated islands, the stories accommodate these anxieties by occurring in discrete settings. Yet the limited space does more than accommodate the anxieties; the setting magnifies and distills fundamental conflicts that arise from changing circumstances. As Locke says to Jack in the first season episode "White Rabbit" (1.5), "This place is different. It's special. The others don't want to talk about it because it scares them. But we all know it. We all feel it." The islands provide a discrete exploration of the mysterious — a framework for successful adaptation to the unknown on our frighteningly vast home where the safety once provided by distance has begun to disappear. The islands, like Earth, are not actually endlessly vast in space, but they seem to contain infinite possibilities.

## *Time*

Both *Lost* and *The Tempest* use narrative complexity in ways that relate to cultural anxieties about changing perceptions of time. In discussing narrative uses of time, I borrow two important ideas from Gerard Genette: his explanations of *order* and *duration* in narrative. In short, Genette's *order* refers to correspondence of events as they are told to the listener (narrative) and events as they occur within the chronology of the events in the story (story).

*Duration* occurs to the relationship between the length of time it takes to tell an event (narrative) and the time it takes for the event to happen (story) (Richardson 25).

*Lost's* approach to narrative time has helped to define the series. The first three seasons function by vacillating between two narratives per episode: the continuing story of the Oceanic flight survivors struggling with daily life on the island, interlaced with a "flashback" (or *analepsis*) story that usually focuses on one character at a time. Upon receiving their desired end-date from ABC, producers made even more complex use of temporal manipulation. Starting with the final episode of the third season, *Lost* seemingly folded the flashbacks over "island time" and began presenting "flash-forwards" (or *prolepses*) by depicting events that transpire *after* some main characters achieve their rescue. Alone, this interplay of narrative order is not particularly innovative. As Genette points out, storytellers at least as long ago as Homer played with order in similar ways (Richardson 26). In looking at narrative complexity on television, Jason Mittel points out various ways in which many recent television series experiment with narrative order. But *Lost's* manipulation of narrative order was central to the series in a manner unlike other television programs. Shuffled narrative order marked *Lost's* default episode structure, and alterations to that distinctive convention shaped the meaning of later seasons.

Following the fourth season that primarily consisted of prolepses, *Lost's* fifth season emphasized the significance of narrative order beyond any ordinary consideration by introducing shuffled order into the story itself. No longer merely a narrative device, the story events included characters and the island *itself* traveling through time. Eventually, a core group of characters "lands" in the mid–1970s and experiences dramatic action during an analepsis that is set in the past for both the audience *and* some of the characters. Meanwhile, the relatively stable temporal location is what started as the previous season's prolepsis: three years after six of the castaways were rescued from the island. These season-by-season changes, ever accelerating, *themselves* mark a unique narrative complexity.

*The Tempest* plays with narrative order less overtly, but with relative complexity. As Barbara Mowat points out: "*The Tempest's* 'story' stretches over more than twenty-four years," while the play itself is "constricted within a plot-time of a single afternoon" (187). The second scene of the play mainly consists of Prospero exposing the past through narration. While not strictly complex ordering, this exposition extends well beyond what is typical in Shakespeare's work. As Mowat explains, "the second and third scenes of the play (I.2 and II.1) contain close to half the lines in the play and over half of *those* lines are past-tense narration" (187). These scenes provide background stories on a large number of characters — both onstage and off: Sycorax's journey to the island, Antonio's betrayal of Prospero, Prospero and Miranda's shipwreck, etc. They also impose serious challenges for actors and directors; delivering exposition written by great playwrights is *still* delivering exposition. It seems unlikely that the playwright's choice to include so much exposition is the result of tedious playwriting. In fact, as if to anticipate and fend off such a charge, Shakespeare gives Prospero a line to remind us of the exposition's necessity in saying to Miranda:

> Hear a little further,
> And then I'll bring thee to the present business
> Which now's upon's, without which this story
> Were most impertinent [I.ii. 161–164].

This moment draws attention to the taxing amount of exposition and resembles the self-reflexivity of numerous moments in *Lost*. For example, Mittel cites the moment following the viewing of the first Dharma initiative video. Locke says to Jack: "We're going to have to watch that again!" ("Orientation" 2.3). Mittel terms this "operational reflexivity"— the character says something that is certainly true for the viewers. In later seasons, Miles and Hurley are utilized in similar ways, often with great humor. This operational reflexivity is the kind of functional self-awareness complex narrative encourages. It also serves to emphasize the thematic significance of narrative complexity. For example, Prospero's line not only asks the audience for patience; it also reminds the audience of just how much exposition there is. In this way, complex narrative order not only entertains, it also magnifies the connections inherent between past and present, present and future, and past and future. Prospero's conjuring of the tempest is only justifiable because his brother usurped his dukedom in the past. Without that knowledge, we—nor Miranda—would understand his actions. His explanation of Caliban's origins prepares the audience for Prospero's foiling of Caliban's plot later in the play. Similarly, *Lost*'s analepses allow its audience to understand the actions of its characters in the contexts of their previously separate lives.

The events on both islands also carry greater dramatic significance for the audience *because* the islands' temporary inhabitants have such interesting pasts. As Mowat explains, "The pressure of the past and the future on a present moment [...] makes believable that which is normally suspect: instant repentance and inner transformation" (189). She cites Alonso's repentance in *The Tempest*, but her observation might just as easily apply to Charlie's final destruction of his heroin stash or Mr. Eko's acceptance of his identity as a priest. Without the unfolding past, these transformations might feel unbearably trite and almost certainly too easy.

Both stories intensify these associations by stretching the duration of time on their respective islands. Unlike most of Shakespeare's other works, the duration of *The Tempest* essentially matches narrative and story time. In the closing scene of the play, Alonso refers to the three hours that have passed since the storm — not far from the approximate stage time for the full play. The duration of *Lost* is more difficult to identify due to its complicated narrative order. However, if one considers the story's duration as occurring between Jack's eye opening on the island following the crash and his parallel death on the island, then the duration of the narrative (almost six years between the September 2004 premiere through the May 2010 finale) eclipses the duration of the story. From this perspective, both stories magnify the duration of time on the island. *The Tempest* defies convention by matching narrative time and story time, while *Lost's* story time is shorter than its narrative time.

In stretching or slowing the duration, the stories increase the significance of the events dramatically portrayed. One reason for doing so may be in part to justify particular dramatic action. For example, the audience ought to believe that Miranda and Ferdinand are truly in love, just as Christian Shephard explains to Jack that the most important moments of his life (which lasted over the course of decades) took place during his few months on the *Lost* island. But in addition to the dramatic justification, the stories' durations reassure their audiences that in an increasingly complicated world, individual moments and actions still have great meaning. By slowing the duration of particular events, these stories reassure their audiences that they still have agency in a rapidly changing world. Extensive pasts and frightening futures do not dull the significance of actions in the present. Changing understandings of what "here" and "now" might mean do not remove the meaning and consequence of the "here" and "now." In both stories, happiness through marriage and redemption through sacrifice are not only possible, but also enabled by the complex interactions among the past, present, and future.

## *The End of the World*

Finally, I suggest that both works' narrative complexities stem in part from particular interests and anxieties often associated with historical crisis: the end of the world and the afterlife. Such concerns are, of course, usual in popular storytelling. Boyd points out that humanity's self-awareness provides evolutionary advantages, yet also "carries costs, including the ability to envisage our own death and absence from the ongoing world" (404). Many stories — especially religious ones — derive from our desire to cope with our own mortality. *Lost* and *The Tempest* address individual death and the possibilities of humanity's end in both their dramatic content and form.

For *Lost*, the notion of the end of the world first entered into the story during the show's second season when some of the survivors felt compelled to "save the world" by typing in a series of numbers and pushing a button once every 108 minutes. From that point forward, numerous characters in the story believed the fate of the world to rest in their hands. In the series finale, the uncapping of the mysterious power at the center of the cave threatens the stability of the island, and by association, the world itself. It was at the end of the fifth season, however, that the narrative began to address most prominently the notion of the end of the world. In the final moment of the season, Juliet seems to detonate an atomic bomb on the island in an attempt to create a new future in which the initial Oceanic crash is avoided. *Lost*'s sixth season ensues with a familiar shuffling of narrative order: an island-present narrative alternating with what was called the "flash-sideways" of a timeline beginning with Oceanic 815 *not* crashing. In the series finale, it became clear that, rather than being an alternate timeline, this narrative line takes place in an afterlife of sorts that followed each of the characters' individual deaths. This purgatorial afterlife within the narrative order introduces a future beyond the physical. In this metaphysical world, the island's characters first exist without knowledge of their physical lives but, over the course of time, they come to understand where and when they are.

In her book *Last Things and Last Plays: Shakespearean Eschatology*, Cynthia Marshall argues that *The Tempest* exhibits a duality of "time and timelessness" that addresses the afterlife. She considers Ferdinand's statement in act four, scene one, in which he says that he could live on the island forever, as a prompt to consider the island in terms of "Paradise": a word that, for Marshall, connotes both the biblical Eden of pre-fall humanity and the New Testament "heaven" of afterlife reward. She points out that the island is essentially timeless for its inhabitants and that Prospero's final departure from the island essentially marks him for death (88). Thus, his declaration at the end of the play that after one further trip into the past his future will focus on his mortality:

> Sir, I invite your Highness and your train
> To my poor cell, where you shall take your rest
> For this one night, which part of it I'll waste
> With such discourse as, I not doubt, shall make it
> Go quick away: the story of my life
> And the particular accidents gone by
> Since I came to this isle. And in the morn
> I'll bring you back to your ship, and so to Naples,
> Where I have hope to see the nuptial
> Of these our dear-beloved solemnized,
> And thence retire me to my Milan, where
> Every third thought shall be my grave [V.i, 358–369].

*The Tempest* is also imprinted with the pending retirement of its prominent playwright. A frequent — if often oversimplified — reading of the play locates Prospero as a stand-in for the playwright. If *The Tempest*'s story is Prospero's farewell to his magic, then the play is Shakespeare's farewell to the theatre. In the same way that Prospero gives up his magic in order to return home and live in quiet retirement, it is widely accepted that Shakespeare left London to retire in his hometown of Stratford near the time in which *The Tempest* was written. Hopefully, *Lost*'s creators are not similarly considering a retirement. However, the relative luxury of a termination date gave the producers every incentive to focus on the ending of the show. In some ways, by asking for a termination date, the producers fostered the expectation that the show's ending would hold much of its total significance. Therefore, external circumstances may contribute to each story's focus on the notion of endings. Nonetheless, I submit that the emphasis on endings also derives naturally from the stories' approach to the rapid changes in the world around us.

Technological innovation and cultural change reshape human conceptions of and assumptions about space and time. These island stories are manifestations of and responses to the anxieties and questions caused by these changes. As I have described, *The Tempest* and *Lost* play with conventional approaches to time and space in order to foster our ability to adapt to changing times. Significant loss necessarily accompanies drastic change. The focus on both individual and cultural endings promotes acceptance of this kind of change. In the end, these stories explore time and space, then undermine their significance in order to preserve the value of what has been lost. They alter space and time, then they try to transcend them.

In one of *Lost*'s final scenes, Jack Shephard asks his dead father Christian about what is real. He also asks whether or not all of his friends from the island are "here now."

Christian responds, "Well, there is no 'now,' here."

Jack inquires, "Where are we, Dad?"

Christian explains, "This is a place that you — that you all made together — so that you could find one another. The most important part of your life was the time you spent with these people. That's why all of you are here. Nobody does it alone, Jack. You needed them and they needed you" ("The End" 6.18).

*Lost* thus concludes by demonstrating how space and time, however complicated, can be ultimately transcended. By utilizing time so prominently both in experimental narrative structure and as content itself, both island dramas drive toward a timelessness that can only be found in three places: the afterlife, dreams, and the imagination dramatic fiction provides — and these are where the dead and gone regularly appear.

In *The Tempest*, Prospero concludes the wedding ceremony with a famous line:

> We are such stuff
> As dreams are made on; and our little life
> Is rounded with a sleep [IV.i. 156–158].

Changing understandings of space and time necessarily lead to fundamental questions that transcend those that are immediately prompted by technological innovation. Perhaps in times of profound change we return to eternal questions that transcend time and space. In the end, both stories end with hopeful thoughts about inevitable death — the state that we innately fear — where, so far as we know, space and time are completely meaningless.

## Works Cited

Boyd, Brian. *On the Origin of Stories: Evolution, Cognition, and Fiction*. Cambridge, MA: The Belknap Press of Harvard University Press, 2009.
Marshall, Cynthia. *Last Things and Last Plays: Shakespearean Eschatology*. Carbondale, IL: Southern Illinois University Press, 1991.
Mittel, Jason. "Narrative Complexity in Contemporary American Television." *The Velvet Light Trap*. 58 (Fall 2006): 29–40.
Mowat, Barbara. "The Tempest: A Modern Perspective." *The New Folger Library Shakespeare Edition of William Shakespeare's* The Tempest. New York: Washington Square Press, 1994.
Richardson, Brian, ed. *Narrative Dynamics: Essays on Time, Plot, Closure, and Frames*. Columbus: The Ohio State University Press, 2002.
Shakespeare, William. *The Tempest: A Norton Critical Edition*. Eds. Peter Hulme and William H. Sherman. New York: W. W. Norton, 2004.

*Part Two*

# Lost Philosophy

# *Lost* and Becoming: Reconceptualizing Philosophy
## *Jason M. Peck*

Browse the philosophy section of any major chain bookstore today and there are, overtaking more "canonical" philosophy texts, any number of books that take popular culture as exemplary moments for philosophical reflection (*Seinfeld* and philosophy, *The Matrix* and philosophy and, yes, *Lost* and philosophy). Setting aside the tricky questions regarding the commingling of "high" and "low" texts, it is the conjunction "and" that must be critically engaged in this particular formulation. With the dueling reified concepts of "philosophy" and whatever popular text falls after the "and," these books often fail to alter our understanding of either popular culture *or* philosophy. As if afraid to truly ask philosophically *what* this influx of popular texts does to our term "philosophy," these volumes are content to mark off the appropriate intertextual references, thus insuring that the intercourse promised by this new strain of philosophical inquiry remains unfulfilled.

Within this context, I wish to place an "as" where an "and" is found. While *Lost* does ask us to pay attention to its myriad intertextual references, from the names of the characters to the books they read on the island, it uses these references not merely to highlight the educated pedigrees of the show's writers but to demonstrate the ways in which philosophy, encountered in a new space, reconfigures knowledge yet again. Further, philosophy is used in its broadest sense: it encompasses the empiricist triad of John Locke, David Hume, and Jeremy Bentham as well as the science fiction of Philip K. Dick. This essay attempts to answer the following question: if *Lost* does not simply remain an appendage to the phrase "and Philosophy," then what kind of philosophy does *Lost* embody? That is, I do not ask to which type or school of philosophy *Lost* subscribes, rather, what *is* the concept of philosophy after *Lost*?

Philosophy seemingly appears in three ways within the show: the first and perhaps most obvious being the use of proper names: John Locke, (Desmond) David Hume, Danielle Rousseau, and other characters are named after famous philosophers. This has led to a number of articles and essays that address the significance of these figures for the show: *i.e.*, how much (or how little) is the historical John Locke similar to the Locke on the show? What role, if any, does empiricism play in Desmond Hume's metaphysical conundrum?[1] The show offers its own reading of this recourse to proper names in the fifth season episode "The Life and Death of Jeremy Bentham" (5.7). After the character John Locke has left the island to convince the "Oceanic Six" to return to the island, he is eventually picked up in Tunisia by Charles Widmore, the shady capitalist who was once the leader of the on-island tribe of "Others." During a conversation in which Widmore instructs Locke on how to find his fellow castaways, Locke is given the alias "Jeremy Bentham" so that he may be safe while trying to find them. Locke, not knowing who Bentham is, asks Widmore about the significance of the name:

> LOCKE: Jeremy Bentham?
> WIDMORE: He was a British philosopher. Your parents had a sense of humor when they named you, so why can't I?

In a typically lengthy discussion on his now (sadly) defunct blog, J. Wood analyses the distinction between the historical John Locke and Jeremy Bentham's conflicting philosophical views:

> Locke is now confirmed to be Jeremy Bentham, another in the *Lost* list of Enlightenment philosophers. And he's an interesting choice: When forging his ideas of utilitarianism and legal positivism, Bentham forcefully broke from the theories [of] natural rights and social contracts put forth by the philosopher John Locke. Island Locke's name change introduces a narrative and metaphysical break that gives rise to all kinds of fun new complications, particularly when it comes to island Locke's uncertainty between faith and reason.

Thus, the "sense of humor" that Widmore suggests in his comment is simultaneously the joke that Locke's parents played at his expense—that John Locke, as the man of faith, is fundamentally at odds with his historical namesake—and the joke that Widmore is playing at Locke's expense—that Bentham and Locke were at odds with one another with regards to man's natural state.

However, the viewer could potentially perceive a third joke being played here: a joke at the expense of those who read the proper names in *Lost* as containing a fundamental truth about the show's philosophical content. Proper names on *Lost*, as in most fictional narratives, are arbitrary things devised either by an external author or, as in the case with this scene, devised by a character within the narrative. That Widmore points out this very construction (*i.e.*, that he is the one "naming" John Locke in the same way his parents did), as well as the nature of the construction as a joke (*i.e.*, the creator is ultimately "playing a joke" on the character who is being named), begs the question as to how meaningfully we should take the other proper names on the show.

The second instance of philosophy on *Lost* is the appearance of books within the show itself. The producers and show runners of *Lost*, Damon Lindelof and Carlton Cuse, have championed books since the very first season of the show. Although there has been only one canonical philosophical text shown on the show — Søren Kiergegaard's *Fear and Trembling*— there have been other books on the series that, arguably, stand on the margins of philosophy (Fyodor Dostoyevsky's *Notes from the Underground*, Carlos Castaneda's *A Separate Reality*) as well as fiction that exhibits a certain philosophical bent (Philip K. Dick's *Valis*, Adolfo Bioy Casares' *The Invention of Morel* and, perhaps the most referenced works in the entire series, Lewis Carroll's *Alice* books).

While these (literal) intertextual moments are significant, it is questionable as to whether or not they contribute to the hermeneutics of the show as a whole. A case in point would be Flann O'Brien's *The Third Policeman*, a novel whose abstract plot has several points in common with *Lost* and whose appearance on the show, according to a then-current article in the *Chicago Tribune*, would contain "key insights into [*Lost*]."[2] Yet, when the episode containing the book was finally aired, there was no discussion of the book itself and it was later revealed that while the episode's writer, Craig Wright, was a big fan of the book, none of the other show writers, directors, producers, or creators had actually read the book. While one could posit that these books are shown in order to "guide" the viewer towards certain conclusions, they hardly add up to a cohesive philosophy or hermeneutics of *Lost* that would offer significant insight into the show's "deeper" meaning. Indeed, as J. Wood so ably demonstrates in his *Lost* blog (and, to a lesser degree, the column writer Jeff "Doc" Jensen demonstrates in his weekly columns on *Lost* for *Entertainment Weekly*) there is no shortage of intertextual references in the show (both diegetic and non-diegetic).

The third instantiation of philosophy on *Lost* is the repetition of certain themes, topics and tropes that have been addressed at length throughout the history of philosophy: empiricism and rationalism, reason and faith, free will and fate, the concepts of good and evil. Questions regarding sense certainty, for example, have been prevalent on the show from the very opening shot — an extreme close-up of Jack Shephard's eye. This consistently recurring shot among the characters foregrounds the show's emphasis on the perceiving subject's — and, by extension, the viewer's — ability to trust what he or she sees. Further, it affects the mode through which most viewers have watched the show; part of the mystery of *Lost* is not that there *is* an ultimate answer to be had but, rather, the viewer's constant *aporiatic* relationship to the show mirrors the character's relationship both to the island and to the other characters on the show. One episode in particular, "Dave" (2.18), made the connection between the two explicit by both presenting the character of Hurley as fundamentally perplexed at the appearance on the island of his imaginary friend Dave from his previous life incarcerated in a mental hospital, and concluding the episode with a shot of Hurley at the mental hospital from the point of view of Libby, a fellow castaway and Hurley's love interest. Thus, the character of Hurley embodies a type of epistemological crisis: prior to the final shot of the episode, the viewer is inclined to believe that either Hurley really has hallucinated the events of the island and, therefore, the reality we are watching can be discredited, or there is some other evidence of psychic trauma causing Hurley to fantasize Dave's appearance. Yet, the final shot of the episode widens the narrative frame to suggest either (a) there is a "reality" independent of the island and that all of the castaways, indeed, have crashed (and, moreover, knew each other before the crash) or (b) there is some kind of collective hallucination represented on *Lost*. The *aporia* of meaning created by this particular episode extends to the viewer's ability to ground a definitive understanding of the unfolding narrative.

Perhaps the most significant philosophical debate that informs the *Lost* narrative may be grouped under the auspice of contingency and necessity. Something that is contingent might take place through a series of events, as an adjunct or a result of something else. Something that is necessary is determined by a series of events, the outcome of which is unavoidable. *Lost* plays with the seeming contradiction of these two terms throughout the course of the show, terms that inform all of the significant leitmotivs that *Lost* thematizes: *i.e.*, reason and faith, science and religion, etc. As with the epistemological questions addressed above, the viewer may desire some kind of answer with regard to this seeming binary. Yet, the show resists any definite answer,[3] only emphasizing the need for the two terms in so far as our perception structures the reality of the island according to these terms.

By way of an example, the cause of flight 815's crash on the island may represent the show's essential *aporia* of contingency and necessity. In the second season episode "Live Together, Die Alone" (2.23 and 2.24), we discover that Desmond, whom the survivors of 815 find living inside a hatch on the island and who enters a series of numbers into a computer every 108 minutes, had decided on the day of the plane crash not to enter the numbers into the computer. Desmond's refusal to enter the numbers causes a massive amount of electromagnetic material to be released from the island. This would be the contingent explanation of the crash: had Desmond not had a crisis of faith, with said crisis being brought on by his finding out that the man who introduced him to the hatch had been lying the entire time, he would have continued to enter the numbers and the flight would not have crashed.

Contrast this interpretation of the crash with the one offered at the end of season five into season six: many of the castaways on flight 815 had been "touched" by Jacob, the island's protector, who has metaphysical powers to affect the lives of those he touches and brings people to the island as candidates for the role of the island's future protector. Ergo, regardless of the course of action taken by Desmond at the end of season two, those people whom Jacob touched would always be "fated" to come to the island, necessitating the crash of Oceanic 815. This is the necessary interpretation of the crash. Although this latter interpretation (given its dominance in the final season) would seem to trump the earlier, contingent explanation for the plane crash, the creators of the show never give us a definitive answer, presenting Jacob's metaphysical powers as limited and contradictory, ultimately portraying him as equally affected by contingent forces upon his arrival to the island. He too crashed on the island, was raised by another, and only became the island protector after his surrogate mother lost her other, more beloved son.

The constant indeterminacy demonstrated above is a key aspect of the fabric of the *Lost* narrative, as well as an essential element of *Lost*'s philosophical commitment. Bringing this particular strain of thought to bear on the epistemic questions raised in the first part of this section, it is significant that when the seemingly binary terms of contingency and necessity are expressed by the characters on the show, it is often in concert with a particular mode of perception. One of the common phrases spoken by the characters after season two is, "Don't mistake coincidence for fate." Mr. Eko first says this to John Locke in the episode "What Kate Did" (2.9), Locke repeats the phrase to Mr. Eko in the episode "The Cost of Living" (3.5), and Jack tells Locke that he might be mistaking coincidence for fate in the episode "What They Died For" (6.16). In all of these instances, the characters shift back and forth between the two possibilities that they are on the island for a reason and that they are on the island arbitrarily. In all of these instances, emphasis should be placed on the word "mistake" since it is the characters' perception of the terms "coincidence" and "fate" that matter, not that the two terms can ever be resolved. The process of perception, so essential to the *Lost* narrative, becomes the dialectical movement between the two terms over the course of the entire series.

While proper names and philosophical debates demonstrate the show's knowledge of philosophy's history, these characteristics do not suggest that the show can re-conceptualize philosophy. It is not enough to ask what philosophical issues are addressed, as if one were making a laundry list; rather it is essential to ask how these discrete philosophical units are conceptualized within the series. In describing the essential philosophical content of film, for example, few theorists simply refer to moments of film, say, in which a particular philosophical text or a philosophical argument is referenced. Starting with the history of film analysis at the beginning of the twentieth century, philosophy has been an essential resource in understanding how film shapes our cognitive world. Many of the so-called *auteurs* of film (Sergei Eisenstein, Orson Welles, Jean Renoir, Alfred Hitchcock, Jean Luc Godard, David Lynch, et al.) become philosophers insofar as they explicate the world through their films. These explications come to be regarded as examinations in their own right, rather than echoes of moments of philosophy that have already existed. Though a filmmaker such as Godard might actually use quotations from this history of philosophy in his films, a filmmaker such as Hitchcock will not. Yet, no one would argue that Hitchcock's films are any less philosophical than Godard's insofar as they reflect on the nature of consciousness, morality, and desire, often redefining the parameters of philosophical issues.

Additionally, philosophers have been willing to use film as an exemplary mode of philosophical reflection since the early part of the twentieth century. Whether using the example of film as a new cognitive construction and radicalization of aesthetics (Walter Benjamin), as evidence of the reification of culture as well as the instrumentalization of consciousness (Theodore Adorno), as a new example of ontological formation (Stanley Cavell), as philosophical conceptualization (Gilles Deleuze), or as ideological and psychoanalytic analysis (Fredric Jameson, Slavoj Žižek), film has become as essential an object for philosophy as literature continues to be.

Television, however, seems to remain outside this realm of analysis, essentially remaining off limits to philosophy.[4] To this end, it would be fruitful to analyze *Lost* as a philosophical text along side of the work of the French philosopher Gilles Deleuze.[5] In a letter to the French film critic Serge Daney, Deleuze diagnoses the fundamental disjunction between television and film with regard to the traditional realm of philosophy:

> For if cinema looked to television and video to "relay" a new aesthetic and poetic function, television for its part (despite a few early experiments) took on an essentially *social function* that disrupted from the outset any relay, appropriated video, and substituted altogether different forces for the potential of beauty and thought [Deleuze, "Letter to Serge Daney" 71].

The social function that Deleuze describes is symptomatic of a society based on surveillance and control, not of aesthetics and philosophical reflection. If film allows a "supplemental" aesthetic reflection that goes beyond a mere presentation of reality, analogous to a philosophical reflection that examines perception beyond what is, then television is denied the ability to enter this aesthetic realm:

> Why not allow television this same supplementary force of creative preservation? There's nothing in principle to stop it adapting its different resources

to this same end, except that TV's social functions (seen in game shows, news) stifle its potential aesthetic function [...] For how could professional training, the professional eye, leave any room for something supplementary in the way of perceptual exploration? [Deleuze, "Letter to Serge Daney" 74].

Moreover, Deleuze argues, "a relay [between television and film] could only be set up in a form of television that had a non-communicative supplement" (74). If perceptual exploration is the space in which philosophy and the visual image intersect, marked by a "non-communicative supplement" that is endemic to film, then television (despite being a visual medium) is denied, according to Deleuze, this exploratory function due to its cooptation in training and social control. It is as if television were simply a panopticon or brain-washing machine that simply creates a "socially engineered eye through which the viewer himself is invited to look" (74).

*Lost* self-consciously inserts the medium's function as surveillance every time a television, or, by extension, a screen, is shown. In the second season, one of the various "stations" built by the Dharma initiative, the Pearl station, which is symbolically represented by a hexagonal shape reminiscent of Jeremy Bentham's drawings of the panopticon, functions as a means of both observing workers in other stations as well as of conducting a psychological experiment on the workers in the Pearl station doing the observing. This observation, both inside and outside, is accomplished by a series of television monitors. In the third season episode "Not in Portland" (3.7), the viewer sees the inside of room 23, a large space originally constructed by the Dharma initiative but subsequently used by the Others, which projects a series of films with suggestive images, sounds, and messages that will ostensibly brainwash potential viewers. The presentation of these images and sounds recalls other representations of brainwashing films in other television shows (most notably *The Prisoner*) and films (*A Clockwork Orange* [1971] and *The Parallax View* [1974]).

By contrast, the "non-communicative supplement" of the show traverses its entire surface from the opening shot of the entire series (a disembodied eye, the context for which is only revealed after several subsequent shots), to the constant symbols, glances between characters, and shots of inessential content that may or may not become canonized "Easter eggs," which fans of the show pour over for clues to the show's overall meaning. Indeed, the often concurrent fulfillment and disappointment viewers experience after an episode has aired is manifested in the reaction to the non-communicative supplement: that is to say, how a certain scene does or does not relate to, or solve, the show's mystery.

Deleuze appears here not merely as a willful evocation of the cultural pessimists' dismissal of television, nor as a stand-in for philosophy's derision of television (while celebrating the ascension of film into philosophical analysis). Rather, Deleuze and *Lost* share a set of texts and concepts that inform the creation of "philosophy." Two philosophical concepts that are prominent and interconnected in the show are the twin concepts of "becoming" and "repetition." The concept of "becoming" informs Deleuze's book *The Logic of Sense*, which, among other things, is an extended reading of Lewis Carroll's two *Alice* books, books that, as was mentioned above, are significant for *Lost*.

"When I say," Deleuze begins, "'Alice becomes larger,' I mean that she becomes larger than she was. By the same token, however, she becomes smaller than she is now" (Deleuze, *The Logic of Sense* 1). This process is "the simultaneity of a becoming whose characteristic is to elude the present. Insofar as it eludes the present, becoming does not tolerate the separation or the distinction of before and after, or of past and future" (1). This simultaneity of becoming (becoming larger and smaller at the same time) results in a paradox: "good sense affirms that in all things there is a determinable sense or direction (*sens*); but paradox is the affirmation of both senses or directions at the same time" (1). There is a parallel, of course, with the narrative structure of *Lost*: each season of the show has presented its own "simultaneity of becoming." The first three seasons show the past and present of the individual characters on the island, the fourth and fifth seasons show the present and future stories of the individual characters, while the sixth and final season produces something entirely different (to be discussed below). What ultimately connects *Lost* to this Deleuzian sense of becoming is the "affirmation" of both at the same time: both narratives are shown to the viewer simultaneously, unfolding over the course of the episode. Thus the affective status of this narrative form is to present the viewer with a neither/nor paradoxical logic insofar as we are neither to assume that the island narrative brings closure to the events of the past nor to the potential events of the future.

"The paradox of this pure becoming," continues Deleuze in his analysis of the *Alice* books, "with its capacity to elude the present, is the paradox of infinite identity" (Deleuze, *The Logic of Sense* 2). This "infinite identity" has "one consequence: the contesting of Alice's personal identity" (3). This paradox, produced through the simultaneous affirmation of both directions (coming and going, past and future, more and less, etc.), removes the foundations for the subject's identity:

> [P]ersonal uncertainty is not a doubt foreign to what is happening, but rather an objective structure of the event itself, insofar as it moves in two directions at once, and insofar as it fragments the subject following this double direction [3].

This fragmentation leads to Alice's constant confusion in discerning her own identity and finding her orientation within Wonderland and the Looking-Glass World.

The passages of *Alice in Wonderland* to which Deleuze refers in his first chapter come from the beginning of the book wherein Alice first falls down the rabbit hole. This section of the book is quoted directly in *Lost* itself. In the season four episode "Something Nice Back Home" (4.10), after the introductory title sequence, Jack is seen reading chapter two of *Alice in Wonderland*, "A Pool of Tears," to Aaron.

> Alice took up the fan and as the hall was very hot she kept fanning herself all the time she went on talking. "Dear, dear! How queer everything is today! And yesterday things went on just as usual. I wonder if I've been changed in the night? Let me think: *was* I the same when I got up this morning? But if I'm not the same, the next question is, 'Who in the world am I?' Ah, *that's* the great puzzle."[6]

The framing of the scene is significant: it is shot from Aaron's perspective (over his shoulder as he lies in bed) and Aaron's body makes up most of the foreground. Jack is in the middle on a chair reading the book and Kate, framed in the doorway, is in the distant background. Both Aaron and Kate are out of focus, while Jack remains in focus. The framing of the shot presents us with the typical nuclear family: mother, father, and son, but Jack is not Aaron's father, Kate is not Aaron's mother, and Jack and Kate are not married. Moreover, because Kate and Aaron are out of focus and Jack is in focus, the camera emphasizes that Jack is the primary character in the scene. Thus, the passage he reads from *Alice in Wonderland* is meant for him (not for Aaron) and it is he, not the two spectral figures in the foreground and the background, who must ask himself, "Who in the world am I?" This indication is further accentuated by the fact that after reading this line aloud and glancing at Kate in the doorway, Jack is framed in a medium shot that excludes the two other figures.

Aside from this explicit Carroll reference, there are several implicit references to the Alice books and to Jack Shephard's mutable identity in the sequence prior to the aforementioned scene. At the beginning of Jack's flashforward, we see him awakened by a phone call from the hospital where he works. Jack gets out of bed, shirtless, and walks into the kitchen. Although the viewer assumes that he is in his own home, there is no context for the scene. Much has been made of Mathew Fox's lack of chest hair in this sequence (previous episodes where the character is shirtless show him to have chest hair). Though this could be easily explained by reasons having nothing to do with the show (another role, for example), the creators of the show have used this (possibly) non-diegetic explanation for diegetic ends: his lack of chest hair causes him to resemble the actor Josh Holloway, who plays Sawyer, the other figure in the Kate-Jack-Sawyer love triangle on the island. Sawyer, who has no chest hair, is often, to an almost parodic level, placed in situations where he must take off his shirt. As Jack enters the kitchen, he trips over something on the floor. It is revealed to be a toy copy of the Millennium Falcon, the ship that Han Solo commandeered in the original three *Star Wars* films. In the numerous intertextual references to Star Wars throughout *Lost*, Sawyer is most often identified with Han Solo: the sarcastic anti-hero. Given the passage of *Alice in Wonderland* that Jack reads to Aaron in the aforementioned scene, coupled with the fact that the plot of the episode will revolve around Jack's jealousy regarding a promise that Kate made to Sawyer before leaving the island, the entire scene might be read as a meditation on becoming (Jack is no longer Jack but not yet Sawyer) and the concomitant loss of Jack's certain identity.

This insinuation is continued in the scene immediately following, wherein it is finally revealed that Jack has spent the night with Kate. There is a close-up of Jack's face as he enters what the viewer assumes to be the bathroom due to the sound of a shower off-screen. In what is at first a disorienting effect, Jack walks directly past the camera and emerges in a medium shot reflected in the bathroom mirror. The subsequent conversation between Jack and Kate (who is not yet revealed to be the person in the shower) is shot entirely from inside the mirror: a mirror image of the scene that is now unfolding. From the shower door, Jack walks up to the mirror, reminding the viewer that the entire previous conversation between Jack and the shadowy figure in the shower stall (another form of optical mediation) has been from the mirror's perspective. As Jack moves closer to the mirror in order to pick up the razor Kate has purchased for him, the shot changes from a medium shot to a medium close-up of Jack, again shot from the perspective of the mirror, although this time Jack's back is in the right-hand side of the frame so that the viewer is aware that Jack is framed by the mirror. The camera pans down from focusing on Jack's face in the mirror to the razor and when it pans back up Jack briefly looks at himself in the mirror before turning away. This "mirroring" of the scene is a more oblique reference to Carroll's other *Alice* book: *Through the Looking-Glass, and What Alice Found There*. If the passage that Jack will read to Aaron in the following scene ends with Alice, perpetually moving back and forth between various states of being, asking "who in the world am I?" then the scene prior to this shows Jack being displaced in the double of the mirror. The camera's evocation of disorientation mimics the back and forth of becoming in the next scene: we are never sure if we are watching the "real" Jack in the frame of the shot or his mirror image. This disorientation will be used to significant effect in the sixth season's flash-sideways, as each character looks at his or her reflection in the mirror throughout the "sideways world" story over the course of the season.[7]

The Carroll reference extends itself beyond the scene in question, however. The last Jack-centric episode prior to "Something Nice Back Home" is entitled "Through the Looking Glass" (3.22 and 3.23). Instead of representing an individual character in the process of becoming, in a Deleuzian sense, it is the entire show which experiences (and reflects upon) the temporal displacement engendered by becoming. In the final minutes of the show, the viewer learns that the entire off-island story, which the audience had been primed to interpret as a flashback, has in fact been a "flash-forward" of Jack's life after being rescued from the island. This temporal displacement, which, like a mirror reflection, will be the dominant narrative device of the next two seasons, is created initially out of disorientation. The first three seasons create a temporal dialectic of before and after: narratives of characters' lives before the plane crash inform and amplify their lives after the plane crash. After peering into the looking glass, much like Alice, the show enters an inverted world: the fourth season will move in reverse from the imminent rescue of the Losties on the island coupled with their unhappiness in the future in the first episode of the season, to witnessing their violent rescue on the island coupled with their eventual desire to return there in the season four finale. In other words, the show appears to move temporally forward on the island and temporally backward in the off-island story, like a mirror (since the viewer has already seen the scene that temporally takes place prior to the first scene of the final episode of season four). This disorientation "through the looking glass" manifests itself in the narrative of the fifth, science fiction–influenced season wherein time travel, as well as a complete temporal indeterminacy, is the dominant mode.

This temporal manifestation of becoming — the show's refusal to rest either in the past, present or future — eventually transforms into a final temporal metamorphosis of repetition in the final season of the series. In the season premiere of the sixth season of *Lost*, Hurley, having just discovered the temple where a majority of the others have been hiding, descends down a secret passageway and discovers a group of skeletons along the way. The viewer knows from the episode "The Little Prince" (5.4) in the fifth season that this group of skeletons was once Danielle Rousseau's group, which had been pulled into the temple by the so-called smoke monster. As Hurley pauses to observe one of the skeletons, he notices that a book is lying beside it: a French-language edition of Søren Kierkegaard's *Fear and Trembling*. Although much has been made of Kierkegaard's influence on the theology of *Lost*, with many attempting to read the tragic tale of the show's John Locke as an allegorical retelling of Kierkegaard's concept of the knight of faith, the volume's appearance in the episode "LA X" (6.1 and 6.2) points to a more significant development in terms of the temporal displacement discussed above.

Kierkegaard published two books on the same day, February 20, 1843;

one was *Fear and Trembling* and the other was *Repetition*. Though *Fear and Trembling* is the book shown in the episode, the narrative structure of the episode (and of the entire season) suggests that the volume's appearance obliquely refers to *Repetition*. In the final season of *Lost*, the viewer encounters scenes from the first season with variations — some trivial (Jack is handed one bottle, not two, by the flight attendant Cindy on flight 815, Kate has not killed her father but wounded another man and is thus still a fugitive) and some significant (the island is at the bottom of the ocean, the plane never crashes on the island). Although it might be seductive to simply understand this as a narrative ploy, a hook for the longtime viewer as well as those who might have nostalgia for the earlier, better seasons of *Lost*, given the appearance of Kierkegaard in the first episode, this temporal change in the narrative is presented philosophically.

Repetition is the final resting place of the becoming in the entire series of *Lost*. Kierkegaard is the figure who best explicates repetition as the "answer" to the temporal confusion of the previous five seasons. In *Repetition*, Kierkegaard's pseudononymous author, Constantine Constantius attempts to show how "the whole of life is a repetition" (132):

> [H]e who does not comprehend that life is a repetition, and that this is the beauty of life, has condemned himself and deserves nothing better than what is sure to befall him, namely, to perish [132].

Elsewhere, the narrator adds that repetition forms a paradoxical dialectic: "for that which is repeated has been — otherwise it could not be repeated — but the very fact that it has been makes the repetition into something new" (149). Again, the movement of repetition mirrors the paradox of becoming articulated earlier: just as Alice was becoming larger at the same time she is becoming smaller — a movement in two directions — the act of repetition has already taken place but is taking place for the first time as well. Kierkegaard contrasts repetition to both the concepts of recollection and hope. "What is recollected has been, is repeated backwards," and results in an unhappiness, a "pretext for stealing out of life, alleging [...] that he has forgotten something" (131). Hope, on the other hand, is "cowardly [...] a beckoning fruit which does not satisfy" (132). In contrast to both this backwards movement (recollection) and forward movement (hope) repetition is the choice for one who "really lives" (132).

Obviously, there is a parallel between this passage in Kierkegaard and *Lost*. Seasons one through three of the series function as a narrative of recollection in the Kierkegaardian sense: all of the characters are merely the sum of the recalled choices that they had made prior to the moment of arriving on the island. With the end of the third season, the viewer is introduced to the concept of the flash-forward storytelling device, thus mimicking the "unsatisfying fruit" of hope. The fruitlessness of hope is made most manifest in the earliest episodes of season four in which the anticipation of leaving the island is contrasted with the melancholic realization of what happened once the characters left. The final season, in which the off-island stories are repetitions of stories that we have seen previously, with certain changes, seems to offer the Kierkegaardian solution to the problem of recollection and hope in repetition: it is neither what the characters have forgotten in their previous lives nor what they hope will happen after leaving the island that matters, but the subtle displacement that occurs in experiencing that which has already taken place.

Repetition as a narrative device, however, haunts the entire series: scenes in flashbacks between characters often repeat one another (the scene of Jack and Desmond running in the sports stadium in the first and last episodes of season two), certain shots within the series repeat themselves (the various shots of eyes opening being the most obvious example), and certain motifs within character episodes (Patsy Cline songs appearing in Kate-centric episodes) suggest that repetition is something that goes beyond the final season of *Lost* and, moreover, could be understood as an essential narrative element to the entirety of the series. In the overall hermeneutics of the show, repetition becomes an end in itself, a way of understanding the overall meaning of *Lost* without a necessary teleological conclusion.

Finally, repetition insinuates itself into the mode of reading/viewing presented by the show. Throughout the series, characters suggest that films should be reviewed (the orientation film for the Swan station in the episode "Orientation" 2.3) and books should be reread (Philip K. Dick's *Valis* in the episode "Eggtown" 4.4) or have been reread (the young Ben telling Sayid that he had read Carlos Castaneda's *A Separate Reality* twice). What is it in the re-watching and re-reading that produces new meaning? *Lost*, perhaps more than any other show, rewards multiple viewings by being both rich in narrative content and by offering a seemingly greater understanding of the convoluted narrative with repeated viewings. However, like the characters in the final season who come to understand the significance of their lives through the immanent repetition of events (*i.e.*, John Locke's multiple epiphanies in the episode "The Substitute" 6.4), the act of reviewing and rereading (both within the show and by those watching the show) suggests that viewers can make the text into something new through repeated re-examination.

Ultimately, this act of examination is already a form of philosophy. *Lost* does not merely recollect a list of proper names, nor does it simply revisit a series of debates. In representing and embodying concepts such as repetition and becoming within the narrative itself, *Lost* moves beyond being a mere storehouse of cultural references or a type of educated parlor game and offers a working-through of philosophy on the conceptual level. Returning to Deleuze for a moment, at the conclusion of *Cinema 2*, the second volume of his books on film, Deleuze writes:

> [T]here is always a time, midday-midnight, when we must no longer ask ourselves, "What is cinema?" but "What is philosophy?" Cinema itself is a new practice of images and signs, whose theory philosophy must produce as conceptual practice [Deleuze *Cinema 2* 280].

If we substitute "television" for "cinema," then *Lost* offers a new practice of images and signs — the supplemental element that Deleuze analyzes elsewhere — that contributes to the re-conceptualizing of philosophy itself.[8]

## Notes

1. See, for example, Sandra Lee, "Meaning and Freedom on the Island," *Lost and Philosophy: The Island Has Its Reasons*, ed. Sharon M. Kaye, the Blackwell philosophy and pop culture series (Malden: Blackwell Publishing Ltd., 2008), 63–77.

2. Quoted in "Lost Writer Interviewed on Irish Radio," *Lost Media.com*.

3. I am writing this section shortly after the airing of the final episode of *Lost*. Though it appears that the writers have seemingly given us a final answer to this question by placing the final scene of the series in a church with our characters moving on to the afterlife, such seemingly simple conclusions should be resisted. Since any real work on the final episodes of the series will require time and reflection, I will keep my remarks on the final episode to a minimum.

4. Some notable exceptions are the work of Raymond Williams, Marshall McLuhan and Paul Virilio: Raymond Williams, *Television and Cultural Form* (New York: Schocken Books, 1975) and Marshall McLuhan, *Understanding Media* (Cambridge: MIT Press, 1994) and Paul Virilio, "Cyberwar, God and Television: Interview with Paul Virilio" in *ctheory.net*, Arthur and Marilouise Kroker, Eds. <www.ctheory.net/articles.aspx?id=62>.

5. For a different comparison between Deleuze's work and *Lost* see Matthew O. Cory and Wendy C. Cory, "Is the Island a Body Without Organs?" *Lost Online Studies* 1.2. Lost Online Studies.

6. The passage is changed somewhat on the show. The original quoted in full:

> Alice took up the fan and gloves, and, as the hall was very hot, she kept fanning herself all the time she went on talking: "Dear, dear! How queer everything is today! And yesterday things went on just as usual. I wonder if I've been changed in the night? Let me think: *was* I the same when I got up this morning? I almost think I can remember feeling a little different. But if I'm not the same, the next question is 'Who in the world am I?' Ah, *that's* the great puzzle" [*The Annotated Alice* 37].

The most significant elision in Jack's reading is the sentence: "I almost think I can remember feeling a little different" (37). The acknowledgement of the movement of becoming, that one remembers the process by which one feels estranged, is, in this scene, hidden from Jack. This begs the question, why can't Jack be privy to this transformation or becoming? Does this episode prefigure the final episode of the series wherein Jack is the final person to realize that he is, indeed, dead?

7. One of the popular theories about the "sideways world" before the final reveal in the last episode of *Lost* was that the "sideways world" represented an alternate universe, a "mirror world" in which the characters, all having certain flaws in the "real" world of the show, find a type of fantasy fulfillment in the other world. The scenes in which each character looks into the mirror had been read as an explicit acknowledgement of this assumed narrative device.

8. I would like to thank Jason Middleton and Jennifer Creech for all their help in working through the issues addressed in this article.

## WORKS CITED

Carroll, Lewis. *The Annotated Alice*. Ed. Martin Gardner. New York: Wings Books, 1998.
Deleuze, Gilles. *Cinema 2: The Time-Image*. Trans. Hugh Tomlinson and Rober Galeta. Minneapolis: University of Minnesota Press, 1995.
\_\_\_\_\_. "Letter to Serge Daney: Optimism, Pessimism, and Travel." Trans. Martin Joughin. *Negotiations 1972–1990*. European Perspectives: A Series in Social Thought and Cultural Criticism. Laurence D. Kritzman, ed. New York: Columbia University Press, 1995. 68–79.
\_\_\_\_\_. *The Logic of Sense*. Trans. Mark Lester with Charles Stivale. Ed. Constantin V. Boundas, New York: Columbia University Press, 1990.
Kaye, Sharon M. *Lost and Philosophy: The Island Has Its Reasons*. Malden, MA: Blackwell Publishing, 2008.
Kierkegaard, Søren. *Fear and Trembling and Repetition*. Trans. and ed. Howard V. Hong and Edna H. Hong. Kierkegaard's Writings Vol. VI. Princeton: Princeton University Press, 1983.
Wood, J. "Of Myths and Pisteutics (or When the Waves of Faith Crash Against the Rocks of Reason)." Powells.com. 2008. Web. 3 June 2008.

# *Lost* in Theory: Everything You Always Wanted to Know About *Lost* but Were Afraid to Ask Lacan, Derrida, and Foucault

*Giancarlo Lombardi*

Dante Alighieri opens his *Divine Comedy* with a pilgrim lost in the woods, prey to a mid-life crisis: from his perspective, a voyage through Hell, Purgatory, and Paradise will be told. Centuries later, Jack Shephard's open right eye is the very first image shown to viewers of *Lost*. Like Dante's pilgrim, Jack finds himself lost in the woods of the island where his plane crashed. Through his vantage point, much of *Lost*'s narrative gradually unravels, and although the lives of many other characters are portrayed, his mid-life crisis is foregrounded as exemplary.[1] When Richard Alpert screams to a group of characters in "Ab Aeterno" (6.9) that they are all dead, viewers could consider the island, with its green hills, as Dante's Purgatory, the island-mountain where dead souls repented for their sins as they earned their ascent into Paradise. This reading is supported by the final episode of the show ("The End" 6.17 and 6.18) where Jack's father tells him that, like all other passengers of the Oceanic 815 flight, Jack is already dead. Narrated along two parallel axes, the final episode of *Lost* ends with an alternate montage which portrays Jack together with his fellow survivors, eyeing the door of a church which opens on a bright white light, and alone in the woods, walking frantically before falling on the ground, as the camera zooms one last time on his left eye, this time closing and not opening.

This is, of course, one of the many interpretations that *Lost*'s intricate text authorizes, despite the apparent closure provided by the final episodes. Ranked by Networked Insights as the program generating the highest volume of social media interactions,[2] *Lost* has capitalized on its ability to invite diverse readings. Its polysemic textual gaps have galvanized viewers all over the world, making it the ideal example of Umberto Eco's text, the "lazy machine asking the reader to do some of its work" (3). My reference to Eco's famous definition bears particular relevance in this context when related to the title of the work from which it is excerpted: *Six Walks in the Fictional Woods*. The woods are, in fact, another metaphor employed by Eco for the narrative text, and the reading process (and the process of interpretation it inevitably engenders) is seen as a promenade in the woods, along paths that constantly bifurcate. While each text, according to Eco, provides signposts that direct the reader toward a "proper" reading, many readers will likely follow different directions and find themselves *lost*. On *Lost*, much of the action revolves around the long walks taken by the many characters of the show, on search, recovery, or flight missions. Each one of these adventures into the woods thus stands as a metaphor for the hermeneutic process engaged in by the viewers and the survivors of the Oceanic flight alike.

This essay will not aim to provide an all-encompassing theory aimed at analyzing *Lost*'s grand narrative: it will seek, instead, to shed light on certain textual areas through key theoretical concepts borrowed from Jacques Lacan, Jacques Derrida, and Michel Foucault. As a show in which several core characters bear the names of influential Western philosophers (Locke, Hume, Rousseau), *Lost* has lent itself to countless analyses informed by a philosophical framework. In 2008, Sharon M. Kaye edited *Lost and Philosophy: The Island Has Its Reasons*, in which the ABC show was read against the work of a most disparate group of philosophers, ranging from Aquinas to Sartre. The common purpose of these essays was to identify the ways in which *Lost* engaged some of the most highly debated philosophical questions:

> The ABC hit drama *Lost* speaks to our deepest fear: the fear of being cut off from everything we know and love, left to fend for ourselves in a strange land. This fear is a philosophical fear because it speaks to the human condition. It forces us to confront profound questions about ourselves and the world [3].

Published before *Lost* revealed its peculiar mythology, this volume now appears dated because it fails to address significant philosophical issues, among which the question of free will is particularly important. The same applies to Christian Piatt's *Lost: A Search for Meaning*, a volume that investigates the spiritual and religious overtones of the series. Published in 2006, this study fails to address the biblical references lying at the core of the show's mythology, its peculiar re-writing of the figure of Jacob and of the story of Adam and Eve. Simone Regazzoni's *La Filosofia di* Lost: *Philosophy Fiction* is the most recent addition to the studies in this field and, although it has not been translated into English, it bears testimony to the transnational power of *Lost*. Regazzoni's engagement with the first four seasons of the show (his book appeared in early 2009) is deeply indebted to the works of Heidegger and Derrida; the former informs his reading of "truth" in the show, while the latter is evoked to discuss the symbolic role played by the island and by the figure of the survivor. Freud figures prominently for his theorization of the oceanic feeling described in *Civilization and Its Discontents*. Possibly because of its time of production, Regazzoni's essay does not address the role played by another Derridean core concepts: the *pharmakon*.

Derrida's *pharmakon*, together with Foucault's *panopticon*, and Lacan's *nom du père* are the key concepts that guide my reading of *Lost*. Each concept will be applied to the entire textual narrative of the show but will stand, eventually, to represent one of the three mythological figures that cross Jack's path during his life on and off the island. If the final episode seems to tell us, in fact, that the entire show revolved around the life and death of Jack Shephard, it behooves us to ask what role key figures such as Jacob, Man in Black, and Christian Shephard come to play in the economy of the narrative. This is where, I believe, Foucault, Derrida, and Lacan become particularly useful.

## *Panopticism: Jacob Is Watching You*

During the last episode of season four ("There's No Place Like Home, Part 2–3" 4.13 and 4.14), flash-forwards portray the apparent sole survivors of the crash (henceforth called the Oceanic Six) discussing their encounters with a character previously unmentioned: Jeremy Bentham. Viewers soon realize that this name is indeed an alias used by another survivor of the Oceanic crash. Only at the very end of the episode, however, does the camera zoom inside Bentham's open casket, revealing his true identity. It is John Locke, the character often pitted against Jack as counter-protagonist of *Lost*: while Jack, the spinal surgeon, has been portrayed as a Man of Science, John, the invalid who recovers the use of his legs after the crash thanks to the healing powers of the island, plays the role of the Man of Faith. When, in season five ("The Life and Death of Jeremy Bentham" 5.7), John Locke asks Charles Widmore the reason for his new alias, the British millionaire who once led the group in charge of the island (the Others) responds that he is showing considerable irony in re-naming him after a different philosopher. It is the web of reference evoked by Bentham's name that informs this section of my argument.

One of the fathers of utilitarian thought, Bentham is a historical figure closely associated to his architectural work and to his creation of the Panopticon, a prison where light and full visibility replaced the darkness and vertical depth of medieval dungeons. We owe to Michel Foucault, and to his analysis of the Panopticon as symptomatic of a culture of discipline and punishment, a possible interpretation of Locke's new identity.[3] A building complex comprised of a circular set of prisons with a tower of central surveillance at its empty center, the Panopticon is a structure that insures complete exposure of the inmate while guaranteeing absolute invisibility to the warden — all this, thanks to a set of facing windows strategically placed in the individual cells so that excessive light forbids external visibility. Showered with light, the inmate cannot perceive the gaze of the warden; the warden's presence, however, is always known and felt. It becomes internalized to the extent that surveillance is felt even when the controlling tower is empty. From mere architectural structure, the Panopticon, according to Foucault, becomes a metaphor for the constant vigilance experienced in modern society.

Season two of *Lost* introduces viewers into the hatch, plunging them into a world that is not dark, but full of light. Soon revealed to be one of many Dharma stations,[4] the hatch exerts a form of central control over the entire island — the numbers that need to be regularly entered into the obsolete computer bespeak a world whose norms can neither be grasped nor controlled. It is in season three, with the apprehension of Jack, Kate, and Sawyer, that many Dharma stations are finally uncovered, and with them a world of surveillance cameras, currently controlled by their captors, the Others. Responsible for the genocide of all the Dharma members, the Others do not derive their power from their physical (or technological) ability to monitor the movements of their prisoners, but from their knowledge of the background of each survivor of the Oceanic Flight. Knowledge is power, Michel Foucault reminds us.

The two facing cages holding Sawyer and Kate recall the panoptical structure: like most animal cages, they are placed outside and thus showered with light, subject to the gaze of passersby. They are also surveiled by a camera placed right outside, and the images captured by the camera are projected onto one of the many screens from which Ben, who replaced Widmore at the helm of the Others, controls the behavior of the entire group. There are at least eight monitors in Ben's room, and each one provides different vantage points on a community that is held under tight surveillance. Another camera is placed on Jack, monitoring his actions in a different cell, placed inside one of the hatches, but still set up in a way that allows full visibility to the warden and a sense of false open space to the inmate: one of its walls is completely made of glass. All other cameras reserve equal potential for surveillance on the community ruled by Ben — of its members, Juliet is the only character that viewers come to know in depth. Like Jack, Kate, and Sawyer, she is held hostage on the island by Ben, who controls her movements and bribes her with information on her family. Foucault tells us that the panoptical structure is particularly effective because of its ability to be internalized: this is evidenced by the temporary taming of *Lost*'s most rebellious cast member, Sawyer, who is led to believe that his captors have injected an instrument into his body that will make his heart explode when it reaches a high number of heartbeats.

Such awareness radically alters Sawyer's behavior, effectively contained by what is revealed to be a hoax: the panoptical tower might be empty, yet we still feel conditioned by its controlling presence.

In season four, the flash-forwards that replace the flashbacks used in the previous three seasons show us the Oceanic Six dispersed around the globe, but still held captive by a controlling presence they seem to have internalized. All those flash-forwards portray them only in an apparent state of freedom, paranoid about the possibility that someone might be controlling their actions, or guilty for abandoning their fellow survivors on the island. The voices that order them to go back to the island, repeated since the very end of season three, are those of the three known leaders of the Others: John Locke (as Jeremy Bentham), Charles Widmore, and Benjamin Linus. Both Ben and Charles have exerted direct or indirect surveillance over the Oceanic Six since they first left the island: Ben has followed their every move and Charles Widmore, upon renaming Locke as Bentham following his exit from the island, provides him with the exact location of all six survivors exactly because, like Ben, he has kept close vigilance over them. And while Bentham fails in his mission, unable to convince them to return to the island, Ben succeeds by manipulating Bentham, killing him and later staging his death as a suicide. And what does the suicide of the alter ego of the Panopticon's creator tell us, at this point? Is it a testament to the enduring symbolic power of the panoptical structure that continues long after the death of his creator? Is it a prelude to the tragic destiny awaiting Jacob, the mythological guardian of the Panopticon?

*Lost* is a show where competent viewers have come to learn that abstraction is fundamental to a proper comprehension of the events narrated. Like the *Divine Comedy* and *The Name of the Rose*, *Lost* can be read at several levels, and gradual abstraction ultimately provides a higher level of viewer satisfaction: after all, the final episode of season five and the entirety of season six have proven that, behind the story of the passengers of Ocean 815, that of the Dharma Initiative, and that of the Others, lies a story that harks back to the Classical era, that of the enmity between Jacob and his nameless twin brother, whom we will call, following the common practice of *Lost* bloggers and commentators, Man in Black. The last episode of season five ("The Incident" 5.16 and 5.17) shows that ageless Jacob once touched the lives of a handful of survivors; he met them at pivotal points in their lives, when they were about to exercise their free will in ways that would change their lives forever.[5] When the first episodes of season six reveal that the survivors had actually been summoned to the island by that same higher power because they were candidates for his replacement as guardians of the very island, the ghost of panopticism is directly evoked. While the panoptical structure had been mainly felt, until then, through the power of modern technology or through the supernatural omnipresence of Jacob, it is suddenly evoked at the end of the fifth episode of season six by a lighthouse, where Jack is summoned by Jacob so that he may perceive what role the future guardian will be asked to play. At the top of the mysterious structure, whose presence was hidden from sight until then simply because, as Hurley says, they "weren't looking for it," Jack sees a surveillance instrument which works similarly to Jeremy Bentham's panoptical tower: the guardian gains insight through a set of mirrors placed against one another, just like the facing windows located in the cells of Bentham's inmates. What Jack sees in the mirrors as he reorients the wheel that holds them together is his childhood home, basking in the sun. It is then that he realizes the extent of Jacob's surveillance and, suddenly angered, smashes the mirrors to little pieces. The placement of the facing mirrors inside the surveillance tower instead of in the (non-existing) prisoner cells demonstrates that the role of the guardian is the one carrying the deepest solitude. As he monitors others, Jacob is himself prisoner in a role that, as "Across the Sea" (6.15) tells us, he did not choose for himself. By smashing the mirrors, Jack might be attempting to exit a role that is about to become his, thus exercising his free will, yet it is painfully clear that, like Jacob, he has no other options. As an appendix to this discussion, it is worth noting that Hurley's final choice to replace Jack as guardian of the island (once Jack commits the ultimate sacrifice to keep the island afloat) is indeed quite appropriate, since Hurley, like Jacob, has been characterized by his ability to *see*. For a long time, in fact, he is the only survivor who can actually see and communicate with the dead, and in particular with Jacob.

On a different note, I believe it is important to discuss the role played by the lighthouse in *Lost* at a macro-structural level. When the viewers see, along with Jack, the images of his childhood home reflected in the facing mirrors, they are invited to see this particular episode as a commentary on the entire narrative process of the show. If we follow the metaphor of the moving flashes of light sent by the lighthouse, which through its mirrors reflects images of the lives of an individual character, we might come to identify each individual episode of the show as portraying the images reflected by a single individual flash of the lighthouse. When Jack smashes the mirrors, there is no doubt that *Lost*'s narrative is soon to come to an end.

## *The Pharmakon: The Poisonous Power of Medicines and Other Gifts*

In the opening episode of season six ("LA X, Parts 1 & 2" 6.1 and 6.2), a near-fatally wounded Sayid is rescued by Jack, Hurley, Kate, and Jin, and, following Jacob's directives, is taken to a location previously unknown to viewers and survivors alike: the temple. In order to access the temple, our protagonists descend into a hole and find themselves lost in a maze. This is, of course, one of many descents that have characterized their journey; such downward movement should be read as equally symbolic as the frequent crossing of the woods. The vertical dimension already invoked by the discovery and incursion into the hatch, Ben and Locke's descent into the Orchid, and Juliet's fall into the pit next to the H-bomb (all events appropriately used as season-ending cliffhangers, and reprised in season-opening episodes) takes on new significance as we follow the characters into the caves of the temple, because this descent symbolizes with renewed impetus the viewers' necessity to "dig deeper" into the mythological background of the narrative. Much of the focus of season six, in fact, lies on the disclosure of the story of Jacob and Man in Black, and viewers learn of the centrality of these two characters in gradual and often confusing fashion, lost in a maze recalled, at a visual level, by the recess of the temple, whose walls are inscribed with those same hieroglyphs often associated to Jacob and his world.

Seized by the inhabitants of the temple, the Oceanic survivors are granted hospitality and Sayid is given the chance to be healed only after Hurley offers proof of his connection to Jacob. He opens the guitar case he has carried since his return to the island, containing a wooden object in the shape of an *ankh*, an Egyptian symbol that recurs frequently in hieroglyphs, as a pendant, and as part of the statue towering over the island in its early days. Embodying life and immortality, the large *ankh* was Jacob's gift to Hurley, yet it is revealed as merely another container: once cracked open, it discloses a foreboding message from Jacob, who instructs his men to keep Sayid alive. It is only then that Sayid is taken into the central hall of the temple and immersed in waters that have suddenly become muddy. Although the temple's waters are meant to heal him, they initially poison him to death. When Sayid eventually comes back to life, he appears to be a changed man. The oxymoronic juxtaposition of remedy and poison, paired with the double-binding nature of all gifts, brings me to a theoretical examination of *Lost* informed by the Derridean concept of the *pharmakon*.

Deconstruction, as theorized by Jacques Derrida, teaches us to appreciate contrasting forces of signification at work within different typologies of texts. Composed of a rich texture, the narrative of *Lost* is the fruit of a complex interweaving of threads visually recalled by Jacob's activity at the loom. Within such a texture, the deconstructive lesson teaches us to tease out the threads that run counter one another, the places where splicing might occur and the thread might seem to break in two opposite directions. Deconstruction teaches us to practice *splicing* and *grafting*. The former encourages us to pay close attention to individual terms which may be the site of discordant polysemy, while the latter process requires us to superimpose profoundly diverse texts onto one another in order to achieve a thicker reading of both texts.[6] Although the *pharmakon* belongs to the realm of Derridean splicing, its application to *Lost* can be further complicated, as I will demonstrate at the end of this section, by the eventual grafting of another text, Michelangelo Antonioni's *The Passenger* (1975).

In "Plato's Pharmacy," an essay on Plato's *Phaedrus*, Derrida discusses the splicing inherent to Plato's use of the Greek term *pharmakon* which, defining *writing* in its binary relation to *logos*, evokes the two opposite meanings of the word: *remedy* and *poison*. In asking us to take both meanings into simultaneous consideration, Derrida brings into play two other terms etymologically adjacent: *pharmakos* (scapegoat) and *pharmakeus* (magician).[7] Images evoking all these terms appear in the episodes that open the last season of *Lost*, culminating with the destruction of the temple in "Sundown" (6.6). When Sayid is immersed in the pool of muddy water, he is healed *and* poisoned at the same time. Initially mistaken for dead, he comes back to life, but his body is slowly deprived of his old personality, and possessed instead by the same darkness that corrupted Claire during her time in the wilderness. Responsibility for the corrupted healing process is placed upon newly-reborn John Locke, whose body has been invaded by Man in Black, also known as the Smoke Monster. Both scapegoat and magician, John Locke takes under siege the very place of his expulsion: the man who is forcefully kept away by the inhabitants of the temple is in fact the last incarnation of that Smoke Monster which terrorizes the island from the vents located in the dark recess of the temple itself. The ambiguous healing power located in the temple first appears in season five ("This Place Is Death" 5.5), when Rousseau's partner emerges physically unscathed from his first encounter with the Smoke Monster, yet prey to the same dark presence which later possesses Claire and Sayid. For this reason Rousseau is eventually forced to kill him. A few episodes later, young Ben is shot by Sayid and taken by Kate and Juliet to the Others so he can be healed. Richard's remarks upon receiving him announce his imminent metamorphosis: "If I take him, he's not ever gonna be the same again [...] his innocence will be gone. He will always be one of us" ("Whatever Happened, Happened" 5.11). Responsible for the murder of his father and the genocide of the Dharma community, Ben becomes the most ruthless leader of the Others. He believes he can summon the Smoke Monster at his own will, unaware of his subjection to the very power that shaped him: "It's where I was told I could summon the monster. That's before I realized that it was the one summoning me" ("What They Died For" 6.16).

In *Given Time*, Derrida traces another etymological splicing in the German word *Gift*, where he locates a Latin root that likens the gift to the *pharmakon*, the dose (*dosis*) of poison he calls "poisoned present" (36). Gifts often acquire poisonous overtones in *Lost*, as witnessed by the past history of many core characters of the show. After winning millions of dollars at the lottery, Hurley falls prey to constant bad luck. When Jin agrees to work for his father-in-law, he forfeits his moral integrity in exchange for financial security. Charlie's pursuit of a successful music career causes his fast descent into drug-addiction. In order to secure advanced cancer treatment for her ailing sister, Juliet exiles herself on the island, where she eventually dies. On a much larger scale, the very gift of life is poisonous on the island of *Lost*, where all pregnant women mysteriously die before reaching the third trimester of pregnancy.

At the very core of the mythology of the island lies a gift that a mother makes to her two children, Jacob and Man in Black: a wooden box containing a white and a black pebble. No script accompanies the box, no rules are provided for the game. It is up to the two children to establish their own rules. This should be read as a *mise-en-abyme* of the entire process of myth-production accomplished by the authors of *Lost*. Although much has been written about the possible referents lying behind the mythology of *Lost*, no precise referential framework can or should be properly identified. Although biblical and classical references are obvious, the foundational myths of *Lost* are unique and original, just like the rules created by Man in Black and his young brother for their new game. The white and the black pebbles carry a legacy of division and enmity, separating the two players in irreconcilable roles. Indeed, the very giver of the gift eventually suffers the consequence of the rivalry she has fueled: she is killed by the bearer of the dark pebble, Man in Black, soon after investing her other son Jacob as new guardian of the island and of its magical powers. This last gift to Jacob, staged again through water, is a gift of knowledge, power, and infinite solitude. The same gift is eventually passed on to Jack, and later to Hurley.

I will now conclude this section by returning briefly to John Locke, who truly experienced the power of the island as *pharmakon* after the plane crash. The paralyzed man who starts to walk upon crashing on the island is forced into a role, as a result of his healing, that eventually leads to his death. For Locke, however, I wish to return to the Derridean concept of the textual graft, whereby two widely diverse texts assume new meaning through their juxtaposition. I believe that, although much has been written about Locke's association to the philosopher of the *tabula rasa*, another "Locke" should be brought into conversation with *Lost*. It is David Locke, the protagonist of Michelangelo Antonioni's *Professione: Reporter*, a film known in the U.S. as *The Passenger*, and made famous by Jack Nicholson's masterful interpretation of this particular character. The story of a journalist who changes his name and assumes the identity of a dead man he accidentally encountered during a *reportage* in Africa, *The Passenger* portrays a man who trades his life of passive spectatorship for one of active involvement. Just as John Locke arrives on the island a paralyzed man, but discovers that he can walk and provide for himself and others, Antonioni's David Locke leaves behind the journalist's role as "seer" in order to become a "doer." What he does not know, however, is that the man he replaces is an arms trafficker and that he is trading one form of slavery for another. Similarly, the John Locke who lands on the island with a suitcase full of knives discovers that his newfound active role is limited by the external constraints placed on his actions by Jacob. Moreover, off the island, as he assumes the new identity of Jeremy Bentham, the ultimate "seer," he walks towards the same impending doom encountered by Antonioni's protagonist. Both characters, in fact, are murdered, yet the cause of their death is made uncertain by their clearly suicidal intentions.

The reference to the title of Antonioni's film casts a much wider shadow on the ABC series: *Lost* is the story of many *passengers*, men and women who assume new identities on the island which are functional to the roles their survival on the island necessitates. In a flash-sideway of "LA X, Parts 1 & 2," John Locke considers the human soul as passenger in the empty shell of the human body during a conversation with Jack at the Lost Baggage counter. While Locke lost a suitcase full of knives, Jack lost a very different piece of baggage: his father's coffin. When the two meet and discuss their incident, Locke says to Jack, "They didn't lose your father [...] they just lost his body." In this light, we should read the figure of Man in Black as that of the ultimate, evil *passenger* who inhabits the dead bodies of Christian Shephard (season one through five) and John Locke (season five and six). Reborn as anathema to the people around them, Christian and John personify the poisonous nature of Man in Black as Derridean *pharmakon*.

## *Enter Lacan: Of Phalluses, Fathers, and Names*

In season one, Jack and Kate venture into the heart of the island and, as they are about to jump into a waterfall, they discover two skeletons, later identified as belonging to a man and a woman ("House of the Rising Sun" 1.6). The two gemstones that adorn one of the two skeletons, one black and one white, gain much relevance five seasons later, when the story of Jacob and Man in Black is revealed. It is only then that the identity of the two skeletons, humorously called by Jack "our Adam and Eve" in both episodes, becomes clear to viewers alone: these two people were not a couple, but they were mother and child. To be precise, the mother was only an adoptive parent, since she had usurped the role of the biological mother after killing her at childbirth, and the son (Man in Black) was left lying next to her by his own twin brother (Jacob), who had killed him after Man in Black had stabbed to death the woman who had long pretended to be their mother. This confusing, disorienting tale lies at the very heart of the mythology of *Lost*: it is the *originary* tale staging a peculiar *originary* sin. Remnants of a unique restaging of the Freudian primal scene, the two skeletons signify the profound subversion of the incest taboo that Lévi-Strauss marks as the threshold into the symbolic network. The incest taboo distinguishes nature from culture, ushering the child into a world of rules shared by our entire society. The rules of the island, however, like the rules of the game invented by Man in Black, are mysterious and unique. Like the island itself, the island's inhabitants are secluded and estranged from the rest of the world in a place where, despite repeated attempts at colonization, nature still coexists with advanced technology.

In his re-thinking of Freudian psychoanalysis, Jacques Lacan comes to the conclusion that, just as the primal scene can be experienced merely at a symbolic level, the maternal and the paternal role actually gain even further strength over the subject when not played by actual parents. The Symbolic Father and the Symbolic Mother thus become central to Lacan's rethinking of the family romance.[8] In *Lost*, the murder of the Symbolic Mother acts as a "myth of origin" and, as such, it prepares the ground for the advent of a patriarchal community. As Elizabeth Grosz points out, according to Lacan, "one must postulate an earlier 'event' at the origin of patriarchy which explains the father's pre-eminent position. This is less likely to be a parricide than a matricide" (69).

No viewer would question the fact that, despite the presence of such an influential female role in the "myth of origin," *Lost* portrays a universe that is heavily male-centered. The struggle of power between Jacob and Man in Black parallels equal struggles between Charles Widmore and Benjamin Linus as well as Jack Shephard and John Locke. Although their strength and propensity for violence make them *phallic* women, characters such as Kate, Juliet, and Sun are never truly placed at the core of the narrative. The first two, in particular, are sequestered in roles of fetishistic commodities circulated between two male lead characters of the show, Jack and Sawyer. The most recurring question raised about Kate and Juliet's fate on the show centers on their eventual "choosing" or "belonging to" one of these two male characters. Thus, from a Lacanian perspective, we should read them as *phallic* women not simply because they embrace weapons and kill people, but because, in their relation to their male counterparts, they come to signify the *phallus*, the elusive possession of which would guarantee men a sense of wholeness. As Jacob says in "What They Died For" (6.16), he brought Jack, Sawyer and the other candidates to the island because of their flawed existence. "You were all looking for something that you couldn't find out there." Furthermore, Kate was conveniently excluded for candidacy, according to Jacob, once she became a mother (a Symbolic Mother, since Aaron's real mother was Claire). We should remember here that, for Lacan, men and women are equally yearning for possession of the phallus; however, women may experience such possession through child-rearing, while men can only experience it through partnership with a woman. Yet, the fate reserved to the would-be patriarchs is one of loneliness, and thus of perennial unfulfillment. This is why, when discussing his choice of candidates, Jacob says to them, "You were all flawed. I chose you because you were like me. You were all alone."

The role played by Jacob in the life of the candidates is that, indeed, of a Symbolic Father. Since the island contains a secret source of light that insures that evil will not be unleashed upon the entire world, Jacob's role as guardian places him in a symbolic paternal role for society at large. For a long time, we are told that he has only appeared to Richard Alpert, and when he touches the lives of the future candidates at the end of season five, he does it without identifying himself. They know him as Jacob only after his death, in his ghostly appearances. His evanescent presence makes him, then, the ultimate representative of the elusive yet powerful paternal presence common to the lives of most characters of the show. Jacques Lacan conceptualizes such elusiveness in the Symbolic paternal figure by reducing it to a mere signifier (and signifiers, according to Lacan, are always slippery): a name, the Name-of-the-Father, which is the key concept that will inform the concluding paragraphs of my essay.[9] Following the Lacanian logic of the slippery signifier, whose constant movement places the individual in ever-changing roles, we are better able to understand the shifting paternal role in the narrative and its eventual co-incidence in the final episode of the show with the figure of Christian Shephard. *Lost* ends its narrative in fact on the poignant rejoining of Symbolic and Real Father through a character whose name evokes clear religious overtones.

The question of naming harks back to the mythological core of the show. When Jacob and his brother are born, their biological mother is surprised to find out that she has given birth to more than one child. As a result, she is only able to name one of them (Jacob) because she never thought of an alternative name. This, we are told, is the reason Man in Black will never have his own name, and for this reason, we might argue, after his death at Jacob's hands, as Smoke Monster he will be able to inhabit different bodies and take on new identities. Names, and the obligations they carry in relation to their paternal ascendance, are very important for the economy of the show, so the character's namelessness places him in the ultimate position of abject trickster, defiant of all rules and separated since birth from social belonging.

At the intradiegetic level, the fatherlessness of Jacob and his nameless brother is revisited in many different ways: most survivors of Oceanic 815 are either fatherless or have been deeply traumatized by the death of their father. Kate has never met her father, and goes to jail when she kills her mother's abusive new husband. Claire is a single parent who has only recently met her biological father. Jin hides his poor father's existence from his rich wife, who herself suffers from the profound interference of an emotionally abusive paternal figure. Sawyer and Locke experience interconnected paternal trauma, since the former witnesses the violent death of his parents, swindled by the absentee father of the latter. Spending the rest of his life seeking revenge, Sawyer eventually accomplishes it on the island, when he murders his nemesis as a favor to John, who was once cheated out of a kidney and put on a wheelchair by his abusive father. Once an elusive figure to both characters, then an abusive presence in his son's life, John's father assumes extreme symbolic relevance upon his death, because his son is invested as new leader of the Others only once he is able to carry his corpse on his shoulder ("The Brig" 3.19). The same group previously invested Benjamin Linus as their leader after he accomplished another parricide, murdering his own father and the entire Dharma community.

Gaining leadership through ritual murders, John and Ben become Symbolic Fathers of their new community, yet their power appears limited by those very mythic figures which stand at the core of the narrative: Jacob and Man in Black. And while Jacob is enshrined in his role as guardian firmly installed in the Panoptical lighthouse that towers over the island, Man in Black is left to roam and poison the souls of its inhabitants as he seeks to escape an island on which he is forever trapped. Against these two Symbolic Fathers, one benign and the other evil, yet both equally controlling, stands a third figure, the only one that actually can be said to have played that role in real life, Jack's father. The show began with Jack flying to Los Angeles, carrying a coffin with his dead father back home. The father, who is long portrayed as an obstacle in his son's professional and emotional development, is eventually revealed to be worthy of the name Christian Shephard when he acts as his son's final guide towards eternal peace ("The End"). Jack, whose terrestrial shepherding began once he first took over as leader of the crash survivors, finds new meaning in his birth name when asked to replace his namesake, Jacob, as guardian of the island. As his journey through life comes to an end on the very island he just managed to save from the destruction caused by Man in Black, Jack takes one last painful walk through the woods before lying down to die. In the flash-sideway universe, where his afterlife journey has been portrayed since the beginning of season six, he finally comes to peace with his father and his own death when he learns that his act of shepherding has indeed touched many lives. In this moment of ultimate reconciliation (with his father, his friends, and his present condition) Jack learns that his Christ-like sacrifice, for the good of the entire world, was indeed not in vain.

## Notes

1. Jack's central role in the narrative is revealed, at a purely structural level, by the mere fact that he is the subject of two of the first five episodes' flashbacks. In the fifth episode, "White Rabbit" (1.5) we are told that Jack went to Australia to find his estranged father, whose dead body he was carrying back to the U.S. on the plane that crashed. In the penultimate episode of the series, "What They Died For" (6.16), Jack and his three fellow survivors were told by Jacob that they had been brought to the island because of their state of crisis, because they were "flawed and alone." Jack's pivotal presence is once again reasserted in this episode, which opens on another close-up of his open right eye, when he eventually volunteers to replace Jacob as guardian of the island and its mysterious powers.

2. According to the SocialSenseTV network ratings report, *Lost* generates an average of 1,314,000 online interactions per week (Networked Insights 4).

3. For a detailed discussion of the Panopticon and its social effects, see Foucault 195–228.

4. The Dharma Initiative was constituted by a group of scientists who took over the island in the '70s to conduct research in "meteorology, psychology, parapsychology, zoology, and electro-magnetism" ("Orientation" 2.3).

5. In "Ab Aeterno" (6.9), Jacob tells Richard Alpert of his firm belief in letting men choose their path voluntarily, even when this would lead them to their eventual demise. This allows us to reread many of the scenes from "The Incident" (5.16 and 5.17): Jacob gives a pen to little Sawyer right after his parents' death, yet the little kid could have chosen not to write the letter that would drive the desire for revenge that would inspire all his future actions. Similarly, after Sayid's wife dies crossing the road, distracted by her husband who is giving directions to Jacob, Sayid could have chosen not to seek retribution by becoming Ben's gun for hire. Caught stealing in a convenience store, Kate could have equally steered clear of trouble after Jacob paid for the object she had stolen, instead of choosing a rebellious path.

6. For a discussion of splicing and grafting, see Culler 85–156.

7. A thorough discussion of the *pharmakon* is provided in Derrida, *Disseminations* 61–171 and Culler 142–144.

8. For a discussion of the Lacanian reinterpretation of the family romance, see Lacan 179–225 and Grosz 67–74.

9. On the Lacanian concept of the Name-of-the-Father, see Silverman 178–193.

## Works Cited

Antonioni, Michelangelo, dir. *The Passenger*. Sony Pictures Classics, 1975.
Culler, Jonathan. *On Deconstruction: Theory and Criticism after Structuralism*. Ithaca: Cornell University Press, 1982.
Derrida, Jacques. *Given Time: I. Counterfeit Money*. Chicago: University of Chicago Press, 1992.
———. "Plato's Pharmacy." *Disseminations*. Chicago: University of Chicago Press, 1981. 61–171.
Eco, Umberto. *Six Walks in the Fictional Woods*. Cambridge: Cambridge University Press, 1994.
Foucault, Michel. *Discipline and Punish: The Birth of the Prison*. New York: Vintage, 1979.
Grosz, Elizabeth. *Jacques Lacan: A Feminist Introduction*. London: Routledge, 1990.
Kaye, Sharon M., ed. *Lost and Philosophy: The Island Has Its Reasons*. Oxford: Blackwell, 2008.

Lacan, Jacques. *Ecrits: A Selection*. New York: Norton, 1977.
Networked Insights. "SocialSenseTV: Network Ratings Report, May 2010." Web. July 2010.
Piatt, Christian. *Lost: A Search for Meaning*. St. Louis: Chalice Press, 2006.
Regazzoni, Simone. *La filosofia di* Lost: *Philosophy Fiction*. Milan: Ponte Alle Grazie, 2009.
Silverman, Kaja. *The Subject of Semiotics*. Oxford: Oxford University Press, 1983.

# "So This Is All in My Mind?": Hugo Crash-Tests the Contemporary Crusoe

*Matthew Pangborn*

Almost three centuries before viewers began to rearrange their television-watching schedules around the mysterious goings-on of the lost passengers of Oceanic Flight 815, a novel about a shipwrecked sailor put into fable form nothing less than the reorganization of the world. Drawing heavily from the thinking of English empiricist John Locke, *Robinson Crusoe* (1719) so inspired Jean-Jacques Rousseau that the French philosopher made it the only book he allowed the pupil in his own novel of education, *Émile* (1762). The scores of unauthorized sequels *Crusoe* spawned and the thousands of readers who strove to emulate its hero's independent-minded pragmatism attest to the novel's influence over the long period of the West's rapid modernization. Defoe's novel has been read for a long time as *the* parable of modernity. Celebrated early on as an origin tale of the adventurous *homo economicus* whose popularization was necessary for the rise of capitalism, the novel has been more recently read as a whitewashed preview of the brutal colonization that was to go hand-in-hand with that economic system's taking hold of the globe.[1] *Lost*'s popularity is likely due to the Crusoe myth's persistence even today, despite studies that have elaborated in great detail on the ethnocentric and exploitative consequences of its central fantasy.

Not only has *Robinson Crusoe* been continued to be remade, as in the Tom Hanks' vehicle *Cast Away* (2000), entire institutions of mind depend upon the book's basic premise. BBC's *Desert Island Discs*, for example, one of the longest-running radio shows on the planet, invites each guest to score a soundtrack suitable for his or her own shipwrecking. And the reality of today's seemingly innumerable reality TV shows appears to consist solely of their adherence to the concept that to be a successful member of this culture requires that one be ruthlessly alone. This is true whether one desires to command an island, a stage, or merely a boardroom seat a little closer to The Donald's strange tonsorial swoop. Crusoe-ism even permeates American politics, where its ideal of resourceful self-determinism has played up to the crowds on welfare reform and a health-care status quo, all the while fomenting the isolationist dreams of third-party libertarians. Indeed, one might say the economy's recent downturn has only brightened the appeal of the idea that Americans, like Crusoe, would be much better off if simply left to their own devices. The wreckage that *Lost* has displayed each week scattered across its idyllic beaches thus signifies both a loss of faith in those steering the airliner of state and an increased cynicism about where that vehicle has been heading. It also holds out, however, even still, the promise of a newer, even more photogenic New World, whose setting might finally guarantee the secure home for our Western hero that the first New World has failed thus far to deliver. Better than any other post-apocalyptic imagining current today, then, *Lost* captures the feelings of Americans who, living the modern myth to its westernmost drift, both dream about and fear the prospect of starting all over again the very same story.

In this way, *Lost*'s updating of the Crusoe myth makes its central crisis of stranding a communal experience, which is perhaps a closer reading of the novel than that given it by so many eager Crusoe emulators. Overlooked in Crusoe's popular application as the imagined heaven of one for the social Darwinist, after all, is the fact that quite a lot of the novel takes place off the island Crusoe himself views as a "prison." He battles Barbary pirates, makes his fortune on a Brazilian plantation, and hunts with his best mate, Friday, the wild beasts of the Pyrenees. For Crusoe, as for so many of the stranded sailors who served as his author's inspiration, being separated from society is a debilitating trauma, one whose downward course is spared Crusoe by his timely sighting of a footprint in the sand. Yet there is something to the character of a solitary inhabitant of an otherwise deserted island that is so fundamental especially to the contemporary American's conception of himself that it is nearly impossible to imagine the nation embracing another archetype. But if Defoe's novel casts a long shadow over Jeffrey Lieber, J. J. Abrams, and Damon Lindelof's TV show, it is because *Lost* asks us to think about the role in our own daily lives of that fictional sovereign of his own little world. That is, *Lost* pursues in its own labyrinthine and frenetic way an interrogation of the Crusoe fantasy alive in each of its viewers, exploring at the same time the possibility that there just might be an alternative to the culture's long fascination with Crusoe-ism.

## *Cue Backstory*

The TV show does this first of all through an acknowledgement of the influence of the novel on modern Western thought. *Lost*'s list of characters reads at times like a *Who's Who* of theorists who have systematically studied, each in his own way, the implications of the novel's modern subject. The show openly references Locke, Rousseau, and David Hume, for example, but it also invokes through its names Edmund Burke, William Godwin, and Thomas Carlyle. If *Lost* presents to its viewers, then, a return to the very moment of conception of the modern world, it does so self-consciously, almost heavy-handedly. The island upon which its various plots unfold resembles in its uniqueness those Utopias and Erewhons dreamed of by Western thinkers who imagined a New World both of geography and of knowledge: new lands, that is, whose rate of discovery was to be matched only by the pace of modern breakthroughs in the sciences. The island of *Lost* thus hovers somewhere between real location and rhetorical construct. Such a place was necessary for the pronouncements of theorists who wanted to imagine that the great upheavals of their time had been lying in wait for people wise enough simply to notice them. Bound up in the age's self-declaration as an Enlightenment, of course, is the notion that all the modern citizen has to do is open his eyes, and the world is changed. But this half-constructed place is also where we still find ourselves today.

When Locke famously declared in his second *Treatise on Government* (1689), for example, that "in the beginning all the world was America," he was referencing the barter system of the Native Americans, which he claimed underlay the more complex financial markets of the modernizing West (section 49). But he was also creating, rhetorically, a setting for the Western individual that he, like so many others, wanted to believe was beholden only to his own powers of seeing and thinking for his connection to a demonstrable, objective reality. If the individual was a *tabula rasa*, that is, a blank slate ready for self-inscription, the world was its necessary complement: a vast storehouse awaiting that individual's possession and cultivation. The demonstrable, objective reality Locke put forward was thus one that from the very start needed only the right surveyor to tease out its secrets. The island Defoe set within sight of the New World, then, is the true homeland, conceptually, of every modern citizen. It is a place whose area matches its sovereign observer's horizon of view, which can thus withhold no secrets from his piercing, rational, and systematic gaze, but which presents easily recognizable objects only awaiting his organization and use. All of these assumptions about the Western individual's fundamental relationship to the world have directed our development of technology towards very specific ends. It is no accident, that is, that the activity for which Crusoe seems to be designed sounds rather like watching a TV.

Defoe's novel did much to popularize the Enlightenment's prioritization of a first-person epistemology and morality by encouraging its readers to copy its hero's basic approach to a world that revolved around that hero's "I." Like Crusoe, but also like early scientists such as Isaac Newton, who drew the curtains over his living-room windows in order to study the basic properties of light, the modern citizen was to decide himself, through his own secluded eye-witnessing, what was real in the world.[2] Like Crusoe, but also like England's early census-takers, who judged the most important knowledge about the nation's population to be that which was apparent from an abstracting distance, the modern citizen was someone who was to hold the world at arm's length in order to study it from afar.[3] And, like Crusoe, but also like the first explorers of the New World, who sought out mountain tops in order to lay claim to a greater prospect of land, the modern citizen was to judge his sight as a means of taking possession.[4]

This latter characteristic was to prove most important in the Crusoization of the West. Few had the education, leisure hours, and specialized equipment to spend their afternoons tracing the skitterish movement of prismatic refractions across the patterned paper of their living-room walls. The lust for possession, however, was much more easily universalizable. The Americans of the early republic might inveigh against the irreligious mania of fashion and fortune, but eventually they too succumbed. They too came to celebrate the visual ecstasy Charles Baudelaire was to describe, strolling through the first multi-windowed shopping arcades in Paris.[5] In the world with which *Lost* confronts us, however, that early queasiness has returned. We spend our every waking moment, it seems, staring through (Microsoft) Windows and at TV or film screens, but only after the illusion of that individualist, social–Darwinist heaven has been popped by countless communal catastrophes. Now that acquisitive individualism has created a first-world of big-box retail and a third-world of these hulking stores' corresponding sweatshops — with an ecological disaster swamping every ocean in between — our participation in the Crusoe fantasy has devolved into a guilty pleasure.

Who has not dreamed of having wealth and power thrust upon him rather than it being bought through his own rapine? Who has not dreamed, in other words, of winning the lottery? What *Lost* asks us to consider is thus our continued involvement in a dream no longer held together by the self-sufficient, self-assertive Crusoe. At the center of our fantasy, in stark contrast, we find *Lost*'s much more enigmatic Hugo Reyes.

## *Whatever, Dude*

Hugo is a character who in the truest postmodern sense would be skeptical of any grand narrative of history, even — or perhaps especially — a reading that asserts his own significance. Crusoe goes to sea against his father's wishes in order to follow an inner drive for discovery but also for dominion; Hugo is a character guided, when he appears to be guided, by the desire rather for an absent father's approval. Yet, like Crusoe, his chance to fulfill that Western fantasy of the solitary observer on an easily surveyable plot of earth comes as the result of something like supernatural intervention. Crusoe regularly reflects upon his abandonment as the workings of providence, designed to teach him a moral about his life — but also to enrich him in a much more literal fashion. He is a prodigal son, whose "fall" is "fortunate" in that it brings him great wealth and power, so that he might return home and reintegrate at a higher level in society.[6] Hugo differs from Crusoe in suspecting that the supernatural intervention resulting in his abandonment is not divine. More important, however, is the nature itself of his exile: not only is he not alone, but there does not seem to be any benefit to be gained by his conceptual shipwrecking. At the slightest hint from another character that the society around him is a solipsistic illusion, he is ready to commit suicide. And, more than for any other character, Hugo's attempts at homecoming in the last seasons find him traveling over the same territory, with hardly anything having been changed. There is the wealth that is a burden to him, a family that "just doesn't get it," and friends who seem not wholly there.

Whereas Crusoe suffers isolation in order to prove his resourcefulness and thus serves as the mascot for philosophers seeking an individualist rather than a social account of humanity's origins, Hugo is a determinedly other-oriented person. Indeed, when we first meet him, he suffers from the guilt of having caused harm to others through the pursuit of his own pleasure. Not until episode 18 of season two, "Dave," however, are viewers given sufficient information about his past to make out his story. Hugo, who is overweight, is haunted by the thought that he caused the death of two people at a party by stepping onto an already overcrowded outdoor deck which then collapsed. Hospitalized for his resulting depression, he meets a fellow patient, Leonard Simms, who mumbles over and over a particular sequence of numbers. Another patient, "Dave," functions as his alter-ego, drawing Hugo deeper into his depressed state through what seems on the surface only a fun-loving rebellion. Once he is released from the institution, Hugo uses Simms' numbers to play the lottery and wins. His good fortune proves of that peculiar Monkey's-Paw variety, however. Although the millions of dollars he wins allows him to buy the fast food restaurant in which he once worked and to move into a mansion with his mother (attracting the return of his long-absent father), he also comes to believe that he is responsible for several seemingly related catastrophes, including the death of a TV reporter whose name provides the title of episode 10 of season three, "Tricia Tanaka Is Dead." Hugo finds himself on Oceanic Flight 815 as the result of an attempt to visit the source of Simms' number sequence in Australia and thus lift the curse harming others that seems to have accompanied his streak of luck.

The character of Hugo thus presents from the start a very different conception of human personality than is demonstrated by Crusoe. Hugo's history, like those of all the other characters, emphasizes the aleatory nature of his entanglement with others' lives rather than any notion of his own remote self-determinism. Much more passive, other-oriented, and empathetic in his approach to the world than Crusoe, Hugo also has to do very little to accomplish his own fortune. If he is the modern individual updated for our times, the differences between Hugo and Crusoe reflect our contemporary dream of a guilt-free wealth, but also the fact that the luxuries of today's world are, for a select few (who are, not coincidentally, most addicted to the Crusoe myth), so easily come by that these few might remain blind to the fact that their comfort requires the exploitation of others. It takes a meteorite landing on a TV reporter outside a chicken restaurant to make Hugo reflect upon the consequences of his native good fortune but also, pointedly, his overconsumption. Whereas Crusoe is the mascot of a culture that has an entire world to exploit, hungry and hustling in his ambition and audacity, Hugo is that hero's mirror image: oversatiated, isolated, numb. His is not the adventurous dawn of history but seemingly its inglorious last whimper.

Yet once a moment of trauma forces Hugo to recognize the connections between his own privilege and others' pain, the character is determined to do something about it. The idea that his good fortune might be causing others' suffering makes him want to give up that easily found fortune in his life off the island. On the island, Hugo's wealth takes the form of the Dharma Initiative food he repeatedly stashes away. And the possibility that his overconsumption is hurting himself as much as it cheats others provokes him into a similar giveaway of his food stores. Rather than measuring his status through acquisition, as a Crusoe, no matter what harm it does himself and others, then, Hugo begins to grope for a healthier, more responsible means of asserting himself. And although his plans to give all of his money away seem to be motivated by nothing more complex than a simple care for himself and others, the gesture does evoke the possibility of another system of measuring social status. It brings to mind, for example, the potlatch of many northwestern Native American tribes, which has been investigated as a counter-modern alternative by such thinkers as Georges Bataille.[7]

The idea that a person might be judged by what he gives away rather than what he hoards is a very basic refutation of the Crusoe character. According to Locke, after all, even human nature may be defined in terms of possession: one's life, figured as one's freedom, is one's most basic possession. In these terms, the slavery of Locke's era was simple theft; but in the terms in which Hugo relates to others, such a crime is almost incomprehensible. His conversation with Jack in which he voices his opinion about the futility of such a dream of security as their food-rationing plan envisions presents, however, not just a compelling case for acknowledging responsibility for others. It argues against the idea that other people might be supervised without their cooperation, never mind their consent. It would be possible to spend many pages on the subject, as the idea of governing through consent is a central issue of Enlightenment political science and especially important in the American and French revolutions. I would only want to point out that for Hugo no consent can take the place of participation. In other words, without the cooperation of his fellow passengers in the rationing plan, any attempt to supervise them is necessarily doomed. Unlike Crusoe's notion of himself as a patriarchal sovereign topping a vertically arranged power structure, Hugo's vision of (the island's) society is resolutely horizontally organized, with all of the members on the same level. Such an organization, rather than appealing to an ultimately self-destructive ideal of self-security and self-stability, rather calls upon every kindergarten graduate's ability to share. Hugo's corresponding vision of government is accordingly non-representative and directly participatory, made up of small, everyday actions, rather than a few paper chads one enters a ceremonial isolation box in order to punch through every forty-eight months.

If Hugo thus appears as something of an idealist, even something like one of the Enlightenment's famous naïfs — Candide, say, whom Voltaire pictures as being guided catastrophically through a vicious world by a philosopher whose rule is "Everything is for the best in this the best of all possible worlds"— his seeming naiveté serves rather to defamiliarize for the viewer the rest of the cast's aggressive individualism.[8] In other words, even as the other passengers around him begin to enact all of the predictable and melodramatic plotlines of the assertive ego — the struggle for leadership, the love triangle, the inevitable war against others who may or may not threaten harm — Hugo's focus remains fixed upon a very basic problem of his own perception. The revelation that "Dave" from the hospital might just be a symptom of his own sickness, and the persistent experience of seeing and communicating with what seem to be ghosts, help Hugo revisit one of the central problems of the Enlightenment's foundation on the seeing "I." This may be put into two questions: If the "I" is the basis of all that is real and provable, then who are these others I see around me? And, just what is my responsibility or connection to these beings, who at times seem only as real as ghosts?

## *Of Lockean VW Buses and Cartesian Flat-Screens*

*Lost*'s setting on an island with all the qualities of a Purgatory, populated by beings caught between life and death, only allegorizes this basic problem of modern personhood. Descartes at his window, overlooking the street below him, wondered after dreaming into being the standard of the *cogito*: Who were the strange creatures on the street below? They appeared to have the shapes of men, but for all he knew they might only be automata. And although Locke wants to base his own philosophy on direct experience rather than sequestered meditation, he too is left pondering a similar conundrum at the end of his monumental *Essay Concerning Human Understanding*, because he too appeals to the objective judgment of a detached spectator.[9] Countless thinkers after Descartes and Locke will argue there exists some kind of natural connection between the seeing, thinking I and the others this I sees, just as they will argue for the existence of a natural law that has led to so many individuals giving up what is supposed to be their native independence in order to form a society. None of these arguments is very convincing, but all are necessary, because the society in which they are forwarded will do anything to avoid taking seriously the insight (provided by thinkers such as Hume) that individualism is not such a black-and-white issue: an independent, self-knowing subject as the near epistemological extreme; an objectified, unknowable other at the far side of the spectrum. Acting as if it were a black-and-white issue, of course, produces a lot of green. Theorists from Bernard Mandeville to Adam Smith very quickly identify the power and wealth generated by the myth of a self-made individual, whose headlong chase after fortune and fame — but also, sadly, community — keeps the machine-like forward course of Western culture on track.[10] On track toward what, of course, is the question raised by the extinction and enslavement of so many of the world's native peoples, unfortunate consequences of progress that were supposed to be offset by those fables of discovered utopias.

And though there has been a lot of philosophy written since Descartes and Locke, our daily lives still revolve around the basic assumptions and questions that came into being with Crusoe. *Lost*, however, does not merely complicate that too-easy tale of the individualist utopia still told in our own day, showing us the violent, chaotic communal hell that is its other half. It also explores the devices produced in order to support the Crusoe myth that motivates people in the half real place / half rhetorical construct in which we play out our own lives. The basic worry that comes from viewing the world as a collection of objects — even one's own life as an object — all of which might be possessed in a competition for acquisition, is that one does not or cannot possess them, that they might become lost. If every possession were taken away — by a plane crash, say — what proof of self-assertion would then satisfy a contemporary Descartes who can no longer appeal to rationalist arguments about a benign deity? What certificate of ownership of one's own life would calm the contemporary Locke, worried that science has only shed one candle's glow on a universe that seems still to be an overwhelmingly incomprehensible and howling dark? *Lost* and Hugo tell us that the industry of the West has come up with two props for its isolated individual basic to its own self-understanding. These inventions are the automobile and the television set.

If the role offered to the participants in the Enlightenment is that of a hero visually navigating a world that opens itself up wholly to his gaze, the automobile is that conveyance that seems the perfect fulfillment of that Lockean relationship to the world. There is something so cinematic to the experience of driving that perhaps owes much to the two technologies' simultaneous development and domination of the culture. In many past films, of course, the rear window of a car has served as the background screen for the conversation of driver and passenger who, without that un-scrolling landscape behind them, might seem to be doing nothing but sitting there and talking. The great boom in American living standards that occurred during the 1950s happened at the peak in production of the automobile but also during a golden era for Hollywood. And while the combination of the two in that iconic American experience of the drive-in may not be as common today, the interstate system laid down over this stretch of the continent under Eisenhower still provides an exhibit A of our culture's drive to make the Earth submit to the demands of the impatient eye. The highway system's geometric regularity, its promise of orderliness and safety but also almost instantaneous speed, all serve in many an automobile advertisement as the climax of an individualism entitled to such power as its birthright. And as the wars in Afghanistan and Iraq have shown, nothing is so important to Americans' ideal of themselves as evangelists of freedom throughout the globe than the cheap gasoline that allows them to drive all over God's creation.

It should therefore come as no surprise that our contemporary Crusoe, Hugo, is a character whose life revolves around automobiles. As a child, his dream of a healthy relationship with his father takes the form of the suggestion that they might someday take a road trip to the Grand Canyon, in a Camaro they repair together. Later on, after the return of the Oceanic Six, he will be presented just such an opportunity but will refuse after recognizing in the car's odometer his cursed lottery numbers. In between, back on the island, he finds a Dharma van in the jungle and talks his fellow castaways into trying to jumpstart it. In one of the show's more whimsical scenes, Sawyer and Jin help push the van down a steep hill, with Hugo and Charlie inside. Just as the duo seem doomed to crash, Hugo repeats to himself, "You make your own luck. There is no curse" ("Tricia Tinaka Is Dead"). The van starts, and the two inside avoid a grisly death. There is, of course, no real use for the van in the wilds of the island, but utility is beside the point. The near-death experience helps to jolt Charlie out of his own depression, which had been caused by Desmond telling Charlie that he is going to die, and it helps all of the characters to bond with one another. Rather than celebrating the typical representation in car advertisements of the solitary driver hogging a road seemingly built just for him, the scene presents the lesson of the car as being one of communal identity. And instead of fulfilling a personal dream, Hugo's experience of fixing a car solidifies his relationship to others — a relationship that does not "go" anywhere specific, that is about process rather than product and about moments rather than destinations. Meanwhile, the van's eight-track plays Three Dog Night's "Shambala," a song about a mythical Eastern place where "Everyone is helpful, everyone is kind."

If *Lost* critiques, through Hugo, a modern misuse of technology that has been employed to prop up a teleological utopian fantasy rather than to investigate and improve communal experience, it pairs this critique with an examination of its own medium. Hugo is not only an avid car buff; he is an inveterate TV junkie. Just as the car mobilizes the fantasy of a world made wholly knowable and navigable, so too does the television present a corresponding Enlightenment dream of the human mind being a separate, securable space away from life's hurdy-gurdy, something with the structure of a *camera obscura* or king's "Presence-room." Whereas with the car one is promised entry into a geometrically organized outside world of objects (the world, say, of Locke), with the television the world is delivered to one, like a pizza, so that one might mediate on it Descartes-like in one's quiet study, fast-forwarding through the commercials. Such a mental space as the TV helps construct is imagined as distinct from the outside world, as the place where the natural tribute of that separate world might be safely sifted through in the easily digestible form of pictures. Accordingly, the first glimpse of Hugo's life back home that is given to viewers is of the character firmly established upon the couch in front of the boob tube. After warning him that he had better not be watching more bikini-clad women, Hugo's mother confronts him with his passivity: "Look at you. It's a Saturday night. A grown-up man sitting at home, watching TV. You should go out, try to find yourself a nice woman." Hugo replies, "Yeah, I'll get right on that" ("Numbers" 1.18).

It is the experience of seeing his numbers come up in that night's lottery drawing that changes things for Hugo. The magic of the numbers lies in their ability to precipitate the possibility of a change for our representative contemporary character, who dreams of possessions and destinations figured by the cherished car in the garage that goes nowhere, and whose dreams of an impossible destination of security and self-assertion assure that he goes nowhere, too. Fantasizing about a relationship with others but fixated on the idea that he might control and dominate his life like a Crusoe, Hugo remains stuck in front of the TV. "Maybe I don't want to change. Maybe I like my life," he offers his mother. She does not buy a word of it. Hearing the telephone ring, she suggests to her son with the same surety as his own statements that it must be Jesus calling. "It is Jesus," she shouts from the other room. "He wants to know what color car you want."

## Dave's Not Here, Man

The possibility that Hugo might change is one of the central issues of the TV series, one that is presented with quasi-religious overtones: a road to Shambala, a world saved by the sacrifice of a new "number one." And though *Lost* presents Hugo and the viewer with glimpses of a future (or alternate timeline) in which he both proves himself the big man at Mr. Cluck's, with a bright yellow Humvee for evidence, and remains the socially isolated viewer of bad TV, the real promise of the character is for something else, something that never gets figured, perhaps because it cannot so easily be pictured. What I want to suggest is that the promise of the character, like the promise of the show, lies not in any unraveling of its mysterious plot, but in its potential to present as a defamiliarizing fantasy the conceptual framework from which its viewers spend so much of their own time staring out at the world. The TV show presents us, then, with Hugo as own contemporary Crusoe, but it also suggests that we viewers are in danger of making ourselves only so many "Daves."

The ride *Lost*'s Hugo takes us all on, in a rediscovery of our own communal identity — the role of solitary starer that, ironically, we are all together enacting — is rather like the experience of one of the many Gothic texts that arose with the height of the Enlightenment. These insisted, against seemingly all available evidence of the time, that within the era's sunniest rationalism was yet something inherently dark and destructive. Today, these Gothic texts are routinely read as exploring the slavery, misogyny, paranoia, and political and ecological violence that went along with modernization's ramped-up activity, all of which dangerous elements the texts found bound up in the same thinking the era was celebrating for producing such an awe-inspiring progress. Gothic texts thus painted the Enlightenment as the return to a darker time and often evoked a medieval setting, complete with monks and ghosts and — sometimes — the "black man," or the devil, himself. *Lost*'s Gothic plays with our own sense of progress and our corresponding trust in a unidirectional time, scaring us with its own "Man in Black"; only, its devices play out not in a haunted house but on the haunted island of modernity. One of *Lost*'s most persistent and effective Gothic devices, then, has to do with the modern individual's doppelganger, or double, who thrives parasitically on a character whose very (nick-) naming suggests a self-doubling. Period Gothic warned of a violent side to the well-intentioned, speculative Crusoe (the echoic Dr. Moreau, for example); the contemporary Gothic of *Lost*, in contrast, warns of an entirely separate personality performed by those whose emulative Crusoe has now become a Hugo/"Hurley."

Perhaps nothing is so common to our daily experience, that is, than the driving of an automobile, with all of the frustration that experience entails. The frustration of driving results from the fact that the existence of other drivers takes up the space we deem our own and impedes what we expect should be our near-instantaneous progress. If this were not so, "road rage" would either be a treatable syndrome or an incomprehensible phrase, not a quotidian cliché. And if any other experience does have as much commonality, it is surely that of watching television, through which performance of sleep-like dullness one separates oneself from others and the world in order to address, paradoxically, an insatiable appetite for society and experience. A self who is the center of the universe wants always to be somewhere else; a self who proceeds from the basic assumption of his isolation is cursed with, but also never satisfied with enough, company. The action required by the genre of the TV show, meanwhile, which is demanded by the viewership in order to maintain ratings, is only a dangerousness or unpredictability of activity that draws us all deeper into that solipsistic fantasy, which suggests there might be in the show an "answer" to a question about ourselves and our own desires that has yet to be clearly articulated. In other words, everything about the world constructed around us on that central tale of modernity assures us that such behavior is not merely unproblematic but logical. When *Lost* reflects this activity back to us, however, it is in the form of a chimera, a symptom of sickness, a mode of self that has so denied its own embodiment in the world — its own responsibility, its own dependencies — that it cannot be said to possess anymore its own body. What *is* "Dave," anyway? The show does not offer us an easy answer; only, his behavior could not be more familiar. In his goading of the contemporary hero for action and adventure — indeed, for meaning — he is our own self-image as quarterbacks of the resolutely armchair variety: shouters at TV screens, self-forgiving blamers of authority figures and other drivers, impatient consumers of others' efforts. He is what the American way, via the Crusoe story, has become.

For our contemporary hero to change, then, he must first recognize and exorcise himself of a parasitic personality that seems, with all of his bizarre behavior, perfectly ordinary. As Hugo remarks to his doctor at the hospital, "Dave's the most normal person in here, man" (2.18). Hugo's decision not to follow Dave outside the hospital in their planned jail break is figurative of the show's own divided loyalties. That is, although *Lost* confines itself to its viewers' expectations of genre and medium, it also betrays an uneasiness with these forms being based on certain conceptual assumptions. And particularly in the interactions between the characters of Dave and Hugo, the show strives to catch a glimpse from outside of these generic and conceptual frameworks of their motivating fantasies. In other words, Hugo's closing the window between himself and Dave reflects the show's own study of what the television is supposed to deliver for its viewer. The epistemological crisis of "Dave," the episode, is only partly resolved by Hugo's decision not to throw himself off the island's cliffs at the suggestion from Dave that everything around him is an illusion. Libby's answer to Hugo, "I'm real. You're real. The way I feel about you is real," and, after kissing him, "And that was real," will only put off Hugo's Cartesian anxiety for so long. Dave will return, and more ghosts with him.[11] *Lost* confesses its inability to provide an answer or solution to the central problems of modern subjectivity but nevertheless points its viewers in a direction: away from the sublime and picturesque catastrophe of cliff-top suicide and toward the insistence of patiently standing still and reflecting; away from the dependence upon visual or painful proof (Dave's shoe, his hitting Hugo with a coconut) and toward an acknowledgement of voice and touch and feeling (Libby's words, her kiss); away, in other words, from "Dave," and toward Libby. Again, there is something perhaps too naïve about these pointers for the knowledgeable and worldly wise viewer, but then again it is Hugo who is up on the screen experiencing love and gaining wisdom at these moments, and the viewer who is sitting all alone in his armchair, watching him.

If at the end of the show Hurley is our "number one," what do we make of our experience as viewers of identifying him as our contemporary Crusoe? The final episodes of *Lost* bring him forward as one of the keys to the show's plot, as he offers in this analysis to serve as the potential for an antidote to a poisonous story. But his value as the plot's potential lynch-pin, the "solution" to its epistemological mystery (What is the show "about"? What does it mean?) pales in comparison, I have been arguing, to his value as an indicator of direction or process (What is my own participation in the myth that is *Lost*'s central story? Who am I, as its viewer?). As the newly appointed guardian of the island (modernity) and its "Man in Black" (the invisible but ubiquitous and purportedly illimitable Individual), Hugo is most meaningful as the possible rewriter of the tale of our darker selves.

Hugo thus shows America's future not merely in a conventionally representative sense — demographically, in other words, as a member of a society that is becoming increasingly Hispanic. He is a kind of scout of the new subjectivity this society must discover in order to survive itself. What is Hugo's finding of an old van on the island, that is, except a demonstration of the ridiculousness of the fantasy of a world so conquered by the eye that it might be traversed instantaneously, without its vista being blotted by the presence of another soul? And what is Hugo's shock at the reading of his winning numbers other than a wake-up call for the mode of self who expects such fantasies to have no bearing on an "outside" world? An era of total globalization no longer holds a quiet corner for the isolated, sovereign self, and a world of widespread nuclear capability *can* be ended by the pushing of a single button. The "desert island" of any world, including the New one, has always already been populated, with people who have always been all too real. Modernity's lone hero has never been alone. That is, the myth of the sovereign individual has always been just that: a myth. We follow the lead of *Lost*, then, when we take over its story, which has been all of this while our own story, and in remaking it in our retelling, remake ourselves.

## Notes

1. For an account of Crusoe as modern *homo economicus*, see Ian Watt's groundbreaking reading of *Robinson Crusoe* in *The Rise of the Novel*.
2. See Newton.
3. For the connection between early English census-takers and the epistemological technology of the prospect view, see Barrell.
4. For an exploration of the eighteenth-century naturalist's and explorer's acquisitive gaze, see Pratt.
5. Baudelaire writes of the pleasures of the "flaneur" in the title essay of *The Painter of Modern Life and Other Essays*.
6. For a thorough examination of Crusoe's "fortunate fall," see Hunter.
7. See Bataille.
8. See Voltaire. The philosopher is Pangloss.
9. Descartes' discussion of the reliability of the senses moves him to tackle the problem of how you know you have seen a ghost at the end of his otherwise very focused *Meditations on First Philosophy*. Similarly, Locke's doubts about the possibility of visually categorizing humans prompts him to consider the differences between men and monsters in his *Essay Concerning Human Understanding* (Book 3, Chapter 6, Section 7). The point is that as soon as each man adopts the stance that the human relation to the world founded on knowledge gained through individual, visual experience, each must confront the strange specter of the self's other.
10. See Mandeville and Smith.
11. In addition to the episodes already mentioned, Hugo sees ghosts in "The Beginning of the End" (4.1) and "The Lie" (5.2).

## Works Cited

Barrell, John. *English Literature in History, 1730–80: An Equal, Wide Survey*. London: Hutchinson, 1983. Print.
Bataille, Georges. *The Accursed Share, Volume 1: Consumption*. Trans. Robert Hurley. New York: Zone Books, 1991. Print.
Baudelaire, Charles. *The Painter of Modern Life and Other Essays*. Ed. and Trans. Jonathan Mayne. London and New York: Phaidon, 1965. Print.

Descartes, Renee. *Meditations on First Philosophy*. Trans. and ed. John Cottingham. Cambridge: Cambridge University Press, 1996. Print.

Hunter, J. Paul. *The Reluctant Pilgrim: Defoe's Emblematic Method and Quest for Form in* Robinson Crusoe. Baltimore: Johns Hopkins, 1966. Print.

Locke, John. *Essay Concerning Human Understanding*. Ed. Peter H. Nidditch. Oxford: Oxford University Press, 1975. Print.

———. *Second Treatise on Government*. Indianapolis: Hackett, 1980.

Mandeville, Bernard. *Fable of the Bees*. Ed. Phillip Harth. London: Penguin, 1989. Print.

Newton, Isaac. *Opticks; or, A Treatise on the Reflections, Refractions, Inflections, and Colours of Light*. Indianapolis: Hackett, 2009. Print.

Pratt, Mary Louise. *Imperial Eyes: Travel Writing and Transculturation*. London and New York: Routledge, 1992. Print.

Smith, Adam. *The Theory of Moral Sentiments*. New York: Cosimo, 2007. Print.

Voltaire. *Candide*. Trans. and ed. Robert M. Adams. New York: Norton, 1991. Print.

Watt, Ian. *The Rise of the Novel: Studies in Defoe, Richardson, and Fielding*. Berkeley: University of California Press, 1957. Print.

# Primitivizing the Island: The Eclectic Collection of "Non-Western" Imagery

*Renee McGarry*

I first conceived of this paper during season five of the popular primetime drama *Lost* when the series' creators and producers began to employ both stand-alone and hybridized primitive[1] imagery. In this season, the morally ambiguous character Benjamin Linus visits a partially decayed subterranean enclosure outfitted with visual allusions to Pre-Columbian and other ancient civilizations. For nearly four seasons, a colossal four-toed statue is repeatedly presented to the audience in a broken and fragmented state. These are only two examples of how ruins and primitive imagery were used to communicate the presence of an exotic other. Throughout *Lost*'s six-season run, a preposterous narrative of the exotic became deeply embedded within its visual culture. The narrative centered on a mix of imagery that could not be pinned down to one specific civilization.

Much of the imagery from seasons five and six can be identified as Egyptian and Greek in origin. In strictly art historical terms, this imagery is classical.[2] In rethinking my paper, I realized two things: I am more interested in viewer response than I am in the actual nature of the imagery itself, and viewer response to Egyptian and Greek imagery[3] is much the same as it is to tribal cultures. To an art historian, Egyptian and Greek art are the very basis of (visual) Western civilization. These civilizations may serve as a basis of the West, but to the average viewer their visual culture is just as *other* as a Cambodian temple, Inca ruins, or a (choose your own location) rainforest. As art historian Peter Mason says in his book *Infelicities: Representations of the Exotic*, "the exotic is produced by a context of decontextualization taken from a setting elsewhere [...] it is transferred to a different setting, or recontextualized" (3). During season six, *Lost* accomplished what I believed was the impossible: it turned the most western of Western civilizations into the *other*.

Often, non-Western imagery functions as a marker of otherness. It is no surprise that when the plane carrying the many characters on *Lost* crashed on an unnamed island in the South Pacific, the survivors were immediately confronted with a glut of otherness. The use of this imagery in *Lost* serves as a means of participating in a prolonged historiography of the primitive in visual culture, using a mish-mash of imagery from Egyptian, South Asian, East Asian, Oceanic, classical, and Pre-Columbian cultures to create a far-flung and alien landscape. I seek to investigate the ways in which this imagery marks both the island and its residents as *other* and exotic. By looking at the ways in which these images combine to form the whole visual culture of the island, I will explore its function in destabilizing the identities of the Others, the members of the Dharma Initiative, and the survivors of the crash, as well as of the *Lost* audience. By using often unidentifiable and unfamiliar imagery, the producers have created constantly shifting power dynamics that allow all residents — and to some extent viewers — to visually move between existences as colonizers and colonized. The island itself becomes a driving force of the visual narrative and must be considered in terms of its actions as a primitive agent and colonial subject.

I have chosen to organize my paper following the structure of one of the most popular resources for the show, *Lostpedia*, an interactive wiki where fans create pages that include established facts from the series and use a separate section to spin theories about the seemingly unending set of open-ended questions. This organizational strategy is useful because it allows for discrete categories of visual phenomena. I will use *Lostpedia* as the primary resource for audience feedback as well.

## *The Statue of Taweret*

The large statue guarding the shore of the island is first seen in ruins in the 2004 episode "Live Together, Die Alone" (2.23 and 2.24) as Jin, Sun, and Sayid sail along the coastline. First Sayid notices the statue and points it out to Jin and Sun who discuss it in Korean. Clearly, the group finds the statue unnerving and remark upon the fact that it is incomplete and the remaining foot has only four toes. They are at such a distance from the site that they must look at it through binoculars. It is no accident that the first sighting of the statue is in ruins. Ruins play no small part in the series, and they often serve to mark an element of the island as exotic or *other*. The writers also made a conscious decision for the group to use binoculars, which provides them with a further authoritative gaze. They can see the ruins in the distance and try to make sense of them, even if they can come to no conclusions. Looking at ruins and attempting to decipher them, particularly through rudimentary scientific tools, further cements the aforementioned role of the survivors of flight 815 as amateur archaeologists, or newcomers seeking to colonize a strange land.

*Lost* message boards and podcasts were abuzz in 2004 about the exact nature of the statue. The role of amateur archaeologist (and sleuth and academic) was then shifted onto the audience. Viewers searched for other four-toed statues and attempted to understand as much as they could from as little evidence as possible. Because the series was relatively new and the plane crashed in the Pacific Islands, viewers immediately and naturally turned to imagery from that region. Some of the most unexplained ruins exist in that part of the world, and viewers latched on to the concept of the Easter Island heads as a possible model for the four-toed statue. The large stone sculptures of Easter Island[4] are perhaps the best known of Oceanic and Pacific Islander art. These large, monolithic sculptures seem to guard the island,[5] stand on platforms, and can be up to forty feet tall. It comes as no surprise, then, that these colossal heads would inevitably find their way into an online conversation about the *Lost* statue. The similarities are obvious: in addition to the previously mentioned size and position of the heads, these are made from volcanic stone similar to the material of the Statue of Taweret. Moreover, the Easter Island heads have a blocky, planar construction that is echoed in the statue's remaining foot. There is one obvious and important difference: the Easter Island heads do not have feet. Still, the discussion of these heads as one possible influence for the statue seemed (and still seems) logical, given the location of the island and the fact that the Others were routinely depicted as a primitive people. Additionally, the "weirdest" thing about the foot—its four-toedness—made it seem equally alien. In its initial introduction, the statue was in ruins, yet it was not completely decontextualized. It looked as if it could belong on the island, and viewers of *Lost* wanted to make the statue belong by any means necessary. In this particular situation, the context that was lacking—the rest of the statue—was the very thing that made the object seem at home.

But nothing on *Lost* makes sense, and in 2009 the statue was revealed in its entirety in a time travel sequence during the episode "LaFleur" (5.8). Even the first time the statue was completely displayed, it was out of context, shown for only a brief moment from behind. This was a quintessential moment of inscrutability for both the characters and the audience of *Lost*: there was no reason to expect this imagery on the island, and it was nearly impossible to identify it. In both an episode re-cap of "The Incident, Part 1" (5.16) and the solution to a puzzle in the May 2009 issue of *Wired*, creators of *Lost* (including J.J. Abrams himself) confirmed that this was the Egyptian goddess Taweret, goddess of birth and rebirth ("The Statue of Taweret"). After this shocking and enigmatic revelation, all perceived context was completely lost. The audience became interested in the question of how Egyptian imagery landed on an island in the South Pacific. In other words, who built this statue? And when was it built? Producer Carlton Cuse on "The Official *Lost* Audio Podcast" went so far as to suggest that the Egyptians themselves were on the island and built the statue.[6] This statement fits into a long and popular historiography of the non–West as strongly influenced by Egypt, no matter its geographic distance and the impossibility of contact with Egyptians.

The Statue of Taweret conforms to some standards of the Egyptian canon. Most noticeably, her pose is fully frontal with her left foot forward. These idiosyncrasies are representative of the Egyptian understanding of three-dimensionality and forward movement. One example of this construction of the human form is the funerary statue, *Menkaure and His Wife* (2490–2472 B.C.E.). The royal couple stands in a fully frontal position, with their left feet forward, as if frozen in space and time. They remain mute and expressionless. Unlike Classical Greek sculpture, there is no shift in the hips to reflect an uneven distribution of weight, and there is not even an Archaic smile to show lifelikeness in the forms. Egyptians also carved the human form with the statue's hands in fists and thumbs pointing forward. The *ankhs* Taweret holds force her hands into this position. Taweret's stance is clearly influenced by the Egyptian royal canon.

Yet, Taweret is carved in the round, which sets her apart from Egyptian funerary statuary.[7] While her rigid pose implies that she is as idealized as an Egyptian pharaoh, she is carved in both the front and the back; she is intended to be seen from all angles. Because the majority of Egyptian sculpture was intended for walls or niches in tombs, the backs of these sculptures were left uncarved; the human form was not yet freed from the block of stone. The intent of Egyptian sculpture as a permanent home for the *ka*, or soul, after death is seen in its timeless form and eternal forward gaze. Taweret may serve a similar function as the home for Jacob (the guardian, or *ka*, of the island) but she is most certainly not funerary statuary.

Outsized Egyptian funerary statue is not at home on the island, and the Statue of Taweret functions as a disconcerting element that causes displacement. The presence of Taweret helps to create the exotic on the island and further creates an alien landscape. The producers of *Lost*, through Cuse's statement that Egyptians may have built the statue (perhaps purposefully, perhaps inadvertently), perpetuate a long-lived myth in popular culture (or conspiracy theories) that all monumental architecture and sculpture can be traced back to Egypt. The series' audience, the survivors of the crash of Oceanic flight 815, the Others, and the members of the Dharma Initiative are confronted with the assumption that iconography, people, and ideas had the ability for pre-globalization travel. Hybridity and syncretism cause confusion, as does the supposition that there is true Egyptian "influence" (or presence) on the island.

## *The Temple Wall*

The Temple Wall demarcates presumably sacred space (the Temple) from the everyday (the island). The structure seems very simple, with two sections of walls covered in hieroglyphs, each with its own false gateway. In my ventures into *Lostpedia*, this is one of the few sections where an author has attempted to stylistically and formally identify an element of architecture, dating it to the Dravidian Period in India, 600–1565 C.E. ("The Temple Wall"). The walls, though, do not fit as easily into those conventions as one might like, and they hold elements of both South Asian and Pre-Columbian architecture. In my estimation, we can forgo identifying this hybrid architecture as a whole.[8] Perhaps we can identify elements of it, but it looks more like a nineteenth-century travel book from an exotic place, where the precise location and elements of the culture do not really matter.

In one of the more compelling events of season five, Ben enters a hole in the Temple Wall to receive his judgment from the smoke monster ("Dead Is Dead" 5.12). In this scene, the smoke monster appears and shows Ben scenes from his life, with many of them focusing on his now-dead daughter Alex. In an earlier episode, Ben chose to sacrifice that which he loved the most, his daughter, for the good of himself and the continuing existence of the island.[9] At the end of his vision, Alex appears to come out of the serpent-shaped smoke monster as she tells him that he is to follow John Locke in whatever he does.

Alex appears to her father as a traditional Mesoamerican vision serpent, providing both prophecy and comfort at a time of critical importance. One of the most famous images of the vision serpent in Mesoamerican art comes from the Classic Maya in Yaxchilan, a Maya site in the Yucatán with some relationship to the better-known site of Palenque. Lintel 25 is part of a series of relief sculptures dating to the eighth century and commemorates important events in the lives of the ruling family. This lintel, which includes the future queen and a vision serpent, was carved in 725 C.E. and commemorated an event that took place in 681 C.E.[10] This image was carved onto a door lintel in Lady Xoc's own building, structure 23, using a very distinctive regional style by an artist that is often referred to as "the cookie cutter master" because he carved figures in such detailed high relief. The majority of sculpture at Yaxchilan relates to visions, the world of the ancestors, war, and capture of sacrificial victims.

Lintel 25, also called *Lady Xoc's Vision*, depicts a complex and ornate accession ritual required of all wives before their husbands could take the throne. Lady Xoc's husband, Shield Jaguar, ascended to the throne in 683 C.E., and his wife had this vision in advance of that critical event. In the lintel, she is depicted performing auto-sacrifice, or ritual bloodletting, in order to bring on a hallucinogenic state. She is on her knees, bent over a bowl, with bloodletting tools on her wrist and the floor nearby. As she cuts herself, the blood falls onto bark paper in the bowl, which is then set on fire in a sacrifice to the gods. In this state, Lady Xoc then sees a vision serpent, one of the oldest auto-sacrificial visions in Mesoamerica. When the serpent opens his mouth, a warrior wearing a mask emerges and provides Lady Xoc with the knowledge that her husband will become king. Lady Xoc, like Benjamin Linus, had to perform a sacrifice in order to see her vision serpent. Though Ben is not kneeling when he sees his vision, he is looking up at it, and he is waiting for the head sprung from the jaws of a snake to tell him his future. In Mesoamerica, the vision serpent is a metaphor for smoke and blood. Clearly, we can see the relationship between the smoke monster and the vision serpent, as the smoke monster is just that: smoke. But where is the blood?

On the Island, Ben performs any number of "sacrifices" in order to maintain the integrity of his beloved home. The most obvious of these "sacrifices" is the Purge, when he works with the Hostiles to destroy the Dharma Initiative village in a puzzling episode that results in over a dozen deaths including that of Ben's own father. This is the sort of considerable sacrifice that we can readily parallel with large-scale and ritual sacrifices in the Pre-Columbian world. But in terms of Ben's vision, the most important sacrifice was that of his daughter, Alex. When deciding whether to protect the island from mercenary invaders or save her, Ben chose the island. It is exactly this sort of pain and suffering that brought on hallucinations in the Pre-Columbian world; however, *Lost* puts a modern twist on it by using psychic and emotional suffering rather than focusing on the physical. It was also common practice in Pre-Columbian ritual sacrifices to choose one of the most beloved and important members of a community to sacrifice to the gods. Therefore, Ben chose to sacrifice his daughter for the good of the island. In fact, it makes perfect sense that letting her go would allow for him to have greater standing in his community.

Because I will discuss the use of hieroglyphs later in this paper, I will only briefly refer to the phenomenon as it relates to the other iconography of the Temple Wall. The only readily identifiable element of this mélange is Egyptian hieroglyphs. This creates a further sense of displacement at the Temple Wall and throughout the island. Because the viewer's eye never knows what it can expect and from where to pull references, the imagery at the Temple Wall reinforces the notion of the exotic on the island. Both the jungle landscape and the built environment are completely foreign to the viewer, the survivors of the crash, the Others, and those working for the Dharma Initiative.

## *The Temple*

Ruins are a powerful force in defining the exotic, the other, and the ancient. The wall and the Statue of Taweret were both shown multiple times in ruin, although they were both in constant use through 2009. The Temple itself is not in ruins, though it is overgrown by the surrounding landscape. This is also indicative of the exotic, the other, and the ancient. Exotic plants that seem to have a life of their own take over a man-made structure. The structure does not crumble, but stands among the flora indicating the building's power.

Though some have tried to identify the style of architecture in which the Temple was built, I again assert that this is a futile cause. The creators of the Temple constructed a mixture of imagery that aligns its stylistic elements more with the *Indiana Jones* movies than with any living, breathing, or long-dead cultural tradition. The *Lostpedia* entry refers to the Temple as an

> immense ancient stone ziggurat of some five tiers [...] [with] one main entrance and two small alcoves on either side containing Buddha-like statues seated in a cross-legged position. Above the main entrance a very steep stairway ascends to a dark doorway in the final tier high above. The structure is slightly overgrown with vines hanging down in numerous places ["The Temple"].

In these three sentences alone there are references to two very discrete exotic cultures: the Near East (the ziggurat) and South Asia through the Far East (Buddhism as a homogenous monolith).[11] It is no accident that these are both Eastern, the ultimate exotic, the beginning of orientalism. The most striking element of the description is that the author(s) identifies the structure, yet he does so incorrectly. The Temple is not a ziggurat. Ziggurats are temple-like structures that date to the Sumerian period of Near Eastern art (ca. 3000–2000 B.C.E.) and were built in a desert landscape. These were built with a solid mud brick core and had no interior space. At times they were tiered, like the Temple, but this was certainly not a universal feature. Like many structures used for worship, ziggurats generally had a perishable or permanent structure at the top to bring worshippers and priests as close to the gods as possible. The top of ziggurats functioned as a "waiting room" where Sumerians believed a deity would descend and appear to priests. The remainder of the structure was marker of a holy place and not utilitarian in any way.

Despite the presence of hieroglyphic writing, the Temple is also not an Egyptian pyramid, though it has a stylistic precedent in the Egyptian world. Pharaohs built funerary structures to commemorate their greatness, and the closest relative to the *Lost*'s Temple in Egyptian architecture is known as the *Stepped Pyramid* (ca. 2630–2611 B.C.E., Saqqara, Egypt). The pyramid is essentially constructed out of a series of *mastabas* (benches) each of smaller and smaller size stacked on top of one another amounting to five tiers. The stepped pyramid was the center of a large walled funerary district for King Djoser, isolated from its surroundings like the Temple from *Lost*. Stepped pyramids — as well as the Pyramids at Giza — contained an internal network of tunnels, mirrored at the *Lost* temple. However, the Egyptian tunnel system was only used by souls in the afterlife.

Egypt and Sumeria are generally thought of as distant and ancient desert relatives. Yet, the Temple is built in a jungle landscape. Certainly there is an element of the exotic in moving structures intended for a specific landscape into its exact opposite ecosystem. But the Temple's jungle habitat makes viewers consider other origins for its iconography. Maya religious and burial complexes are most frequently located in cleared jungle settings. Though they are not walled, this environment calls attention to many similarities between the *Lost* Temple and Maya pyramids. It is possible to consider any Maya site for influence. Sites such as Tikal, Palenque, and Copán are relatively well known and feature large, sometimes tiered pyramids. (Of particular note, Pakal's burial temple at Palenque had a series of underground passages that lead to the king's tomb.) Much like these Maya sites, the *Lost* Temple is arranged around a large open courtyard. These well-known archaeological sites were also the subjects of nineteenth- and twentieth-century expeditions to Mesoamerica that resulted in exotic and foreign pen-and-ink drawings by such artists such as Frederick Catherwood. In nearly all of Catherwood's images the temples were vine-covered and surrounded by lush wildlife. This romanticized notion was then transferred into the popular imagination and repeated at the Temple in *Lost*.

While Buddhist *stupas* dating to the third century B.C.E. in Southeast Asia seem an unlikely source for the Temple, there is the *Lostpedia* reference to "Buddha-like" statues in the alcoves above the door that remains to be discussed. *Stupas* are Buddhist sanctuaries housing relics, but unlike the *Lost* Temple they are round. The presence of these "Buddha-like" statues in a non–Buddhist sanctuary is coupled with the bizarre combination of influences on the architecture of the Temple to create a very *othered* location in the jungle. As usual, this fusion of visual references in a single building poses more questions than answers.

The pool area is also an interesting mix of cultural antecedents, with influences from Greek architecture, Egyptian hieroglyphs, the Egyptian site of Karnak, and ancient South Asian civilizations. The similarities to the Great Bath at Mohenjo-daro, Pakistan (ca. 2600–1900 B.C.E.) create an interesting parallel with the Temple Wall, identified in *Lostpedia* as dating from the Dravidian period. This structure dates to the Indus civilization and is one of earliest examples of sophisticated sewage and water distribution facilities. This central bath required steps down into it and was made of bricks, much like the *Lost* Temple pool. The columns in the poolroom are notably influenced by both Egyptian and Classical Greek architecture, and they are covered in hieroglyphs. Decorated columns are also found in the hypostyle hall at the temple of Amen-Re at Karnak, Egypt (15th century B.C.E.). Like some columns found at the *Lost* Temple, the columns at Karnak are structurally necessary and have a long vertical shaft that ends in fluting rather than a capital. The columns at Karnak are communicative like those in the poolroom, decorated with painted, sunken relief sculpture. While the types of decoration are different, it is easy to see the precedent set at Karnak. A final influence on the pool room can be found in Greek architecture dating all the way back to the Archaic period (ca. 650–480 B.C.E.) with the Temple of Aphaia, Aegina, Greece (ca. 500–490 B.C.E.). Generally, rooms surrounded with structurally necessary columns are associated with classical architecture, and complexes such as the Acropolis in Athens (447–438 B.C.E.) provide the most obvious examples. A variety of Corinthian, Doric, and Ionic columns abound in this complex, and it is likely that the creators of the poolroom were wittingly or unwittingly influenced by that combination of structures.

In only two very limited areas of the *Lost* Temple complex we can readily see the hybridizing of (at least) six cultural and historical traditions of art and architecture. The unbridled mixing of these forms, taking pieces of Greece, adding it to pieces of Egypt and subtracting pieces of Buddhism, creates a wholly unfamiliar structure, one that the eye cannot readily identify. This immediately becomes exotic to the viewer and the residents of the island, and it serves to displace all the aforementioned groups. It remains unclear, even at the end of the series, who built these structures and their intended uses. This uncertainty subverts the idea of colonialism, calling into question whether newcomers to the island were even capable of colonizing it. The island has a history and a life of its own, and it is possible that in its role as primitive agent it was also the colonizer, exerting control over those who were called to it.

## *Hieroglyphs (or, Writing with and Without Words)*

Hieroglyphs are the most common visual thread running throughout the series, and *Lostpedia* dedicates one of its longest entries to a discussion of these signs and symbols. The wiki identifies the following occurrences of hieroglyphs: the countdown timer, Ben's secret door, the frozen wheel chamber, Ajira airlines, the Temple wall, Danielle's map, the statue of Taweret, Paul's necklace, the Cerberus chamber, the Dharma Initiative classroom, the tunnels leading to the Temple, Jacob's tapestry, inside the Temple, and inside the Lighthouse. These are fourteen distinct locations of hieroglyphics both on and off the island ("Hieroglyphs"). Most importantly, hieroglyphs are clearly spread throughout visual narrative of the series, and they are somehow integral to understanding its secrets.

Fans have put a great deal of effort into translating and identifying the various hieroglyphs, and *Lostpedia* offers an interesting explanation of how difficult it can be to understand this writing: "To further complicate translation, each symbol can mean something on its own (ideogram), represent a sound (phonetic), or give you a clue about the word written before it (determinative)" ("Hieroglyphs"). The author(s) of this statement demonstrate a rudimentary understanding of the problematic of picture-writing. First and foremost, he understands that it is writing. He also seems to understand that he is specifically looking at Egyptian hieroglyphs, and these are fundamentally different from other cultures' writing systems. He also understands basic glyphic forms, from pictograph to ideogram to phonetic. Thankfully, this author understands hieroglyphic writing on a level not yet demonstrated by *Lost* co-creator and producer Damon Lindelof, who indicated "there are many interpretations of hieroglyphics [*sic*], that's what we were going for" ("Access: Granted").[12] This is a profound misunderstanding of picture-writing. Hieroglyphs are open to interpretation in the same way that words are: their meaning is dependent upon context. Just because hieroglyphs are images does not mean that they are subject to multiple decontextualized interpretations. The creators, producers, and writers of *Lost* demonstrate a lack of knowledge about hieroglyphs and writing in general that is then passed on to the amateur archaeologist audience who is left to decode it.

In her introduction to *Writing Without Words,* Pre-Columbian scholar Elizabeth Hill Boone argues for a more comprehensive view of writing — one that includes both glottographic[13] and semasiographic[14] symbols (13–17). It is essential to understand that Egyptians could read hieroglyphs. Interpretive difficulties came about in modern times with the Western "discovery" of Egyptian tombs and writing. This distinction is not made fully clear on *Lost.* The confusion causes a misinterpretation of primitive cultures as somehow less literate than our own because they read in a different way. Lindelof and Cuse's related statements imply that hieroglyphs were chosen as a means of communication on the island precisely because they produced a non–Western vibe. They have literally marked the island with hieroglyphs when they could have chosen any number of pictographic systems, or even made up their own. For the first five seasons of the series, the creators were primarily interested in posing a series of (semi)unanswerable questions. Their goal, or the result of this quest, was to position the audience as amateur archaeologists functioning in a colonial system: Egyptian hieroglyphs were recognizable but not translatable. The viewer and the survivors of crash 815 (albeit with far fewer resources) were then left with the task — and the power — of decoding. The island was foreign, and it was their job to domesticate it with "real language."

In addition to hieroglyphs, there is some Greek writing on the island, often quoting Homer. While the references are compelling quotes about the nature of good versus evil, the interweaving of ancient Greek with Egyptian imagery merges classical cultures with the exotic and reinforces the affiliation of anything old with the primitive.[15] The mingling of classical languages with pre-classical Egyptian visual culture and a variety of unidentifiable architectural structures creates a boggled and boggling landscape that cannot be easily read or understood. This bewildering setting plays a very active role in creating the world of *Lost*; there is constant uncertainty about how and when it was created and from where it originated. The mixing of classical and Egyptian visual and written traditions with imagery from any number of non–Western and tribal sources creates panic about whether the island can be controlled and colonized. Ultimately, the island has much more agency than its residents.

## *The Barracks (or, The Familiar Is Never at Home)*

Theorist Homi Bhabha tells us "to be unhomed is not to be homeless" (13). Indeed, while members of the Dharma Initiative, the Others, and the survivors of Oceanic Flight 815 are repeatedly unhomed, we learn in the final season that they are in fact never homeless, that all of the events in their lives were meant to lead them to the exotic landscape of the island (and, more importantly, each other). "To be unhomed is not to be homeless," but the desire to create a home does not stop with surrounding oneself with people one loves. Rather, as envisioned by the Dharma Initiative, to be unhomed but not homeless involves the creation of a village that mirrors that of daily life in the real world. The Barracks was built not long after the Dharma Initiative arrived on the island in the 1970s and consisted of a group of simple, functional, and middle-class homes inhabited by scientists, Dharma Initiative staff, and their families. The Barracks is an entire community that consisted of work and play, secretive and public lives.

Through multiple characters' time travels we see that life in the Barracks is fairly mundane. While working for the Dharma Initiative, Sawyer and Juliet fall in love and create a home together. We see Charlotte playing on a swing in one of Faraday's travels, and we realize that children are born and raised there. Young Ben Linus is shown with his abusive and alcoholic father who works as a janitor. The Dharma Initiative went to great pains to make the Barracks as normal as possible in an effort to help with assimilation to this alien landscape. It is just this level of normalcy that punctuates a sense of displacement. The Others took over the Barracks after the Dharma Initiative Purge and continued an everyday existence. They lived in these homes and formed relationships with one another, occasionally donning costumes that made them look like "natives" to scare off the survivors of the plane crash. Again, we see Juliet in a relationship, in love, paralleling her time travel with Sawyer. There is a book club; there are CDs and other products that indicate ties to contemporary consumer culture. But the Others cannot maintain this normal existence. They are in a constant state of warfare with other inhabitants of the island, and with the island itself. There is an elaborate sonar security system built by the Dharma Initiative that wards off the smoke monster, but it is not long before the Barracks is attacked from the outside during season four.

For the final two seasons, the audience and the survivors of the crash only see the Barracks in ruins, with the swing set empty and blowing in the island breeze. But one specific episode in the series finale demonstrates just how commonplace and unexciting the Barracks was. When Ben takes Charles Widmore and his assistant, Zoe, into his closet to find a hidden stash of explosives, viewers are struck by the very ordinariness of his house. Even his closet is well ordered and clean, stocked with clothes more at home off the island than on it. The Barracks in general and Ben's house in particular are the definition of run-of-the-mill.

The Dharma Initiative model for the Barracks appears to be middle-class housing of the 1950s and 1960s, with just enough space for a post-war family and just enough amenities to make life easier and more comfortable. This, the viewers can assume, made the exotic location more familiar, more like home for those forced to live there. The members of the Dharma Initiative may have been unhomed, but they were not homeless. This normalized existence, the very plain homes and lawn, underlines the exotic landscape that surrounds the Barracks. The Barracks is familiar, ordinary, and safe. It substitutes for home. The rest of the island is exotic, primitive, scary, and uncomfortable. The island must be kept out, and the Dharma Initiative claims the sonar fence will do that, keeping the island's wildlife at bay. Of course, the exotic flora and fauna are the least of their problems ("The Barracks").

The context of the island forces the plain and middling homes of the

Barracks into the same category as much of the other imagery, for "the exotic is produced by a context of decontextualization" (Mason, 3). Everything on the island is unstable, and it becomes clear that "the exotic is never at home" (Mason, 6). The Barracks may create a temporary home for the Dharma Initiative, the Others, and the survivors of flight 815, but the Barracks and its residents are not at home. This highlights the question of perspective on the island and provides the audience with a contrast to exotic imagery. The context produces the categories of colonizer and colonized and then tears them apart.

## Notes

1. I have struggled with labeling this imagery. Throughout this paper I will use primitive, tribal, and non–Western fairly interchangeably as generic labels, since none of them is absolutely correct. When I can cite a cultural tradition more specifically, I will do so.

2. The linear progression of any college-level art history survey class moves the human figure in particular from Egypt to Greece to Hellenism as it becomes more and more veristic. Ancient Egypt, though a part of the African continent, is therefore understood as a classical (visual) culture.

3. Particularly writing — hieroglyphs and the Greek alphabet are used heavily in the show.

4. I have chosen to eschew the appropriate names of these constructions (*moai*) and the island on which they were found (*Rapa Nui*) in favor of Easter Island and heads because that was largely the language used in any conversation on internet fora, blogs, and podcasts.

5. One of the prisoners on the *Black Rock* believes that Taweret serves the same guardian-like function, claiming "el Diablo" (the Devil) guards the island.

6. The nature of this statement seems as if the intent was to further confuse the audience and keep the island shrouded in mystery, even as the series came to a close. Yet internet audience conversation suggests that the statement was taken to be earnest.

7. My colleague Andrea Ortuño suggested that the statue may also reference the *Colossus of Rhodes*. Unfortunately, I did not have space to adequately consider this hypothesis.

8. At first glance, I readily shifted between agreeing with the author about Dravidian influence on the arches and viewing them as corbel vaults, which are a Maya convention. This slide between cultures — it could be one or the other or both — further emphasizes the *other*ing nature of hybridization. The imagery just *is* exotic, no matter where it came from, if it came from anywhere.

9. I am purposefully ignoring the references to Christianity, as they seem obvious.

10. We know the exact dates of these lintels from the explanatory hieroglyphs on them. I will discuss the relevance of hieroglyphs vis-à-vis *Lost* later in the paper.

11. There are many alternate theories about these sculptures. One is that it is the Hindu Trimurti (Freeman). The preponderance of theories about the imagery reinforces the sense of dislocation on the part of the audience and Island residents.

12. Executive producer Carlton Cuse stated something very similar on "The Official *Lost* Podcast," 7 May 2010.

13. Geoffrey Sampson introduced glottographic as a term in his 1985 book *Writing Systems: A Linguistic Introduction*. This definition is what most scholars have passed on to the general public as writing: marks that represent speech. This includes hieroglyphs.

14. This category was introduced by Sampson as well, and Boone does an excellent job of summarizing his argument. Semasiographic symbols communicate meaning within their own system. This can include conventional semasiographs, such as mathematical and musical notations, which are something most people can agree are read. (I remember as a young child learning to "read music.") This can also include iconic semasiographs, such as the circle with a line

through it that most Americans readily understand as prohibiting something. (The primary example of this being "No Smoking" signs. As Americans we do not have to even translate this into words, it almost goes directly into our brain.)

15. Many characters on the series also speak Latin, including the Others, Jacob, the Man in Black, and both their birth and adoptive mothers.

## WORKS CITED

"Access: Granted." *Lost: The Complete Third Season—The Unexplored Experience*. Buena Vista Home Entertainment, 2007. DVD.
"The Barracks." *Lostpedia*. Web. 20 June 2010.
Bhabha, Homi K. *The Location of Culture*. London: Routledge, 2006. Print.
Boone, Elizabeth H., and Walter Mignolo. *Writing Without Words: Alternative Literacies in Mesoamerica and the Andes*. Durham: Duke University Press, 1994. Print.
Freeman, Bob. "LOST in Translation: The Temple Set." *The Occult Detective: The Official Homepage of Bob Freeman*. 17 Dec 2009. Web. 23 June 2010.
"Hieroglyphs." *Lostpedia*. Web. 8 June 2010.
"Jacob's Rug." *Lostpedia*. Web. 8 June 2010.
Mason, Peter. *Infelicities: Representations of the Exotic*. Baltimore: Johns Hopkins University Press, 1998. Print.
"The Official *Lost* Podcast." 7 May 2010. Web. 8 June 2010.
Sampson, Geoffrey. *Writing Systems: A Linguistic Introduction*. Stanford, CA: Stanford University Press, 1985. Print.
"Statue of Taweret." *Lostpedia*. Web. 8 June 2010.
"The Temple." *Lostpedia*. Web. 8 June 2010.
"The Temple Wall." *Lostpedia*. Web. 8 June 2010.

## Part Three

# LOST MEN AND LOST WOMEN

# The *Lost* Boys and Masculinity Found

*David Magill*

From the opening plane crash and the black smoke monster to time travel and the disappearing island, the science fiction pyrotechnics of *Lost* have bedazzled us with questions of past and present, time and space, energy and particle. But at its heart, *Lost* focuses on questions of good and evil, asking what we should do, what we can do, and what we must do. The show has centered those questions mainly around its male protagonists: Jack Shephard, John Locke, James "Sawyer" Ford, Hugo "Hurley" Reyes, Sayid Jarrah, Daniel Faraday, and the central antagonists Benjamin Linus and Charles Widmore. While strong female characters do enter such conversations at times, the central ethical conflicts of the show are dramatized through these male figures. As a result, *Lost* places in dialogue the social construction of contemporary masculinities and the cultural determinations of ethical behavior. In particular, *Lost* interrogates various possible formations within contemporary masculinity as a means of supporting a vision of ethical manhood that uses the authority and power associated with masculinity in a socially responsible manner. However, *Lost* articulates this progressive vision within a narrative of wounded white masculinity that recapitulates traditional patriarchal ideals. While the show mainly focuses on Jack, Locke, Sawyer, and Hurley to construct this vision, the secondary characters (both male and female) provide compelling support as well for this vision of American manhood.

## *Real Men Don't Ask for Directions*

One reason we can read *Lost* as a meditation on masculinity is that its male characters have many of the markers of traditional masculine identity and authority. For example, their real world professions are often traditionally masculine in nature. Charlie is a guitarist for *DriveShaft* and a successful rock star, Sayid is a soldier and torturer for the Republican National Guard in

Iraq, Sawyer is a machismo-driven con man, Jin is a businessman working for Sun's father as a mafia-type enforcer, Locke is a businessman and a hunter (using knives, a phallic symbol of power), and Jack is a surgeon who is incredibly successful at what he does. *Lost*'s character development narratives place the men in positions associated with "masculinity," even though, as in Jack's case, there are women whom we also see as doctors (Juliet, for example). But Juliet's focus on obstetrics and gynecology clearly demarcates her as focused primarily on women's issues, such that she must participate in Jack's kidnapping in order to access his surgical abilities for Ben and the Others, thereby demonstrating his medical superiority.

*Lost* also denotes its men as heterosexual — a compulsory component of white American manhood — through relationships on and off the island. Charlie's rock star days of wine and roses come with women, often several at one time, but he also begins a relationship with Claire on the island. Sayid has lost one love in the real world, but redeems his humanity by connecting with Shannon after he tortures Sawyer. Jin is married to Sun and reclaims his romance with her through their time on the island, leading several reviewers to label them the Romeo and Juliet of the island. Locke is engaged in the real world, Desmond searches for and reunites with Penny, and Hurley dates Libby. Compulsively, the island's men engage in romantic relationships that clearly define them as heterosexual. Glyn Davis and Gary Needham compellingly argue that the only character who even suggests homosexuality is Boone, but the clues are subtle and he is killed off in the first season after being linked to incest (269–70).[1]

Perhaps the two most important men in this regard are Sawyer and Jack, each of whom has multiple heterosexual romances, including relationships on the island with Juliet and Kate. Sawyer makes love to Kate when they are trapped in the Others' cages, and kisses Kate before jumping from the helicopter that will take them to a boat offshore and, they believe, to freedom. When the island jumps to the 1970s, we find Sawyer living with Juliet in marital harmony, and her death rocks him to the core. In addition, Sawyer's flashbacks introduce his relationship with Cassidy, a fellow con artist and Sawyer's apprentice. Sawyer is generally played as the "bad boy" on the island, and his persona created much fan interest and media reaction.

Jack's experiences match Sawyer's, except he plays the "good hero" role in the group. Michael Newbury notes, "Viewers of the show know Jack to be the embodiment of almost everything white and Western, but also to be a little rebellious against conventional authority. He is handsome, white, male, a child of privilege, a gifted neurosurgeon, well schooled and practiced in the benefits of technological progress and modern medicine" (201). As such, Jack is the ultimate representative of acceptable white masculinity and thus the recipient of much female attention. In the real world, Jack leaves behind an ex-wife whom he meets after saving her from certain paralysis. Jack's torrid sexual affair with Achara, a South Sea island inhabitant and tattoo artist, also enhances his masculinity ("Stranger in a Strange Land" 3.9). On the Island, we see similar connections. Jack and Juliet connect during his time in captivity with the Others, and have a short romantic relationship. But the show offers Jack and Kate as an important couple. We see much evidence of his on-again/off-again relationship with Kate, including time spent living together when they escape the island the first time as well as the final kiss before Jack saves the island in the season finale and the final connection in the church as they head to the afterlife together. As a result, Jack and Sawyer take on the most masculine positions in the group, as their physical bodies match desired masculine ideals.

The island's men are all devoutly heterosexual, and this extends in many cases to making them fathers as well: Sawyer has a daughter, Jack imagines himself with a son in the final season and helps care for Aaron during his time with Kate away from the island, Jin has a daughter with Sun, and Charlie acts as a father figure to Aaron. Ben and Charles Widmore also have daughters, a trait which is meant to humanize them as well as masculinize them. And we must not forget Michael, a character who ends up shooting Ana Lucia and Libby in order to free Ben from captivity in the Hatch and thereby free his son Walt from captivity and take him off the island. The repetitive link of these male characters to fatherhood and sexuality clearly suggests that we must read these characters as avatars of masculinity, albeit a masculinity in crisis.

The characters access masculinity not only through their social positions but also through their own bodies. Jack and Sawyer's bodies are constantly on display in a manner that confirms traditional visions of muscular masculinity. They both spend much time with shirts off, flexing their muscles or displaying Jack's tattoo and Sawyer's washboard abs. Sayid is similarly dressed in shirts that display his biceps. Davis and Needham state, "Certainly, Sawyer regularly removes his shirt, and his body is framed and lit for viewer pleasure; Jack has a 'soft' (perhaps suspiciously soft?) masculinity, coupled with a muscular torso that is also regularly displayed as spectacle" (272). It is important to note the actors as well when considering Jack and Sawyer, for the casting choices and their real-world work reflect on the show's character development. As Davis and Needham note, "both [Matthew] Fox and [Josh] Holloway have recently featured in advertising campaigns — respectively, for a L'Oreal Men Expert moisturizer and for the Davidoff Cool Water aftershave" (271), campaigns which tally with Jack and Sawyer's personas on *Lost* and further their claims to masculine identity.

These bodies, however, are not just for show; in addition to the displays of manly physique, these men display their muscular masculinity by controlling other men's bodies through violence. Jack and Sawyer fight at regular intervals, throwing punches and threatening bodily harm to one another. Sayid tortures Sawyer's body (incorrectly) in order to find the necessary medicine for Shannon's asthma. Jack and Locke both use violence against the Others, including Ethan (whom the castaways kill) and Ben. Even Michael's violence indicates his manhood, and his desire to save his son from the Others seems to partially justify his violence against two women, including one who is unarmed. Besides these individual instances of one-on-one violence, we also have cases where these men lead others to violence. Ben Linus and Charles Widmore battle one another with the help of armed fighters — they use others as violent means to their ends. Jack and Sawyer both lead their fellow Oceanic victims to war against the Others, who are only too willing to bring the fight. Even Jacob and the Man in Black are at war, in a sense, and Jacob's violent attack on his brother leads to the creation of the Smoke Monster, a vision of evil violence that haunts the show from the pilot. Thus, the violence we see can be individual or collective, but the power to wield it is coded as masculine in the show's vision.

The ability to incite others to action leads us to the final stereotypically masculine quality defined on *Lost*: the authority of leadership. Ben and Charles Widmore represent a leadership defined by financial and emotional power. They battle over ownership of the island, over who will control its power and resources. Jack, Sawyer, and Locke battle as well over who will determine the fate of the Oceanic survivors. Locke and Jack discuss this idea of leadership:

>JACK: How are they, the others?
>LOCKE: Thirsty. Hungry. Waiting to be rescued. And they need someone to tell them what to do.
>JACK: Me? I can't.
>LOCKE: Why can't you?
>JACK: Because I'm not a leader.
>LOCKE: And yet they all treat you like one.
>JACK: I don't know how to help them. I'll fail. I don't have what it takes ["Tabula Rasa" 1.3].

Jack and Locke debate Jack's leadership abilities, but there is no question that the Losties' leader will not be Kate or Sun or Claire. In fact, while women occasionally access the authority and power associated with masculinity in the show, the overall narrative of the show clearly leaves women to focus on reproductive issues — the baby question — while men determine the fate of the island and its inhabitants.

*Lost*, a show which hooked viewers with its myriad "mysteries" that left us "lost," nevertheless is rooted in traditional generic requirements of science fiction and offers a particularly familiar version of white masculinity and its discontents. As a science fiction show, *Lost* uses de-familiarization as a means of placing its regular elements within a new interpretive vision; thus, we see individuals we can easily recognize, placed on an island with mysterious electromagnetic properties and strange denizens, including smoke monsters, polar bears, and teleportation devices that move the entire island in space and time. Michael Newbury describes the island as an "unnamed, unreachable island thoroughly cut off from exchange, migration, and movement" (203), a description that marks its inscrutability even as we can map it and recognize it as "an island." While we are trying to figure out the mystery of the island, we are simultaneously learning more and more about the characters and their sense of being "lost" as well as their pasts and the choices they have made that led them to the island. And the series finale affirmed strongly the show's focus on characters over ideas. *The Washington Post*'s Hank Stuever writes, "It was never about answers, *Lost*'s makers claimed, so much as it was about story, characters—the surviving passengers of Oceanic Flight 815 who deathmarched from one desolately beautiful beach to another, for days, weeks, time-warped decades" (C12). As a result, we see these easily recognizable men and women placed in a fantastic setting which highlights their personalities and allows us to see their identities in sharp relief, away from the traditional trappings of American culture. And while the picture gives us those traditional men in many ways, what we also see in that vision is they are wounded white men trying to heal themselves.

## *The Wounds of War*

An important contemporary cultural narrative that holds much sway is that of wounded white masculinity, which suggests that white men in our culture are currently injured by, among other things, corporate culture, third wave feminism, the advancements of people of color, and domestic losses (Robinson 1–21). Camille Paglia, for example, in a recent *New York Times* op-ed, suggests that "Men must neuter themselves, while ambitious women postpone procreation [...] Meanwhile, family life has put middle-class men in a bind; they are simply cogs in a domestic machine commanded by women" (WK 12). This vision of wounded or victimized white masculinity is an old tale full of sound and fury against feminists and racial minorities who have eroded the traditional power bases and "natural" authority of white men. But the specter of 9/11 must come into consideration here, too, as that moment wounded America in a spectacle of terror. Using a plane crash in the pilot episode references that primal terror; combining the horrors of 9/11 with recent surges in nonwhite immigration provides fuel for those who would see white masculinity as damaged and in need of repair. What continually reappears in various guises across popular culture are recovery narratives of wounded white men resurrecting themselves to a more powerful and authoritative position in culture, often with the help of women or minority individuals. *Lost* incorporates this narrative into its structure as well. Sawyer asks Jacob, "Tell me something, Jacob. Why do I gotta be punished for your mistake? What made you think you could mess with my life? I was doin' just fine til you dragged my ass to this damn rock." Jacob's response suggests these characters' wounded nature: "No, you weren't. None of you were. I didn't pluck any of you out of a happy existence. You were all flawed. I chose you because you were like me. You were all alone. You were all looking for something that you couldn't find out there. I chose you because you needed this place as much as it needed you" ("What They Died For" 6.16). Jacob's exchange with Sawyer summarizes *Lost*'s general approach to its characters, depicting them as existentially flawed and in need of the island to find what they are lacking. This condition, however, is tied to the characters' genders.

*Lost* depicts its male characters as wounded white men through a variety of devices. First, the show's flashbacks and flash-forwards clearly delineate these men as "lost" in ways that connect to their masculinity. James "Sawyer" Ford is a con man searching for the person who conned his parents, leading his father to murder his mother and then commit suicide. This quest reveals Sawyer's inner turmoil and grief, even to the extent that it defines his identity: his nickname Sawyer comes from the con man who swindled his parents (later found to be Anthony Cooper, Locke's father) and whom he is hunting in order to kill. This hunt has disastrous consequences, as it leads Sawyer to become so blinded by his rage that he kills an innocent man in the mistaken belief that it is his father. While Sawyer's damage is completely internal, John Locke evinces external damage as part of his condition. Locke is paralyzed after being thrown from a window by his own father, but he is also emotionally damaged by the events of his life. He works in a cubicle, obviously does not enjoy his job, and spends most of his free time obsessing over his father. Hurley spends time in a mental institution, fearful of the "numbers" that seem to dominate him. Jack is an alcoholic divorcee who can't seem to get it together. Even the secondary characters are damaged: Charlie the heroin addict, Jin the reluctant mobster, Sayid the tortured torturer, and Desmond the insecure loner who must prove his worth in order to be with Penny. Jacob and the Man in Black are at war with one another, as are Ben and Charles Widmore. In short, every man on the show is damaged in one way or another by the events of their lives before coming to the island, and in some cases while interacting with the island.

Another means by which the show reveals the characters' wounded nature is through the male characters' access to primal emotions. Jack, for example, is often seen crying, such as he does after Jin and Sun die on the submarine. We see Damon Lindelof has defended Fox's tears as manly, stating that "Matthew has elevated crying to an art, where somehow it's a form of badassness. He never cries because he's sad. He cries because he wants to hit someone. I can't think of any other hero characters who have cried" (Stein). Lindelof's rationale demonstrates the desire to see Jack as "manly" but it also reveals his damage and his separation from the traditional codes of masculinity. Sawyer also cries at moments of extreme anguish, such as when Juliet dies. But Sawyer's main emotion is anger, and he wields it as a shield to protect himself from emotional intimacy. His machismo and penchant for colorful nicknames serve to hide his sensitive side, which comes out in his relationship with Juliet.

One specific commonality that damages many of these men is the absent or derelict father. Locke, we learn, spends his childhood moving from one foster home to another. When he does finally find his parents, Locke's father Anthony Cooper pretends to desire a relationship with Locke only as long as it takes for Locke to give up a kidney to save Cooper's life. With kidney in hand, Cooper rejects Locke, telling him, "You're not wanted." Locke stalks Cooper and obsessively wishes for a reunion that is not forthcoming, wasting his chance with his fiancée, who leaves because of his obsession. Sawyer's father is dead, killing himself after murdering Sawyer's mother following the con perpetrated by Anthony Cooper, and that loss defines Sawyer's actions and life choices in negative ways. Jack's father, in the most obvious case, is what brings Jack to the island. Christian Shephard has died in Australia, drinking himself to death, and Jack's trip down under leads him to Oceanic flight 815 and the crash that strands him on the island. Michael Newbury states, "He likes the authority he carries with him by virtue of his masculinity, money, modernity, and whiteness. Jack is the avatar of a prosperous, mobile, technologically advanced global order" (202). But at the same time, he is a symbol of the burdens associated with maintaining that order; hence, his rebellion against that order as symbolized by his father becomes a statement of the wounds that order has caused him.

The show highlights this relationship as Jack keeps seeing his dead father walking in the jungle and, in chasing the ghost, finds the empty coffin, the bodies of The Man in Black and his "mother," and water to help the inhabitants of the island survive. Jack's relationship with his father comprises multiple flashbacks that reveal their love-hate relationship and the conflict that drives them apart. For instance, in "All the Best Cowboys Have Daddy Issues" (1.11), an episode whose title makes explicit this issue for *Lost*'s men, Jack recants his testimony to a medical review board and gives evidence against his father for killing a pregnant woman by performing surgery under the influence. The entire episode reveals Jack's angst over his relationship with his father as they go back and forth on whether Jack should protect Christian. Jack at first agrees because Christian apologizes for his lack of fatherly attention. Jack's relationship with his father contains little support; in fact, Christian tells him "You don't have what it takes" to be a doctor, words he repeats when Locke asks him to be a leader. We could grant Christian the benefit of the doubt and decide that he was using tough love and reverse psychology to motivate Jack to prove him wrong. But this decision places Jack and his father in fundamental conflict and ultimately leads to Jack's turning in Christian.

We can see that the main characters have "daddy issues," and this is a fundamental pattern that offers an underlying reason for their flawed existence. Again, other characters mirror these men's experiences. Hurley's father has abandoned them (though he does return), while Ben's father demeans and ridicules him, leading Ben to murder the Dharma workers in retaliation. Aaron's father is gone as well. Even Jacob and the Man in Black are similar in that, while they have a biological mother (murdered by the island's protector who then raises them), we see no father. Bad fathers, it seems, have contributed to this state of wounded white manhood in almost every case. And as we shall see, becoming a better father is a signal of success and healing on the island.

In addition to the lack of fatherly role models, the men of the island have in common a history of losing the women in their lives. Sawyer's mother is dead, killed by his father, and so are the relationships he has had with a variety of women. Locke loses his fiancée to his obsession with Anthony Cooper. Jack's wife has left him for another man. Jin is about to lose Sun, who has learned English and plans to go to America to flee her husband. Sayid's love is dead. This catalogue of women simultaneously verifies the characters' heterosexuality and contributes to our understanding of them as wounded, for they have lost in love and life and are adrift, searching for meaning, just as we are watching the show. Ryan McGee notes, "By exploiting stereotypes and hinting at greater connections between these people, the show was consciously commenting on our fractured world, more connected than ever yet simultaneously more isolated." What these various losses signify is that while we might want to consider the characters of *Lost* as "existentially" lost, the specific characteristics of their downfall are intimately connected to their identities *as men*. Thus, the losses they suffer mark them as wounded and in need of masculine regeneration.

## *Welcome to Fantasy Island*

*Lost*, as I have shown above, draws on both the traditional architecture of masculinity as well as the cultural narrative of wounded white men in constructing its characters. Contemporary men, the show suggests, have lost their way and need to be found. The path home, *Lost* reveals, lies in the adoption of ethical manhood as a recovery strategy that heals the men from the wounds created by a post-feminist, post-racial, post–9/11 culture where, it seems, men must learn to act better in order to live better. Jack Shephard states eloquently, "If we can't live together, then we're going to die alone" ("White Rabbit" 1.5). *Lost*'s tale of candidates chosen to protect the island is set up as a vision of communal awareness, moving from a model of masculine competition to one of masculine cooperation and developing an ethical leadership model based on making the "right" decisions. Thus, the show moves us from macho men battling for supremacy to a fantastic band of brothers who work to defend the innocent, destroy evil, and save the island both physically and metaphorically, the latter making the island a symbol of the community that has arisen between these survivors.

Ethical manhood is posited in *Lost* as a means of recovering a traditional white masculinity reformulated to enhance community and to reduce the conflicts that defined white manhood. Ryan McGee writes, "The point of the show seems to be that what you do is less important than the meaning behind what you do. And moreover, if you live those lives in the correct manner, then the specifics are null and void. In the end, you arrive at the same destination." Learning this lesson allows white men to regenerate their authority, their power, and their manhood. *Lost* resolves the narrative of wounded white masculinity by restoring white manhood through a progressive ethical stance while retaining its traditional characteristics of authority. The narrative progression of *Lost* offers us this fantasy of white masculine regeneration through a combination of primitive escape and ethical reformulation. The men of *Lost* learn to act better as a means of making them feel better. By the end of the show, each major male figure has been recovered and made whole, learning to be good fathers, good lovers, and good leaders.

Contrast, for example, Locke and Sawyer. Locke opens the show by literally being healed — he has recovered miraculously from his paralysis as a result of his arrival on the island, so he alone recognizes the value of the island. Even though he loses his faith temporarily when Jack uncovers the "writing on the wall" and exposes the Hatch as a Dharma experiment, he recovers it again and sacrifices his life to save the island and to bring the other survivors back to the island as well. Locke's entire motivation lies in protecting the island and the survivors on it. He goes on the hunt and lands a huge boar, which demonstrates his masculinity but also his concern for others, as he feeds the group with his kill. Sawyer, on the other hand, begins his island journey with a selfish focus. For example, Sawyer manipulates Kate's goodwill and Ana Lucia's fears of the Others in order to control of the armory ("The

Long Con" 2.13). After stealing the guns from the Hatch, he claims a leadership role, stating, "New sheriff in town, boys. Y'all best get used to it." But this form of leadership is ultimately critiqued on the island as self-serving. While Sawyer obtains goodwill from saving Michael and taking a bullet while trying to keep Walt from the Others, he uses this beneficence cynically to gain power, similar to what we see from Benjamin Linus. Meanwhile, Jack and Locke seek to protect the Oceanic survivors without a similar desire for remuneration. Sawyer, however, develops over time from being a rebellious con man with selfish inclinations to a loving husband for Juliet, a protective fighter for the other survivors, and a determined enemy of the Man in Black. His path to healing and redemption simply takes a little longer.

Hurley's narrative also resolves with his becoming a more masculine figure of leadership in the community. As I noted earlier, Hurley's wound is connected to his belief that he is mentally unstable and cursed by the numbers that won his fortune. Nevertheless, he comes to be a leader of the survivors and the caretaker of the island. Hurley serves as a conduit to Jacob, but his ethical leadership is also a model for the others to follow, and in the series' final episodes he often takes the lead, a trait Jack encourages. Hurley, however, has developed this vision previously, as we see when he is placed in charge of the food supply. Hurley defends it vigorously, making sure that everyone receives a fair share of the food. It is no surprise, then, that Jack turns to Hurley to become the new caretaker after his mortal wounding. Hurley is the show's goodhearted soul, and he does not fit the traditional masculinity in terms of his body or his actions. But he does have money and power in the real world, and his relationship with Libby provides his heterosexual identity that makes him accessible as a masculine figure on the show. However, Hurley's ethical vision pre-empts those characteristics, and allows him to reclaim Benjamin Linus when others could not.

Hurley's adoption of Ben Linus as his second-in-command allows Ben to recover his own ethical vision. They help each other — Ben encourages Hurley to find his own path, telling him that "maybe there's another way" to protect the island, "a better way," and Hurley gives Ben a chance to protect the island ethically. The final scenes reveal that, in fact, Ben and Hurley make a strong team and do their jobs well ("The End" 6.17 and 6.18).[2] Benjamin Linus is also interesting because for most of the show, he has served as a villainous manipulative enemy for the Oceanic survivors. We know he is a mass murderer who helped the Others defeat the Dharma Initiative and who has sought to kidnap several castaways, including Jack. We also see him succumb to the Man in Black's promises, betraying Charles Widmore and then murdering him as revenge for Ben's own daughter's death at the hands of mercenaries sent to re-take the island. The Linus-Widmore agon represents a power-hungry masculine conflict that the show seeks to repudiate through its vision of ethical manhood.

The secondary characters of the show also engage with this narrative of ethical manhood through their sacrifices, including even the sacrifice of their own lives. By doing so, each also demonstrates that he has healed from the wounds that led him to the island. Charlie, for example, embraces the destiny that Desmond forecasts for him, choosing to push the button and drown in order to save Claire and Aaron. He does so after giving up his drug habit (with help from Locke and the island) and beginning a romance with Claire that includes taking on the role of father figure to Aaron. Sayid, after literally dying and being reborn at the Temple, finds his soul and saves the Candidates by taking the Man in Black's bomb away and sacrificing his life for theirs. Much of his past had been about his use of violence to coerce others; however, in this instance he chooses to use his masculine body to protect and defend his friends at the ultimate cost to himself. Jin sacrifices his life to continue helping Sun — he will not leave her to die alone, echoing Jack's sentiments in the opening season as well as his own promise never to leave her again when they are reunited. In each of these cases, the men demonstrate their healing. Charlie is no longer an addict; Sayid is no longer a soulless killer; Jin is now a devoted and tender husband who has reclaimed his love for his wife. As Newbury argues, while the community in *Lost* has friction and conflict, it largely functions as a "multiracial, multinational alliance" in which the social and cultural divisions of the world are forgotten in the fight to survive the island (209). Note, too, that this healing extends into the afterlife. As they confront their limitations and accept their place, their wounds heal. And in a sense, they all escape death, living on in a paradise of community and love that serves as a meta-narrative for the role of our imaginations. We will live on in your memories, the show tells us, together forever in your hearts and in our heaven.

Thus, the story of becoming "found" — of recovering one's identity through this ethical connection to the survivor community — parallels the narrative of a resurrected white masculinity. Jack Shephard is undoubtedly the focal point of these two narratives. We learn more about Jack's issues than any other male character save perhaps Locke, and Jack demonstrates his commitment to the island by killing the Man in Black and then sacrificing his own life to save the island as well as Kate, Sawyer, and the others who escape on the Ajira plane in the series finale. He is the Oceanic Six member who realizes they must return to the island and save the others, and in the final season, he takes charge as the new protector. Even his name makes clear that he will be the shepherd to his flock so that they shall not want. And though he dies at the end, lying down not in green pastures but in a green/brown bamboo forest, nevertheless, he clearly rejuvenates himself through his actions and becomes the ultimate leader that these people need and that the island requires. Jack Shephard's journey is one from wounded white man with no place in the world to restored hero with a divine purpose. He moves from his earlier belief that he cannot lead to a position where he unquestioningly takes on the role of savior:

> JACK: I'll do it.... This is why I'm here. This is ... this is what I'm supposed to do.
> JACOB: Is that a question, Jack?
> JACK: No ["What They Died For"].

Jack's assertive claim reveals that he no longer questions his abilities or himself. His final battle with the Man in Black highlights his restored masculinity. The iconic shot of Jack leaping into the air, fist raised to deliver a mighty blow to Locke's head, highlights Jack as a man of action and power. His battle with the Man in Black clearly demonstrates his superior strength; the Man in Black can only defeat him by grabbing a knife and stabbing Jack, and even that does not stop Jack from saving the island after kicking MIB off the cliff ledge to his death. This wound, unlike the ones in the real world, may be mortal but is not debilitating. *Lost* articulates the end of a traditional white masculinity by offering us a new and improved white masculinity that is still in power but knows how to use that power effectively for the greatest good. The key is that we must trust those in power—the show's narrative seems to suggest that in men we must trust if we want to advance. That is why, over and over again in the final season, Jack asks, "Do you trust me?" The ritual of asking for and receiving trust demonstrates the community's acceptance of Jack's newfound manhood.

Important as well to understanding Jack's central position is the cinematographic closure of the series. *Lost* opens with a close-up on Jack's eye, highlighting not just the idea of perception in general but also of Jack's perception in particular. Indeed, the rejuvenation Jack achieves comes mostly because of a revised sense of his own self-worth. Lindelof and Cuse's decision to end the series with the same shot, only reversed from an eye closed and then opening to an eye opening and then closed, makes clear that Jack's perception and his identity were the central foci of the show. The close-up on Jack's eye privileges his vision. Jack is our hero, our central masculine figure, and he leads the others by word and deed to freedom and resurrection into the world, vanquishes the evil Man in Black, and saves the island, leaving Hurley and Ben as caretakers. He has led them to the promised land, learning to make his decisions not for pride or self-interest but for the good of the island community. The result of the candidate storyline thus reconstitutes white masculinity through an ethical narrative that also leaves in place the traditional patriarchy that demands such ethics to circumvent.

We can further note that the imagined afterlife that gathers the survivors together once again is also centered in many ways on Jack. While Christian tells us that this place has been created by the group, I find it significant that the other characters cannot move on until Jack arrives and that Jack is the last to arrive, marking him as significant. Add to that the placement of Christian Shephard as the guide to the afterlife, and Jack's belief becomes even more central. The iconography of the church in that scene does portray symbols from many different belief systems, but the central architecture and symbology follow the aptly named "Christian" Shephard, as does the kindly white father who leads his followers to salvation. Perception gives Jack further credence as our narrative center, for we see this final reunion through Jack's eyes. For the entire sixth season, followers of the show referred to this time line as the "sideways world," assuming it was the creation of the atomic bomb explosion that killed Juliet in the season five finale and reading it as an alternate universe/timeline contiguous with the central narrative involving the Man in Black. The revelation of this timeline as a purgatory of sorts comes to us as viewers only when Jack realizes it. The final scenes, in fact, switch from Jack dying on the island to Jack learning the truth of this world — the narrative clearly suggests that as island Jack sees the plane fly overhead, affirming the survivors' escape from the island, he also sees the afterlife that awaits with his friends. The opening and closing images of the show, then, focus on Jack Shephard as a means of foregrounding his journey as the central one of the show. While it is visually circular, the narrative of identity we have seen is clearly one of progress and resolution as Jack is resurrected into the afterlife.

## *See You in Another Life, Brother*

So it would seem that *Lost* clearly argues for a kinder, gentler white masculinity that leaves in place traditional power structures but suggests a different way of determining that power's use. To quote the mantra of another troubled hero, "with great power comes great responsibility." *Lost* wants to take that mantra as its guiding light, asserting that responsibility to one's community is central to creating a better world. But this ending is ambivalent, for it leaves women and racial minorities behind and maintains the patriarchal structures of power that define contemporary American culture. It is no accident that Sayid, Jin, and Michael have all died, for they represent racial threats to white manhood. Though we might read Hurley as Hispanic given his family heritage, it becomes clear on the island that he can take on this leadership role because he acts in a way conducive to white masculine authority. Even his name suggests this — we know that his given name was Hugo Reyes, which clearly indicates his ethnic heritage. But he spends much of the show using the name Hurley, which masks his ethnicity and allows him to take on a white masculine position of leadership. Indeed, his lack of confidence in replacing Jack and his adoption of Ben as his assistant (a decision not necessary to protect the island, as Jacob had done so by himself for many years, and his mother for years before that) can be read as an indication of his anxiety over replacing Jack and Jacob as the white masculine authority figures. Ben must tell Hurley that he can chart his own path with the island, leaving behind Jacob's vision and implementing his own. Ben's advice allows Hurley to redefine protecting the island in a way that breaks with the white male tradition established by Jack and Jacob, but it also leaves men in charge and suggests that an ethical masculinity is required for the role.

## *But What About the Women?*

One objection that can be raised involves Kate Austin. Her name is on the candidate list, and she does shoot MIB to save Jack. Therefore, one might argue that the show provides a powerful counter-example that undermines my thesis about men, patriarchy, and power on the island. Fair enough. But ultimately, Kate's narrative spins out in a way that actually supports the overarching narrative of white masculinity in *Lost*. Kate spends the entire series as the focal point of an erotic triangle between Sawyer and Jack. Eve Sedgwick describes the erotic triangle as a literary device where two men actively compete/cooperate to control a particular woman (1–21). Thus, the erotic triangle often positions the woman in a manner that denies her agency and, more importantly, highlights the masculinity of the two suitors. Kate is involved with Jack and Sawyer at different times, and we are given scenes in which each makes love to her. Thus, she is positioned as feminine at key moments in the series.

Further, most of her narrative focuses on questions of reproduction, as do the narratives of most women in the series. Kate delivers Claire's baby, she babysits Sun's child, she rescues Aaron from the island, and her return to the island is for one reason only — to reunite Claire with Aaron. Again, these elements position her outside the realm of masculine authority. While she does take on a role of violence and power at times — such as when she shoots Locke — the show always re-asserts her femininity soon after. Even her name on the list of candidates comes into question:

> KATE: Why did you cross my name off of your wall?
> JACOB: Because you became a mother. It's just a line of chalk in a cave. The job is yours if you want it, Kate ["What They Died For"].

This answer suggests her ability to take on the leadership role but simultaneously negates it through her identity as "a mother." The language of "choice," a loaded term in American culture due to its connection to abortion, suggests that Kate must choose between her femininity and her authority — one cannot have both. Similarly, when she shoots Locke as he prepares to kill Jack, it seems that she takes on a masculine position. But this access is only temporary — in fact, Locke does not die until Jack pushes him off the cliff ledge, which undercuts her role in defeating the villain, and a few minutes later, Jack is kissing her and remanding her into Sawyer's care before he limps off to save the island. The show's reconnection with her position as the feminine love interest at this moment again negates her access to masculine authority — she becomes Jack's lover, feminized into a submissive role, while he becomes the hero once again. In addition, the scene's narrative reconstitutes the erotic triangle, this time in a manner that emphasizes Jack and Sawyer's cooperation in protecting and saving Kate and therefore reasserts their masculinity through her positioning as a feminine damsel in distress. Of course, she has demonstrated her independence and skills at multiple times throughout the show, but the final resolution must return her to a dependent role as a means of developing Jack's position as the group leader and hero of the day.

Let me be clear that the show itself connects masculinity and authority as "natural" partners, which I am arguing creates a blind spot on account of which *Lost* is unable to imagine female ethical authority. Kate is a primary example, but Juliet and Sun also find themselves constrained by their femininity in terms of being effective leaders. Even Jacob's mother, the island's previous caretaker, cannot achieve this goal, for her act of finding her replacements comes through the murder of Jacob and the Man in Black's biological mother, and her maternal instincts appear wanting since they culminate in one son becoming a sociopathic murderer and smoke monster (MIB) and the other becoming a fratricidal protector who nevertheless sacrifices many lives to ensure that his candidates come to the island and take his place. Kate, Sun, Claire, and the other women face similar issues, offered agency for individual decisions but at the same time positioned within a larger social structure that defines them as feminine and absconds with their authority in larger matters. *Lost*'s melodramatic structure, then, creates a romance between various male and female characters that reinvigorates traditional gender relations, then offers men a particular ethical stance from which to determine the actions of all.

## *The End?*

*Lost* might be seen as a melodrama of beset manhood, at least in its flashbacks, with the island serving as a repository for these masculine anxieties to be erased or assuaged through a combination of primitive regeneration and social reconstruction that creates the vision of ethical manhood the show supports while re-asserting the social structures of patriarchy and masculinity that made such anxieties prevalent in the first place.[3] John Locke the character mirrors his philosopher namesake and asserts that "everyone gets a new life on this island" ("...In Translation" 1.17). Characters believe that they should be able to start over. But this reboot looks startlingly familiar in that it replicates traditional norms of gender and race even as it claims to move beyond them. Lauren Berlant has insisted that we must refuse "to elevate the ethic of personal sacrifice, suffering, and mourning over a politically interested 'will' to socially transformative action" (55). Tania Modleski extends this ideal by noting that melodrama often passes male sentimentality off as a socially transformative act when it is actually focused only on reasserting masculinity. *Lost* offers ethical manhood as a potential transformation, but only for individual men—the social milieu remains the same, but the actors in it choose to act differently. As a result, *Lost* offers a fantasy of masculine regeneration that promises a better world through men acting as good men, but that fantasy only appears to come to fruition through Jack's death. We only see the complete success of this vision in the afterlife scenes, where everyone seems to have solved their problems and can live in joyful communion with one another. *Lost*'s fantastic story, then, resolves in a fantasy that it may not believe can exist, one that seems to leave us in the hands of shepherds and con men redeemed.

## Notes

1. Davis and Needham's essay was published before the revelation of Tom Friendly's sexuality in "Meet Kevin Johnson." Nevertheless, Tom Friendly only supports my argument as he is not a castaway but an "Other" and he is not developed as a central character in the development of the island's community or of our heroes' masculine identities.

2. The forthcoming DVD of Season Six promises extended clips of Hurley and Ben's time on the island, scenes that were deleted from the television finale but should offer an interesting glimpse into the relationship between Ben and Hurley.

3. This term comes from Nina Baym's compelling argument on American literature and the exclusion of women writers, "Melodramas of Beset Manhood: How Theories of American Fiction Exclude Women Authors."

## Works Cited

Baym, Nina. "Melodramas of Beset Manhood: How Theories of American Fiction Exclude Women Authors." *American Quarterly* 33.2 (Summer 1981): 123–139. Print.

Berlant, Lauren. *The Female Complaint: The Unfinished Business of Sentimentality in American Culture.* Durham: Duke University Press, 2008. Print.

Davis, Glyn, and Gary Needham. "Queer(ying) *Lost*." *Reading* Lost: *Perspectives on a Hit Television Show*. Ed. Roberta Pearson. New York: I.B. Tauris, 2009. 261–280. Print.
McGee, Ryan. "*Lost*: It Only Ends Once." *Zap2It.com*. 3 June 2010. Web. 19 June 2010.
Modleski, Tania. "Clint Eastwood and Male Weepies." *American Literary History* 22.1 (2010): 136–58. Print.
Newbury, Michael. "*Lost* in the Orient: Transnationalism Interrupted." *Reading* Lost: *Perspectives on a Hit Television Show*. Ed. Roberta Pearson. New York: I.B. Tauris, 2009. 201–220. Print.
Paglia, Camille. "No Sex Please, We're Middle Class." *The New York Times*, 27 June 2010. WK 12. Print.
Robinson, Sally. *Marked Men: White Masculinity in Crisis*. New York: Columbia University Press, 2000. Print.
Sedgwick, Eve Kosofsky. *Between Men: English Literature and Male Homosocial Desire*. New York: Columbia University Press, 1985. Print.
Stein, Joel. "*Lost*'s Sensitive Action Hero." *Time*. 1 February 2007. Web. June 19 2010.
Stuever, Hank. "'Lost' or Not, We're Still at Loose Ends." *The Washington Post* 21 May 2010. A01. Print.

# "It Always Ends the Same": Paternal Failures

*Holly Hassel and Nancy L. Chick*

In "I Graduated from Lost University," Patricia Treble observes that "ivory-tower interest" in *Lost* has flourished since the show's debut, especially among philosophy departments. Indeed, the *Lost* interpretive canon, including books like *Lost and Philosophy: The Island Has Its Reasons* and the online journal *Lost Online Studies*, is preoccupied with the show's ontological and cosmological dimensions. Critics have applied theoretical lenses ranging from Deleuze to Foucault, and analyses of time-travel, spirituality and religion, and creation mythology are popular among academics. However, little work has examined the series through a feminist lens.[1] In this essay, we approach this gap by arguing that paternity is a core concern of the story arc of *Lost* and examine the show's major archetypes of the paternal failure motif from its premiere to its conclusion. Whether absent, abusive, or doomed, the show's fathers force the main characters to grapple with their own fathers' failures or their own failures as fathers, posing questions about parental responsibility and exposing cultural anxieties about fatherhood. Because the motif is so pervasive, we cannot claim to be comprehensive in analyzing all relevant characters, so we instead focus on the characters most representative of each archetype, beginning with the show's creation narrative that highlights the (monstrous) maternal, omits the paternal, and clarifies why the characters of *Lost* are unable either to come to terms with their fathers' failures or fully actualize their own paternal aspirations.

## *Fatherless Origins*

> BEN to LOCKE: You'll never be free until you release the hold your father has on you…. That's why you have to kill your father ["The Brig" 3.19].

From early on, the series unfolds a meta-narrative questioning the origin of the island, the origin of the Others, and issues of destiny, determinism, and free will, but not until late in the final season does the show offer some answer. This late episode, "Across the Sea" (6.15), reveals how these origins, the fundamental theme of individual destiny, and the possible models for paternal identity are interwoven within the show's overarching narrative.

As early as 2006, J.M. Berger argued that *Lost* is "a microcosm or allegory of the universal creation story, following a story of existence from creation to collapse using the tools of this archetypical myth." If this is the case, then it is especially important to critically examine the characters of Jacob and the Man in Black (MIB), whose chess game in which the survivors are pawns (or "candidates") propels the storyline — two gods directing their unwilling aspirants or prototypes and mapping out future generations. Viewers learn the most about Jacob and MIB in "Across the Sea," an episode that clearly draws on allusions to the Biblical book of Genesis,[2] cementing its significance in the *Lost* canon as the show's origin story.

For these two men at the heart of the island's origin story, there is no model of fatherhood, or even manhood. The twin brothers were borne of Claudia, washed up on shore, and helped by a nameless woman known only as Mother. Claudia gives birth first to the boy she names Jacob and then to a second son who remains unnamed. Notably, Claudia is alone with no mention of a father, so the paternal origins of Jacob and MIB are obscured. Similarly, Mother — who murders Claudia shortly after the birth and then adopts the twins — has no male companion to serve as a father to the two boys. Prefiguring what will become a series-long preoccupation, Jacob and MIB come of age on the island with no example of fatherhood. In fact, their exposure to other men is accidental (they run across a group of warriors when chasing a boar), and of these men Mother says only, "They come. They fight. They destroy. They corrupt. And it always ends the same," a speech repeated by MIB to Jacob thousands of years later ("The Incident" 5.16 and 5.17). With an origin story containing no narrative tradition of fatherhood and only this speech about manhood passed down from Mother, the island's inhabitants — including our castaways — seem predestined to fail in their attempts to develop their own stories of paternal identity.

Simultaneously, the notion that the fathers of *Lost* are fated to fail based on the show's origin story indicates a more complex causality than one which can be described as mere determinism, questioning determinism even as it appears to reinforce it. Determinism is problematized in fascinating ways by the early episode "Tabula Rasa" (1.3), in which the castaways propose a contradictory worldview based on the new circumstances presented by living on a proverbially remote island: a rebirth, the opportunity to start over and remake oneself, raising questions about human autonomy. Girard and Meulemans have similarly articulated this dilemma, noting that *Lost* "exploits" the "philosophical cliché" that asks if it is "possible for an individual to act according to his free will without yielding to the influence of determinist factors" (90). For example, Sawyer observes "we can all play a part. Who do you want to be?" echoing philosopher (not character) John Locke's theory of the *tabula rasa*, that humans are born blank slates and that identity, character, and values are not innate but formed by experience. Early on, then, the series (on the surface) appears to propose that this self-determination is a possibility echoed throughout the interwoven stories of the characters.³

Despite this provocative introduction of the free will-determinism dilemma, the show itself subverts its characters' own assumptions through its use of flashbacks, the manner in which characters are haunted by their pasts, and a refrain taken from the title of the episode "Whatever Happened, Happened" (5.11). The tension between the show's deterministic ideology and the characters' attempts to fight it is *resolved tragically*: as hard as they try to define their own identities and leave their pasts behind, the characters' previous narratives follow them — even to a remote island in the Pacific Ocean with total strangers. When it comes to paternal identity, this tension — unknown to the characters themselves — reinforces the origin story's predetermining path toward failed fatherhood, a destiny that is especially tragic for those characters who struggle against this fate.

## *Absent Fathers*

> BEN to JACOB: What was it that was so wrong with me? What about me? ["The Incident"].

A recurring archetype of paternal failure in the series is that of the Absent Father, one that takes on multiple complexities for each character. The Absent Father, for whom the god-like island founder, Jacob, becomes a prototype, is either physically or emotionally absent or both, sometimes neglectful and sometimes rejecting. Some Absent Fathers — prefigured by Jacob's rejection of Ben Linus — reject specific children who fail or challenge their expectations, while others simply reject the role of fatherhood altogether. In each scenario, however, the spectrum of consequences is dire for these fathers and sons — emotional damage on the one end and patricide on the other as sons try to erase the damage inflicted by the Absent Fathers.

Ben Linus and his relationship to Jacob, the island's archetypal father, reinforce the pervasive nature of the Absent Father motif in the *Lost* metanarrative. It is clear from early on that Ben thinks of Jacob as a paternal figure, as when he tells Locke, "I was born here on this Island. I'm one of the last that was. Most of these people you see — I brought them here. So Jacob talks to me, John. He tells me what to do, trusts me" ("The Man Behind the Curtain" 3.20). Much of this episode documents Ben's struggle to connect with Jacob, the father figure who could replace his memories of his own abusive father. However, the invented relationship he has always sought unravels in the fifth season finale, when it becomes clear that Ben has never actually seen Jacob. Instead of choosing Ben, who has been loyal to Jacob for years, Jacob chooses to reveal himself to Locke. Ben's feelings of neglect explode when he finally comes face to face with the man whose physical absence has always tormented him:

> So now, after all this time, you've decided to stop ignoring me. Thirty-five years I lived on this island, and all I ever heard was your name over and over. Richard would bring me your instructions — all those slips of paper, all those lists — and I never questioned anything. I did as I was told. But when I dared to ask to see you myself, I was told, "You have to wait. You have to be patient." But when he [Locke] asked to see you? He gets marched straight up here as if was Moses. So why him? What was it that was so wrong with me? What about me? ["The Incident"].

Dismissing the armed Ben with the question, "What about you?" and forsaking his most loyal son, Jacob mysteriously seals his own death. The rejected son kills Jacob, a moment of symbolic patricide and the ultimate moment of paternal failure that prefigures the way that many of *Lost*'s sons resolve their angst over fatherly abandonment.

For several of the survivors, early flashbacks reveal their literal abandonment by their fathers with less tragic but nonetheless predictable consequences. In "Raised by Another" (1.10), Claire's initial resistance to continuing her pregnancy is overcome by her boyfriend Thomas, who encourages her to have the baby with promises to be the supportive father she never had. A few months later, however, a fight over curtains escalates into abandonment, with Thomas dissolving into self-pity: "How in the hell am I supposed to be a dad, Claire? How about my painting, my life?" Claire's shock is deflected by Thomas's accusations of Claire's "daddy abandonment crap," referring to an as-yet-unrevealed plot detail: Claire was abandoned by her own father, the unfaithful Christian Shephard, whose illegitimate daughter never interested him until he failed drastically with his legitimate son, Jack. Claire is thus doubly haunted by paternal failures in the form of Absent Fathers: her own father's absence and the child she plans to give up for adoption, largely because of Thomas's abandonment. In this case, the rejection is rooted in Thomas's immaturity, but subsequent fatherly absences more vividly echo Jacob's rejection of his specific "child."

Brian Porter, Walt's stepfather, similarly rejects his fatherly obligations, but Brian's rejection comes well after he has established his importance in the life of the child. In a striking scene in which he asks Michael to take over custody of Walt after the child's mother dies suddenly, Brian confesses that "from the beginning," he had been clear with Susan that he "didn't want to be a father. I just don't know how" ("Special" 1.14). Despite Michael's selfless admission that "You're the only father he knows," Brian reveals that "[he] can't be his father," not just because of his lack of abilities or his character flaws; he abandons Walt because the boy is "different somehow" and because "when he's around, things happen." In other words, he is not so much rejecting the general role of father; he is instead, as Jacob does with Ben, specifically rejecting this boy who has looked to him as his only father figure for nine years. Though the island's origin story offers no model of fatherhood — or perhaps because of this situation — these absentee fathers willfully remove themselves from the lives of those who have grown too emotionally dependant on them, as Jacob does with Ben, Thomas with Aaron and Claire, and Brian with Walt.

Unlike Thomas and Brian, David Reyes's abandonment seems motivated by the irresponsible desire for a life made up of gambling, "making" his "own luck," and then living off of his son's lottery money. Hugo Reyes's father echoes Brian's ambivalence and his betrayal of his responsibilities to his son. Instead of a promised trip with Hugo to the Grand Canyon, Reyes goes to Las Vegas and stays gone for seventeen years ("Tricia Tanaka Is Dead" 3.10), returning primarily to avail himself of Hugo's newfound wealth. The symbol of this abandonment is the Camaro they had worked on together, left untouched in Hugo's garage and invoked later on the island in Hugo's discovery of an old Volkswagen bus.[4] Hugo claims that "We make our own luck"— echoing his father's own advice to him as he left for Vegas — and resurrects the bus, as if redefining his past by substituting his friendship with Charlie, Sawyer, and Jin for his failed relationship with his father, providing an example of another character who tries to break the strangling fate of a painful past while ironically showing that that past is still with him. In the end, however, this assertion of free will is at odds with the deterministic bent of the show, as Hugo never fully comes to terms with his father's abandonment, just as David never really compensates for his absence.

A more dramatically absent father is experienced by James Ford, or Sawyer, whose entire life trajectory is predetermined by his father's absence and, consistent with the origin story of absent fatherhood, ends in patricide. His childhood is marred not only by his father's absence, but an absence resulting from his father's murder-suicide (over Anthony Cooper's swindling of Sawyer's mother) that leaves both of his parents dead and Sawyer a young witness to the violence ("Outlaws" 1.16). In this situation, the paternal failure is violent and powerful — not only creating an enormous gap in the child's life because of the loss of his father, but also depriving him of his mother, priming him for a life of violence and loss and betrayal, and leading him to the ill-fated Oceanic 815. Because he cannot let go of the rage he cultivated as a boy and nurtured throughout his life, he finds himself in an endless quest to kill the man who "killed my daddy" ("The Brig"). The rage over his father's murderous act (which Sawyer blames on Cooper) drives him to murder Cooper when Ben brings him to the island. Sawyer's murderous impulses are channeled into surrogate patricide—killing Locke's biological father even as he avenges his own childhood loss.

## Abusive Fathers

> WALT: You have a dad?
> LOCKE: Everyone's got a dad.
> WALT: Is he cool?
> LOCKE: No. No, he's not ["...In Translation" 1.17].

Another recurring archetype of paternal failures on *Lost* is the Abusive Father, more damaging than the Absent Father, and as pervasive. These figures range from authoritative to abusive to murderous but are always dominant, exerting power over their children in ways that leave them emotionally, psychologically, or physically crippled. The Abusive Father is a patriarch, echoing the island's prototype, the Man in Black, whose violent impulses are strikingly at odds with Jacob's passive satisfaction with his lot on the island. MIB murders Mother, attacks his brother, and, as the Smoke Monster, shows no regard for human life in the pursuit of his goal—to leave the island. The Abusive Father echoes sociologist Allan Johnson's definition of masculinity—qualities such as "control, strength, competitiveness, toughness, coolness under pressure, logic, forcefulness, decisiveness, rationality, autonomy, self-sufficiency, and control over any emotion that interferes with other core values (such as invulnerability)" (7), though the figure of the patriarch is taken to the abusive extreme in both the origin story and its manifestations explored by the *Lost* storyline.

The patriarchal, abusive fathers in *Lost*, regardless of culture or class, execute their paternal responsibilities as patriarchs who are flawed and sometimes violent. Johnson explains that, within a patriarchal culture, "men maintain their privilege by controlling women *and anyone else who might threaten it*" (emphasis added, 14) and that "Men are assumed (and expected) to be in control at all times, to be unemotional (except for anger and rage), to present themselves as invulnerable, autonomous, independent, strong, rational, logical, dispassionate, knowledgeable, always right, and in command of every situation, especially those involving women" (14). These characteristics are reflected in the fathers of several *Lost* castaways, including Christian and Jack Shephard, Roger and Ben Linus, and Anthony Cooper and Sawyer and John Locke, whose lack of compassion, invulnerability, emotional distance, and exertion of physical force make them not just patriarchal fathers, but abusive ones.

Christian Shephard, presented almost exclusively through Jack's flashbacks, is the show's quintessential patriarch: a man of authority obsessed with power. He has an inflated sense of self-importance, uses his son, withholds approval, cannot authentically relate to Jack as a loving father, and paradoxically holds both high and low expectations for his son. As a result, Jack's storyline is defined by his efforts to resolve his conflicted relationship with his father. Chief of Surgery at St. Sebastian Hospital, Christian's professional role is central to his identity, even as a father, as the power it gives him defines his relationship with Jack. Flashbacks reveal insights about their relationship, mostly that it is defined by Christian's unachievable expectations for his son and his contradictory belief in Jack's inability to meet those expectations. Two instances in the first season illustrate this paradox. In "White Rabbit" (1.5), Jack remembers a childhood conversation following his efforts to intervene when a friend is being bullied. Christian, drinking, reveals too much about his belief that his son will never measure up to his own inflated self-perception: while Christian has the strength to be in charge, make life-or-death decisions, and be happy "even when I fail" because "I have what it takes," he tells Jack that the boy shouldn't try "to be the hero. Because when you fail, you just don't have what it takes." His father's lack of support clearly haunts Jack, even as he closely follows in Christian's footsteps by becoming a spinal surgeon and working under him in the same hospital. Throughout the series, Jack's storyline on the island is driven by continual efforts to assert his competence while continually believing himself a failure.

Later, the aptly titled episode "All the Best Cowboys Have Daddy Issues" (1.11) documents Christian's fall from grace and his pathological withholding of approval from his son. When a patient dies because Christian performs surgery after drinking, his medical license rests on Jack's willingness to lie for him. Knowing that his son is desperate for his approval, he manipulatively pleads with Jack to defend him:

> I know I have been hard on you, but that is how you make a soft metal into steel. That is why you are the most gifted young surgeon in this city. And this, this is a career that is all about the greater good. I've had to sacrifice certain aspects of my relationship with you so that hundreds and thousands of patients will live because of your extraordinary skills. I know it's a long time coming. What happened yesterday, I promise you, will never happen

again. And after all, what I've given — this is not just about my career, Jack. It's my life.

Jack, of course, agrees in the beginning but later revises his statement about his father's intoxication because he realizes that this approval — finally granted after so many years — is all part of a self-serving, last-ditch effort to save Christian's career. When Jack sees his father employ the same rehearsed gestures of confidence that he used with Jack (a reassuring hand on the shoulder) with the dead patient's husband, he can no longer maintain the charade. He realizes that Christian is unable to authentically relate to him as a loving father and instead is abusive, manipulative, and exploitative — as well as incapable of authentic human connection.

In keeping with *Lost*'s tendency to problematize seemingly simple relationships, season five's last episode calls some of the previous assumptions about Christian and Jack's relationship into question ("The Incident, Part 2" 5.17). Following Christian's interferences in one of Jack's early surgeries, Jack confronts his father: "You know, it's bad enough that everybody in this hospital thinks the only reason I got this residency is because you're my father. But then you ... you put me in a time-out during my first major procedure, in front of my entire team. Dad, I know you don't believe in me, but I need them to," to which Christian replies, "Are you sure I'm the one who doesn't believe in you, Jack?" Though Jack's insecurities are the understandable result of years of his father's emotional abuse, this scene raises questions about the degree to which and for how long filial failures can be attributed to paternal failures, as well as the impact of these insecurities not only on Jack's navigation of the world but also on his own paternal responsibility. In the final season's alternate reality in which Jack has a son with Juliet, this father-son relationship begins as complicated and troubled as Jack's relationship with Christian ("The Substitute" 6.4), suggesting that Jack has continued his own father's cycle with his son David. When David goes to a music school audition without telling Jack, he confesses that he did not want his father to come because "I didn't want you to see me fail," hinting that the pressure of Jack's gaze has led David to live with the legacy of his grandfather's admonition that Jack — and by extension, his own son David — "doesn't have what it takes." Though the relationship between Jack and David becomes an idealized version of fatherhood where they have resolved their conflicts and insecurities, clearly the narrative questions this outcome since the concluding episodes suggest that it is only in an alternative fantasy world that such father-son relationships can exist.

With no healthy paternal model in the island origin story and MIB as his prototype, Christian's failures are predetermined and never redeemed. He later reveals to Ana Lucia that he is in Australia because "I can't apologize to my son. He tries to help me so I thanked him by cutting him off. I thanked him by hating him," but this drunken admission is a cowardly confession made to a stranger, and he never attempts to rectify his paternal failures ("Two for the Road" 2.20). Significantly, it is only in the series finale scene in the nondenominational afterlife that Jack finally appears to receive the love and approval he has been seeking from Christian; however, this moment is too little, too late. Immediately afterward, Jack dies.

Unlike the series-long tensions between Jack and Christian, Benjamin Linus's problems with his biological father aren't documented until later in the series. These early experiences with his father contextualize the complexities of Ben's invented paternal identities with Jacob as his substitute father-figure and with Alex, the child he steals to become his own. A single parent (Ben's mother died in childbirth), Roger Linus is emotionally and physically abusive to his son Ben. Revealed through flashbacks in the appropriately titled "The Man Behind the Curtain" (3.20), Ben's personality is traced to his father's alcohol-fueled abuse. When he wants a better job on the island, Dharma's leader reassures Roger that his son is getting an excellent education, but the father responds, "I don't give a damn about his education," illustrating his disconnection from his son, reinforced later when he not only forgets Ben's birthday but spitefully demonstrates his resentment toward his son: "Sorry I forgot. Kinda hard to celebrate on the day you killed your mom. She was just seven months pregnant. We went for a hike, but you had to come early. Now, she's gone. And I'm stuck here on this island ... with you. Happy birthday, Ben." Later, Roger roughs up young Ben when he catches him befriending the imprisoned Sayid ("He's Our You" 5.10). Notably, his father teaches him early on that human connections — to his mother, to strangers, to his father — are punishable offenses, sealing Ben's adulthood inability to empathize and express compassion. The consequences of Roger's paternal failures are dire, leading Ben to kill his own father and the other Dharma Initiative converts, yet another paternal failure that results in the death of the father, echoing Ben's killing of Jacob and MIB's murderous impulses.[5]

Finally, as the most treacherous father, Anthony Cooper's patriarchal authority takes the stereotypical qualities of patriarchal masculinity to malevolent extremes: he is not just cool under pressure, but also sociopathically disengaged; he is not just in control, but also manipulative and exploitative; he is both tough and invulnerable, but also willing to use others as objects to achieve his criminal ends and for his own gain. Most importantly, he wields this twisted sense of authority over his son John Locke as much as he does over any other object of his con, demonstrating that he has no sense of his paternal identity beyond one of additional opportunities for exploitation. In any estimation, Anthony Cooper's actions seem to determine Locke's life, from his inauspicious birth to a teen mom hit by a car to his ignominious death as a murder victim.

In an elaborate scheme to save his own life, Cooper enters the series by manipulating Locke into donating a kidney, exploiting his son's desperate desire for a fatherly relationship after growing up an orphan in the foster care system ("Deus Ex Machina" 1.19).[6] Even in the hospital bed, Locke believes that fate has brought them together: "This was meant to be," says Locke, and Cooper replies noncommittally, "See you on the other side, son." Locke awakens to find his father has abandoned him and is unwilling to see him, reinforcing Cooper's cruelty. In *Lost*'s most vivid moment of abusive fatherhood, Anthony Cooper pushes his son out an eighth story window, revealing the reason for Locke's off-island confinement to a wheelchair ("The Man from Tallahassee" 3.13). He fails to kill his son, instead merely crippling him, solely for interfering with one of his cons. Like Jack, who is plagued by an unresolved sense that he must know and please his unpleasable father, Locke's relentless quest is also fruitless. The island's origin story has already established the narrative path of fatherhood for its castaways, sealing Locke's fate with his failed father from the beginning, despite his continued, seemingly irresistible efforts to resolve the relationship. In fact, the apparent resolution provided when Locke manipulates Sawyer into killing Cooper invokes his father's own diabolical behavior, suggesting that on some level the father has corrupted the son, providing yet another tragic outcome with no real emotional closure ("The Brig").[7]

## *Aspiring Fathers*

> MOTHER to JACOB and MIB; MIB to JACOB: They come. They fight. They destroy. They corrupt. And it always ends the same ["Across the Sea," "The Incident"].

Although the previous archetypes convey abandonment and abuse, they are debatably less tragic than the final archetype of the Aspiring Fathers who embody—to varying degrees—heart and hope, and ultimately failure. This archetype seems the most persuasive in reinforcing the impact of the fatherlessness of the *Lost* island origin story, in that more fathers on *Lost* aspire to be better than their own fathers or to improve on their previous failures than are Absent or Abusive, and yet they are just as likely to fail their children in profound ways. Neither Jacob nor MIB become fathers themselves, and at the same time, their chess game in quest of human virtue suggests a kind of aspiring paternity—the Aspiring Father archetype is defined by an effort to actualize the best features of successful fatherhood — nurturing, encouragement, hope, optimism, and commitment. Jacob intervenes in the lives of the castaways as seen in "The Incident, Part 1" 5.1, attempting to direct the futures of the *Lost* survivors, and MIB, in the corporal form of Christian and Locke, similarly directs the fates of the castaways. However, neither of these efforts at surrogate fatherhood is successful in the end, just as the *Lost* men who are biological or adoptive fathers — Sawyer, Ben, Michael, Jin, and Charlie — also fail to actualize a successful paternal identity.

In his "Every Man for Himself" brand of individualism, Sawyer believes in no externally imposed rules, responsibilities, or relationships, all of which are visually represented by the repeated motif of being caged ("A Tale of Two Cities" 3.1) or imprisoned ("Every Man for Himself" 3.4). His role as a father begins with his denial of all parental responsibility: "I ain't got no daughter," he tells Cassidy Phillips when she tells him about their baby, Clementine. Given his background, we might assume that he doesn't know how to be a parent and that he is positioning himself as a deadbeat dad, a classic example of the Absentee Father archetype. However, Sawyer constantly reminds us that he is never as one-dimensional as he appears. Shortly after he denies his role to Cassidy, he secretly sets up a bank account for his daughter and later asks Kate to bring Cassidy even more money, but swears Kate to secrecy. Publicly rejecting the fact of his paternity, Sawyer privately accepts at least this easiest and shallowest level of paternal responsibility. (Significantly, Cassidy points out that it is minimal, an act of "coward[ice]" that doesn't require him to "lift a finger" ["Whatever Happened, Happened" 5.11]).[8] Furthermore, in season six's alternate reality, police detective Sawyer has no such paternal obligations. *Lost* ends with Sawyer never meeting Clementine, never publicly claiming his paternity, and never extending beyond the barest of fatherly responsibilities. Any promising narrative trajectory is never actualized, reinforcing the show's belief in the power of creation stories to determine outcomes.

Perhaps the most surprising aspiring father is Ben. The final season's flash sideways in which he is a kind schoolteacher who takes care to nurture his student Alex contrasts with the lack of human emotion he expresses in the regular timeline of the show. For most of the series, we have known Ben as the one who murdered the Dharma Initiative staff in a violent purge, or killed Keamy knowing that in doing so he is sentencing the dozens of people aboard Widmore's freighter to death, chillingly illustrated when Locke laments "You just killed everybody on that boat," and Ben replies "So?" ("There's No Place Like Home, Part 2" 4.14). Ben shows no empathy, compassion, or regard for others, with the sole exception of his relationship with Alex, whom he stole from her mother Danielle Rousseau, raised to believe she was his own daughter, and genuinely tries to protect from danger. Ironically, it is this emotional attachment that leads to one of his rare strategic missteps and one of the most vivid examples of the failure of fatherly obligation on *Lost*: when Keamy has a gun to Alex's head, Ben reassures his daughter, "I have this under control. Everything's gonna be okay," believing he can outwit Keamy and his boss Widmore's rules for their game of cat and mouse. However, his attempt to manipulate the situation is unsuccessful: "She's not my daughter.... She's a pawn, nothing more. She means nothing to me ... so if you want to kill her, go ahead and do it" ("The Shape of Things to Come" 4.9). Keamy calls his bluff, leaving Ben responsible for Alex's death, as well as bringing about the tragic end of Ben's role as father, the single manifestation of his sense of humanity. Blaming Widmore, Ben promises to kill Widmore's daughter in retribution but ultimately kills Widmore instead, so "He doesn't get to save his daughter," enacting island law that all fathers fail — in this case, in their ability to keep their daughters safe ("What They Died For" 6.16).

Efforts by other *Lost* fathers to protect their endangered children end in similarly tragic ways. In "Monstrous Musings, Patriarchal Baddies and Smokey Goodness: Musings on the Monsters of *Lost*," Natalie Wilson illustrates what she calls the show's "white is good, black is evil meme" by listing Michael as the show's "deadbeat dad." On the contrary, despite repeated obstacles, Michael is defined by his persistent attempts to fulfill his parental role with Walt. Admittedly, soon after taking custody of Walt, Michael confesses to his mother that he doesn't think he can "do this" ("Exodus: Part 2" 1.25); however, after that moment of uncertainty, Michael is unwavering in his determination to assume his fatherly responsibilities. More than any other character, Michael wants to be a father — and a good one.

Throughout the series, Michael calls Walt "my son" and "my boy" as often as he calls him by name, positioning himself as always the father. In contrast to Brian, the stepfather who rejects Walt for being "different," Michael puts in the "hard work" of fatherhood, even in the face of Susan's denial of his parental rights and access, Walt's surly rejections, and various external forces keeping him from Walt ("Special" 1.14). When Michael flies to Australia to get Walt shortly after Susan's death, father and son are strangers: Walt asks, "Who are you?" and Michael must tell him, "I'm your father." Reflecting the show's existential basis in which the major players forge their own characters, this central father and son must start from scratch.

In this extended absence from Walt's early childhood and the son's limited perspective of feeling abandoned, Michael resembles the Absent Father archetype, but the show focuses on Michael's perspective rather than Walt's, foregrounding the father's good intentions rather than the son's anguish. Michael even selflessly defends Susan's actions, telling Walt that "She did what she thought what was best for you," presumably to spare the ten-year-old —

already troubled by years of an absent father — resentment of his dead mother ("Exodus: Part 2"). This statement is remarkable, given Susan's pressuring of Michael to relinquish his parental rights and even taking Walt to Amsterdam. In Michael, then, we have a glimpse of redemptive fatherhood, a fatherly foil to both the Absentee Fathers and the Abusive Fathers. His persistence and effort also highlight the ease of Sawyer's minimal sense of paternal responsibility in just sending money.

However, the final episode of the first season reminds us of the series' deterministic meta-narrative that fathers cannot succeed on *Lost*. Just after a moment of reconciliation and tenderness (Walt tells Michael that it was "wrong" for Susan to keep them apart), Walt is kidnapped by the Others, and Michael is rendered powerless, an ineffectual father again kept apart from his son ("Exodus: Part 2"). His remaining appearances in the series document his torment over losing his son and the sense of paternal competence he had finally and fleetingly gained. This torment that leads him to justify doing anything — lying to his fellow castaways, stealing, attacking Locke, even murdering Libby and Ana Lucia — in the name of rescuing his son becomes Michael's hubris and the guarantee that he will continue to fail as a father. As his assertions that "It's a father's right" to do whatever it takes override his sense of right and wrong ("Three Minutes" 2.22), his style of obsessively devoted fatherhood corrupts his moral compass. When Ben frees Michael and Walt, viewers suspect that the reunion is temporary. As Ben suggests, once anyone discovers "what you did to get your son back," no one will trust him, including Walt ("Live Together, Die Alone: Part 2" 2.24). Everyone, including Michael, knows that he can't be around his son because of what he did in the name of fatherhood. When their storyline resumes two seasons later, Walt is no longer with his father, has nightmares, and is living with Michael's mother, who assumes Michael is dead. In a sense, he is. He is suicidal, wracked with guilt over what he has done and over his destruction of his short-lived relationship with his son. His ultimate suicide is not merely the product of his guilt, though; he sacrifices himself to explode the ship to atone for his actions by saving those left on the island and to escape his life as a paternal failure.

Like Michael, Jin Kwon is *Lost*'s other biological father who is continually prevented from assuming his fatherly role. He wants to become a father, primarily because it would "change everything" and "make" their lives "better" by giving him more status in the patriarchal Paik family business ("The Whole Truth" 2.16). Despite his intentions, Jin faces obstacles at every step toward becoming a father. He is initially surrounded by questions of infertility and then paternity when it is unclear who impregnated Sun. Then he is separated from Sun while she is pregnant, spending nearly half of the series trying to reunite with her, and when they finally reunite, they don't live long, and Jin dies before ever meeting his daughter, Ji Yeon. Although Sun is initially blamed for their infertility, we learn that it is secretly Jin, symbolically reinforcing his position as a lesser man than is worthy of the daughter of the wealthy Mr. Paik. This figurative lack of virility — he cannot become a father and establish his own paternal line — is compounded by his status as the son of a mere fisherman, a paternal line that prevents him from breaking into the hierarchical, patriarchal Korean social circles of Sun's family. In fact, paternity is so significant in determining the fate of Jin's character that the fact that his father was a lowly fisherman affects his life more than his mother being a prostitute.

When Sun does get pregnant, Jin's infertility and Sun's affair before the crash make the paternity uncertain, echoing the possibility that — unbeknownst to Jin — Mr. Kwon is not his biological father, since his mother was a prostitute. Sun initially resists telling Jin she is pregnant, denying him his paternal right to know if he is the father. Once Juliet establishes the date of conception confirming Jin's paternity, Jin enjoys his first moments of paternal success. As the island transformed Locke from wheelchair-bound cripple to expert hunter, Jin is rendered virile with a sperm count five times higher than before ("D.O.C." 3.18), as if the island allowed Jin to become a father, finally — only to frustrate any further attempts to fulfill this role. He and Sun are separated when he gets stuck on the freighter and begins the series of time jumps, ending up in the Dharma Initiative (1974–77) for Ji Yeon's birth and first years. They do not reunite until two-thirds of the way through the final season, and because his daughter is in Korea, Jin never even meets her by the time he and Sun die. In contrast to Michael, who briefly gets to act out his aspirations of fatherhood, Jin is allowed nothing beyond conception. Perhaps it is a cosmic punishment for rejecting his own father, claiming the lowly fisherman is dead. On the island, Jin is often shown fishing, suggesting that he is destined to be like his father: ultimately denied, erased from the life of his child. Perhaps it is punishment for initially wanting to be a father for the wrong reasons: status and acceptance by Mr. Paik. Or perhaps it is Mr. Paik's continued power, as if his own monstrous paternity supersedes Jin's. Whatever the reason, the island reinforces the narrative gap of the powerful fathers as Mr. Paik, Charles Widmore, and Christian Shephard wield great paternal authority, while the aspiring fathers like Michael and Jin are continually foiled in their attempts to provide alternative models of fatherhood.

Finally, Charlie Pace begins the series as a bass player who has lost his band, a heroin addict who feels alone on the island, "useless," and treated "like a bloody child"— hardly father material ("The Moth" 1.7). In another of the island's character transformations (Locke gains use of his legs, Jin becomes fertile), Charlie quickly evolves in a heavily symbolic episode appropriately titled "The Moth." With some quick fathering from Locke, who helps him kick his drug habit, and Jack, the island's hero-figure whom Charlie saves in a cave collapse, Charlie straightens up and feels useful, competent, and even heroic. Afterwards, he positions himself as Claire's partner and then her baby's father. In some ways, he is the most successful father figure in *Lost*. Charlie kills Ethan to protect pregnant Claire, but in contrast with Michael's actions, Charlie's are seen as justified. (Claire had even written "Charlie makes me feel safe" in her diary ["Special" 1.14].) When Michael fails to stop the Others from kidnapping Walt at the end of the first season, Charlie rescues kidnapped Aaron and returns him to Claire. Unlike the Absentee Fathers, he is nurturing and involved, as illustrated in the many scenes of his holding Aaron, in some episodes more often than Claire holds her baby ("One of Us" 3.16). In "Can Feminists Applaud *Lost*'s Final Season?" Natalie Wilson notes that "none of the childish males of *Lost* have to 'become men' via parenthood," but Charlie's character arc suggests that he comes into his own identity through his relationship with Claire and Aaron.

But in the world of *Lost*, Charlie's fatherly role cannot be flawless, and it cannot last. After he challenges Claire's parental authority by inappropriately berating her for waking the sleeping baby with her post-nightmare screams, Claire points out, "I don't remember marrying him" ("Abandoned" 2.6), suggesting that his fatherly role is as make-believe as the peanut butter he woos her with in "Confidence Man" (1.8). Later, Claire asserts her maternal authority when she suspects Charlie of using drugs again, suggesting that Charlie is unfit to be a father. He is not using again, but as with all other *Lost* characters, he cannot escape his past, and he does not determine his future. He ultimately works his way back into Claire's favor, just in time to discover that he is destined to die on the island and not to bring Claire and Aaron home with him to live as a family. Recalling the memory of his father helping him overcome his fear of water while teaching him how to swim (perhaps *Lost*'s fondest representation of a father-son relationship ["Greatest Hits" 3.21]), Charlie resolves to give up his aspirations of being a father himself to save Claire and Aaron. His father kept his word and kept him safe, so Charlie will keep his word of protecting Claire and Aaron — but not his vow, "I won't leave you, Claire. I promise" ("Raised by Another" 1.10). Instead, to get them off the island, he sacrifices himself — or more precisely, surrenders to his fate of drowning and relinquishes his future as protector, provider, partner, and father. His unfulfilled identity is represented by the familiar DS ring he has worn throughout the series, passed down through the Pace patriarchs, given to him by his brother Liam, and confirming that Charlie should have become a father. Charlie leaves the ring in Aaron's crib but hides it too well, so it is never found, never recognized, never worn. Again, the island won't let this father figure survive.

## Conclusions

As a show defined by the themes of history, memory, and origins, by philosophical questions about free will and determinism, and by characters' efforts to remake and redeem themselves, the theme of failed fatherhood is inscribed and reinscribed throughout the six seasons. Though early episodes gesture at a belief in the free will of the characters to shape their futures, especially as they are stranded in a place that seems to exist outside of space and time and to provide opportunity for such remaking, the narrative structure calls into question this possibility. Haunted by their pasts through the series' signature use of flashbacks and by alternative realities that are as troubled as their "real" histories and presents, *Lost* is ambivalent about the castaways' abilities to atone for their past sins or to create new lives for themselves.

The theme of fatherhood, however, is less characteristically ambivalent about determinism. The fatherless origin story retroactively explains the inadequacies of fathers on the show and suggests that, whether Absent, Abusive, or Aspiring, fathers on *Lost* are destined to fall short. Even the most extreme efforts to rectify those deficiencies — the patricides executed by Sawyer and by Ben Linus, for example — do nothing to provide closure for these sons, and the show's most successful father (Charlie) is not really a father and demonstrates his ultimate effectiveness by dying. As Mother tells her adoptive sons, the founding fathers of *Lost*, "it always ends the same"— with failure.

## NOTES

1. An exception to this is Meyer and Stern's essay which focuses solely on the character of Sun Paik and focuses on the gendered and racial identity of Sun as a Korean woman.
2. For example, the two brothers' attempts to murder each other invokes the Biblical story of Cain and Abel. Similarly, its conclusion (MIB murdering his mother and Jacob murdering MIB) solves a season one mystery in which the survivors in the cave find two bodies, which Locke dubs "our very own Adam and Eve" ("House of the Rising Sun").
3. Kate's flashback punctuates this theme. As a fugitive, her friend Ray doesn't ask too many questions and asserts, "I get it, you know. Everyone deserves a fresh start." Later, in the island world, Jack prevents Kate from confessing her past, interrupting her with "I don't want to know. It doesn't matter, Kate. Who we were, what we did before this, before the crash. Three days ago, we all died. We should all be able to start over."
4. Significantly (but unbeknownst to Hugo), the VW had been the coffin for Ben's father for over 20 years.
5. The *Lost* writers do attempt to humanize Roger by showing him confessing his regrets to Kate: "I thought I was going to be the greatest father ever ... I guess it didn't work out that way. I tried to do what I thought she'd want me to do, but I guess a boy just needs his mother" ("Whatever Happened, Happened"). As with Christian Shephard, to whom the *Lost* writers also offer moments of redemption late in the series, it is simply not enough to compensate for the profound ways both fathers have inflicted damage on their sons in any of the *Lost* realities.
6. In the end, his lack of kidney is a blessing because he only survives Ben shooting him because he is missing the organ ("The Man Behind the Curtain").

7. It should also be noted that Kate Austen similarly commits patricide with no emotional closure. She burns down her mother's house with her (faux) stepfather/biological father inside, and in the end it secures her mother's hatred, a life as a fugitive, and a continued internal agony over both her fathers' failures.

8. The series also suggests greater ambiguity in Sawyer's ability and desire to grow into a fatherly role. In "The Greater Good" (an episode named after the philosophy most opposed to his public "Every Man for Himself" stance), a different side of Sawyer is revealed. When Aaron's crying can't be quieted by Claire, Charlie, Hurley, or anyone else, Sawyer alone soothes the baby. Without effort, he merely has to speak (even reading from a car magazine), and Aaron stops crying, suggesting that he has a natural ability with children and may in fact be the most capable parent in the group — a role he is never able to fulfill.

## WORKS CITED

Berger, J.M. "The Split/Join Theory of *Lost*." *Lost Online Studies* 1.3 (2006). Web. 13 July 2010.

Girard, Charles, and David Meulemans. "The Island as a Test of Free Will: Freedom of Reinvention and Internal Determinism in *Lost.*" *Lost and Philosophy: The Island Has Its Reasons*. Ed. Sharon Kaye. Oxford, England: Blackwell Publishing, 2008.

Johnson, Allan. *The Gender Knot: Unraveling our Patriarchal Legacy*. Philadelphia: Temple University Press, 1997.

Meyer, Michaela D.E., and Danielle M. Stern. "The Modern (?) Korean Woman in Prime-Time: Analyzing the Representation of Sun on the Television Series *Lost*." *Women's Studies* 36(2007): 313–331. *Literary Reference Center*. Web. 14 July 2010.

Treble, Patricia. "I Graduated from Lost University." *Macleans*. 1 February 2010. Web. 21 July 2010.

Wilson, Natalie. "*Can Feminists Applaud Lost's Final Season?*" *Ms. Blog*. Ms. Magazine. 9 March 2010. Web. 17 July 2010.

_____. "Monstrous Musings, Patriarchal Baddies and Smokey Goodness? Musings on the Monsters of *Lost*." *Womanist Musings*. 25 February 2010. Web. 17 July 2010.

# Lost Children: Pregnancy, Parenthood, and Potential

*Deborah Davidson and Wayne Jebian*

## Introduction: A Tale of Two Cities

The image of a pregnant woman having contractions on a beach greets the viewer in the early minutes of ABC's *Lost*. Not only is this character, Claire Littleton, carrying a life inside her, she is also a symbol of life, one juxtaposed against all of the death surrounding her. Here the creators of *Lost* establish their earliest and sharpest contrast of overarching themes in a television program that will quickly reveal itself to be all about dualities: faith/science, choice/destiny, in-group/others, male/female — the list goes on. Claire and her pregnancy become a driving force behind the plot of the first season, both as a central figure in the castaways' attempts to create a community and as a magnet for the Others' disruptive efforts. In episode 20 ("Do No Harm" 1.20), the life-or-death theme reappears with the birth of Aaron playing out against the backdrop of the death of Boone, creating a moment of decision for the show's doctor, Jack Shephard.

From Lucille Ball's first on-screen pregnancy in *I Love Lucy* through portrayals of expectant action heroes by Lucy Lawless in *Xena: Warrior Princess* and Jennifer Garner in J.J. Abrams' own *Alias*, pregnant actresses have challenged writers to integrate pregnancy and birth plotlines into existing formulas. There have been shows in which actresses' pregnancies were concealed (*Seinfeld* comes readily to mind), perhaps to avoid a hackneyed prime time stereotype: birth as an indication that writers have run out of ideas. Television has definitely expanded its treatment of the subject since the early 1950s when the *Quarterly of Film, Radio and Television* reported, "The subject of birth [in scripted dramas] is avoided altogether except for one instance of pregnancy" (Head 189). In the half century since that article, *Lost* may be the first television action drama to make pregnancy intentionally pivotal in the series and omnipresent as a metaphor from the show's inception.

Fans engaged from the first moment by the dazzle of special effects, the esoterica of physics and time travel, and the gravitas of philosophers' names and religious symbols might need a reminder about the proliferation of birth imagery in the show's six seasons. We see Claire giving birth to Aaron (three times!), Sun and Ji Yeon, Danielle Rousseau and Alex, Jacob's birth mother, a pregnant Ana Lucia, the births of Locke, Ben, and Ethan, Walt's pregnant mother, Charlie's pregnant sister-in-law, Juliet's sister, Penelope with baby Charlie, Sawyer's off-island baby-mama and daughter (Cassidy and Clementine), Jack's ex-wife, Miles' mother, Eloise Hawking, the patient from Christian Shephard's botched surgery, the birth of the Chinese ambassador's grandchild, and the oft-alluded-to failed pregnancies among the Others. Add to the mix a fertility doctor, a mysterious syndrome that kills expectant mothers, a giant statue widely interpreted to be a fertility god, and yin/yang symbolism, and the observant viewer is left wondering what this huge accumulation of evidence signifies.

Interpretation of *Lost* challenges the audience because the show "broke the rules" of television narrative. More like a serialized novel by Dickens, *Lost* had an ending plotted from the beginning, with an installment format that allowed for flexibility and demanded creativity, although Dickens never had to contend with actors, producers, or strikes. Due to these and other factors, the show quickly took on a life of its own, with the episodes growing organically from one to the next and sometimes headed in divergent directions. The writers found themselves brimming over with ideas in the fertile landscape of the island they had created, much as Jin and the male inhabitants suddenly found themselves five times as virile. New characters and subplots rained down around viewers like so many pallets of Dharma food. In short order, the show that the writers were actually creating diverged from the show they had conceived, so that by the climax, they were left to reconcile these dual trajectories. The final product represented an attempt to meld two conceptions of the show into one cohesive narrative; posterity will determine to what extent the writers succeeded.

The multiple uses of birth in *Lost* illustrate how elusive synthesis can be. Aside from incorporating actual births into plot arcs, *Lost* uses birth in multiple deliberate metaphors, many of which are not pursued to a point of logical conclusion in the final episode. The resolution focuses almost exclusively on the theme of "passing on" to the next stage in a spiritual journey; death as a metaphor is heavily present, and birth takes on a complementary symbolic meaning: a narrow metaphor for *re*birth. A rite of passage intrinsic to women is appropriated by the *Lost* writers to signify a transformative experience for the show's male characters. When the show began, this particular interpretation of the significance of birth on *Lost* was but one of many possible readings, and far from the most conspicuous one. Birth cloaked as metaphor for rebirth and renewal may have been the main point all along, given that the final episode leaves rebirth as the last metaphor standing.

If one's schema is frontloaded with the expectation of a story woven around a male hero, then all of the pregnancies, births, and babies become so much decoration, akin to cherubs on wallpaper, but in a work of this detail, even the chosen decorating scheme is significant. Commenting on the film *Children of Men*, which, like *Lost*, portrays an infertile world, theorist Slavoj Žižek makes this strikingly applicable comment:

> I would say that the true focus of the film is there in the background [...] it's not really that all of this infertility and so on is just a pretext for the hero's inner journey from this apathetic antihero mode to a more active engagement and so on [...] no it's this fate of the individual hero [that] remains a kind of a prism through which you see the background even more sharply.

The isolation and remoteness of the island fit the viewers' expectations of the castaway genre, but the unexpected significance of the setting is in the panoramic views of lush, fertile, expansive greenery and in the intimate views of fish, boar, fruit, and seeds for Sun's garden. In spite of the polar bear threat, with an almost primal instinct, Claire stumbles off into the jungle whenever she has a contraction, and in this fertile embrace, she first labors and delivers. Awareness of this undercurrent of fertility imagery allows the audience to see the abundance of birth-related material not merely as window-dressing. Without this perspective, important information may at first seem like throwaway banter or mundane activity. In the seemingly inane banter category is when Jack's father arrives for his son's wedding and his greeting involves a complaint about the "screaming kid next to me in first class [...] how does that happen?" (1.20). His confusion reveals a lack of understanding of why the best things in life (*i.e.*, first class) might be well suited to the accommodation of mothers and babies. It is not just an offhand comment; it is delivered right before Jack's nuptials, in a conversation in which Jack questions his readiness to be a husband and father.

In the riveting opener of season three, a scene that parallels the isolation and fragile stoicism revealed in the first glimpse of Desmond's life in the hatch (2.1), we see Juliet startled out of her attempt to fortify herself with the ironically upbeat Petula Clark song, "Downtown," by the timer in her kitchen. Rushing to the smoking appliance, Juliet burns her hand as she mis-carries the muffins from the oven. Juliet greets a guest at the door, saying, "I burnt my hand on my muffins." The guest, a sympathetic older woman, gestures toward a partially obscured Ethan, and says, "He still hasn't finished your plumbing yet?" Ethan replies: "It's a work in progress." Could this really be about buns in the oven and faulty plumbing? It turns out that Juliet is a frustrated fertility doctor.

The scene transitions to Juliet's book club meeting where Juliet herself testifies to the weightiness of the prior moment when the fourth wall is broken and the book club banter instructs the TV audience in how to "read" the show, with the following dialogue:

> ADAM: It's not even literature. It's popcorn.
> SYMPATHETIC OLDER WOMAN: And why isn't it literature, Adam? I'm dying to know.
> ADAM: There's no metaphor. It's by the numbers religious hokum pokum.
> SOW: No metaphor?
> ADAM: It's science fiction [...] Now I know why Ben isn't here.
> JULIET: Excuse me?
> ADAM: I know the host picks the book, but seriously, Julie, he wouldn't read this in the damn bathroom.
> JULIET: Well, Adam, I am the host, and I do pick the book. And this is my favorite book, so I am absolutely thrilled that you can't stand it. Silly me for sinking so low as to select something that Ben wouldn't like. Here I am thinking that free will still actually exists on thi... (interrupted by noise and quaking) ["A Tale of Two Cities" 3.1].

Sequences like the one above are revelatory, with the *Lost* writers commenting on the show's themes and plot devices before quickly diverting the audience's attention with some earth-shaking action. In a few short minutes, they run through a checklist of important themes and instruct the audience on what to look for: 1. fertility, 2. readiness, 3. metaphor, and 4. free will. The timing of the introduction of Juliet suggests infertility as an extended metaphor for the island's imbalance and hints at her potential to heal it. A parallel sequence occurs later the same season in "The Brig" (3.19), beginning with Ben listening to Juliet's taped report on Sun's pregnancy and highlighted by Ben's blunt statement to Locke: "It's a metaphor, John!" shortly before questioning Locke's readiness and will to assume leadership.

## *Raised by an Other*

An oft-revisited trope of *Lost* is the healing of one's inner child, and what visual image could better represent an inner child than an actual *inner* child? A pregnant woman conveys this image, while also embodying the future, optimism, and a paradoxical unified state of two human beings contained in one. When the baby emerges, the two may bond, but they will do so as "others" because they are no longer one. How well or how poorly this primary "other" relationship is worked through (Hurley and his mother are at the successful end of this spectrum; Kate and her mother are not) is determined by various contributing factors. Pregnancy, labor, post-partum, and beyond may be profoundly impacted by how those around the mother facilitate or hinder the mother-child bond. Taken to an extreme, the ultimate act of alienation is to separate mother and child entirely.

The season one episode "Raised by Another" (1.10) examines a number of issues that will continue to loom large as future seasons of *Lost* unfold, including the mother-child relationship and the process of "othering" through parental separation. Claire's back story addresses issues surrounding the consensual separation of mother and child through adoption, and her "dreams" introduce the child-stealing conflict. Claire's mysterious nocturnal experiences also give viewers the first sign of the castaways' adversaries, soon to become known as the Others, whose external threat will make the castaways more cohesive as a group. Early episodes show pairs of survivors — Michael and Walt, Boone and Shannon, and most explicitly Sun and Jin (1.6) — regarding their fellow passengers as "others," then abandoning this term once the *other* Others reveal themselves.

Claire's escape from the Others is enabled by Alex (2.5), who is disillusioned with her own group, an other among the Others. Alex, kidnapped as an infant by Ben, resents Ben's attempts to control her sexuality, even though his heavy handed efforts are motivated by the dangers of procreation on the island. Ben himself is an outsider turned insider through paternal abuse and adoption into the opposing camp. Ben's mother dies in childbirth, and in a rare moment of tenderness in "Whatever Happened, Happened" (5.11) his bitter father remarks of young Ben's troubles, "I guess a boy just needs his mother."

The origin story of Jacob and his brother revives the child abduction theme as part of the buildup to the finale. In young adulthood, when the twins learn that the mother who raised them is a murderous usurper, their loyalties are tested. Jacob's brother joins the Others on the island, whom he realizes are "his" people. The parent-child relationship of Jacob's brother and his adoptive mother, and that of Alex and Ben, challenge the soundness of bonds formed in the shadow of parental alienation, echoing the ominous warnings from a psychic stating that Claire should not give Aaron up for adoption and must instead raise the baby herself. Claire's dream vision of John Locke admonishing her ("He was your responsibility, but you gave him away. Everyone pays the price now" 1.10) reiterates the earlier warnings. In Alex's story, we see two possible outcomes of mother-child alienation. Alex comes to a violent, premature demise at the hands of Charles Widmore's mercenaries in the primary scenario where she is stolen from Danielle Rousseau and raised by Ben (4.9). Yet, in the alternate flash-sideways universe of season six, Alex lives her life with her birth mother, with Ben relegated to benevolent mentor, and Alex is headed to a (presumably) preferable fate at Yale (6.6). Whether the viewer interprets the entwined flash-sideways of Danielle, Alex, and Ben as a portrayal of purgatory, as a second chance for the characters, or as an alternate reality, the association between the mother-child relationship and the outcome is clear.

## *Follow the Leader*

"Potential" is a major undercurrent in the plot of *Lost*. A fetus is a potential life, a pregnant woman a potential mother, and two lovers a potential pregnancy. There is additional symbolic potential that permeates the story: the potential energy trapped beneath the island, the potential leaders to replace Jacob, and the chance that any pregnancy might yield a potential savior. Long before the revelation that many of the adult castaways are part of a selection process to replace Jacob, the theme of a potential leader or savior for the group, the island, and possibly for humanity, is introduced in the characters of Aaron and Walt. Aaron's name suggests the story of Moses, as does the prospect of his being separated from his mother and raised by the enemy, while Walt's "special" clairvoyance and his recurring estrangement from his father, further reinforce this metaphor. The messianic theme carries on in flashbacks of the birth and childhood of John Locke. Richard Alpert investigates Locke's origins, visiting the hospital where Locke is born (4.11), seemingly hoping to witness a birth-of-the-hero moment.

Locke's potential elevation to a leadership role gives rise to an exploration of "readiness," a theme frequently associated with major transitions on *Lost*. Examples include being ready to love, to start a family, or to "move on" to another stage of life, and many of the characters confront the question of their own readiness when facing the idea of birth and parenthood. Jack expresses doubts about his preparedness to be a husband and father (1.20). A drunken binge indicating lack of readiness for fatherhood keeps Horace from being present at the birth of his son, Ethan (5.8), just as heroin had kept Charlie's brother, Liam, away from the birth of his daughter (2.12). In "Ji Yeon" (4.7), Jin overcomes hurdles in preparing to visit the Chinese ambassador's new grandchild in a maternity ward, and he comes through by securing the proper stuffed Panda (a two-tone animal with infamous fertility issues).

The portrayal of birth as a test of readiness for an intimidating life change helps explain why it is a template for initiation and rites of passage on paths to personal growth. According to the *Initiation Dictionary*: "Initiation was always spoken of under the metaphor or figure of speech of 'a new birth,' a 'birth into truth,' for it was a spiritual and intellectual rebirth of the powers of the human spirit-soul" ("Initiation"). On *Lost*, one example of a ritual of preparation and readiness occurs when John Locke constructs a tiny sweat lodge, a symbolic womb, when he is seeking new direction in "Further Instructions" (3.3). Locke's rebirth draws upon a Native American ritual, and occurs inside the frame of Mr. Eko's partially constructed church. *Lost* frequently presents the viewer with images and ideas taken from different religions, but rather than relying on conventional religious treatments of rebirth, such as Christian resurrection or Hindu reincarnation, the writers anchor the rebirth metaphor to birth itself, an act that is universal across cultures. Viewers witness a viable facsimile of a New Age rebirth rite when Locke ties up Boone and leaves him to devise his own escape because, in Locke's words, "It's time for you to let go of some things" (1.13).

"Letting go" is among the most frequently articulated motifs in the series, and the phrase is often spoken in conjunction with the idea of readiness to move forward (*Lostpedia*). This concept is demonstrated in scenes when Claire labors. In the first view of the island birth of Aaron, Claire's doubts and insecurities cause her to hold her breath in an attempt to stop the progress of delivery (1.20). In her flash-sideways pregnancy, she allows the doctor (Ethan) to administer drugs to postpone the birth (6.2), in both cases saying "I'm not ready." She repeats the phrase immediately before the final delivery (6.16). For Claire, "letting go" means not only releasing her fears, but also letting the baby come out of her body. Most of the characters on *Lost*, but especially Jack, have something from their pasts that they need to "let go" before they are ready to either move on to the next phase of their existence, enter the nebulous heaven of the series finale, or take Jacob's place in the line of succession.

As famously exemplified by the fertility issues of King Henry VIII, whose quest for an heir went so far as to overturn the power of the Catholic Church and humanity's concepts of God, it is hard to overstate the stakes in some instances of succession. By the end of *Lost*, we learn that Jacob's search for a replacement, and his brother's search for a substitute body, have involved not only the mysterious forces on the island and the rationale for the crash of Oceanic flight 815, but also various interventions in the characters' off-island lives.

Of course, replacement of leadership is only part of the picture. Every society faces the need to repopulate itself, and the infertility that plagues the Others threatens their long-term survival. As the film *Children of Men* shows, the loss of potential to reproduce undermines hope, robbing both society and the individual of their *raison d'être* for advancing civilization. Richard Alpert questions Ben's focus on fertility and reproduction (3.19), but Alpert's own immortality distances him from the cycle of life until his optimism is restored when he finds a grey hair on his head (6.16).

## *Whatever Happened, Happened*

"I was kind of born into it," says Jack of his profession (1.4). This comment hints at the relationship between the circumstances of one's birth and the idea of a fixed destiny. Can the specifics of one's birth and parentage shape a fate from which all of life's details flow? Or, rather, is life an open scenario in which free choice is possible? These questions have been explored in "switched at birth" plots since before the time of Shakespeare. Indeed, birthright and destiny as literary themes go back to the Bible, with passages on Isaac and Ishmael tying destiny to one's birth mother and passages on Jacob and Esau suggesting that destiny begins in the womb.

Daniel Faraday's back-story throws the "birth as destiny" model into question. By having Eloise Hawking as a mother, he was "born into" his profession just like Jack, but in Daniel's flashbacks, self-fulfilling parental prophecy steers the pivotal choice of science over music, and thusly ensures a grim fate that seems otherwise eminently preventable (5.14). John Locke, by contrast, often seems to personify free choice in the moment, rendering the commandeering of his body in the sixth season particularly droll. Locke is one of those characters whose personality and ultimate fate would seem tied to the circumstances of his parentage, much as they are for Benjamin Linus. Locke, however, refuses to accept that his history determines his future, his catchphrase being "Don't tell me what I can't do!" In "Some Like It Hoth" (5.13), Hurley rewrites the "birth as destiny" narrative when he edits *The Empire Strikes Back* so that Luke Skywalker and Darth Vader have a father-son heart-to-heart in lieu of a dismembering duel.

The dilemma of choice versus determinism, perhaps one of the most consistent themes on *Lost*, draws on the Existentialism of Jean-Paul Sartre. The show's flashbacks demonstrate the burdens that the characters' pasts place on them and illustrate how the past informs present actions and future consequences. Frequent comparisons are made between *Lost* and Sartre's *No Exit*, in which the characters are trapped within the selves they have constructed over their lifetimes. An even more apt comparison might be Sartre's *Les Jeux Sont Faits*, in which two deceased characters are given a second chance at life and love. They can choose to be with each other for eternity (like Bernard and Rose) or they can address the unfinished business of their past lives. Sartre is pessimistic about one's ability to alter life's path, but ends his tale on a note of consolation, since his characters manage to help a child and inspire a pair of young lovers. This work shares the optimism of *Lost* in two ways: that choice is indeed possible, and that even when people can't save themselves, they can at least have a positive impact on future generations.

"You can't just change your mind!" shouts Claire when her boyfriend has second thoughts about his commitment to fatherhood (1.10). In the world of *Lost*, pregnancy represents the purest example of how a past choice can limit future options. In the translated words of Sartre: "The chips are down, you see. One can't take back one's bet" (184). Given the advanced state of Claire's pregnancy, abortion may not be medically possible, but the absence of the abortion option in the case of Sun's life threatening on-island conception frames the shows' boundaries regarding the breadth of personal choice. Sun's pregnancy emerges as a *fait accompli* in spite of the presence of a surgeon, a skilled fertility doctor, and available medical facilities. Pregnancy serves as a vehicle, a metaphor about the limitations of choice (particularly for women, although Locke in a wheelchair shows a how a physical situation could impact the free will of a man), rather than simply being an incidental plot point. The centrality and irreversibility of pregnancy in *Lost* as a symbolic vehicle helps to explain why there are no openly gay characters in a very large cast (a brief off-island tryst of Tom Friendly's in "Meet Kevin Johnson" (4.8) being the exception that proves the rule). As a microcosm of society, *Lost* presents a highly improbable sampling, given that the survivors were on a flight from Sydney to Los Angeles. Variables that complicate fertility metaphors, such as abortion and homosexuality, are largely absent.

Although neither Claire nor Sun appear able to undo the past choices represented by their pregnancies, Claire believes she has a choice about what to do with her baby. Life on the island provides an extended opportunity for Claire to reconsider her decision to put her baby up for adoption. Unlike the scene in which a succession of defective pens gives her pause (1.10), season six offers a twist when Claire suddenly discovers that the intended adoption has fallen through, taking away what she thought was her choice, in essence telling her, "what she can't do" (6.3). The change of heart by the adoptive mother demonstrates how choices may have profound impact on others. Mirroring her statement in episode 1.10, Claire shouts, "You just changed your mind!?" as her panic begins inducing early labor contractions. This reaction parallels the magnitude of the impact on her psyche (and therefore mind/body connection) when the plane crashes in the pilot episode, thwarting her plans.

By the conclusion of *Lost*, it is as if the writers have given themselves license to frequently change their own minds on the question of determinism versus free will. The quasi-magical sci-fi milieu of the show, particularly the use of the flash-sideways timeline in the sixth season, released the writers from having to make a philosophical commitment. This dynamic is described by

Žižek as "the growing perception of our reality as but one of innumerable or possible worlds [...] this notion that other possible outcomes are not simply cancelled out but continue to haunt our 'true' reality as a specter of what might have happened" (Davis 225). Thus, Jack and Juliet can fulfill their violent, heroic destinies, have a child together in flash-sideways world, and still find true love with someone else. One of the significant contributions of *Lost* to television narrative structure is simultaneously its biggest cop-out as a story. *Lost*'s writers have exploited the notion of parallel universes to tell a tale more optimistically noncommittal than *Les Jeux Sont Faits,* one in which the characters can find true love and fight successfully for their respective causes. *Lost* is a Christmas story more saccharine than that granddaddy of all alternate reality stories, Dickens' *A Christmas Carol*, with Ebenezer Scrooge never having lost his true love, yet still waking up a changed man. Don't tell the writers what they can't do.

## *Ab Aeterno*

The love stories on *Lost* hold the show together, but the conspicuously melodramatic Jack/Sawyer/Kate/Juliet quadrangle is not the only love story. Other romances that pack punch involve the show's breeding pairs: Desmond and Penelope and Sun and Jin. The stakes are higher with these couples, particularly by the end of the series when potential offspring are in the balance. If lovers symbolize a potential pregnancy, then the extended separation that characterizes both of these stories creates extra tension by holding this potential in an attenuated state as a form of potential energy. The story of Desmond and Penelope places greater emphasis on romance than does the classic template of Odysseus and Penelope, since the characters from *The Odyssey* already had a child.

Not only does the story of Sun and Jin have the requisite separation of lovers; it also involves a fertility hurdle whose resolution bonds their narrative to the island more profoundly than that of other romances on *Lost*. Like Desmond and Penelope, they are star-crossed lovers in the vein of *Romeo and Juliet*, defying parental authority in order to find happiness. With Sun and Jin, *Lost*'s writers achieve much of the pathos of the Shakespearean original, retaining the wistful consolation of escape from a hostile world through death, while mitigating a tragic component of *Romeo and Juliet*: that couple never had the chance to produce offspring. Ji Yeon is a kind of escape pod for the passengers of Oceanic flight 815, as are Aaron, Walt, and baby Charlie. All are shown off-island in their final appearances on the show. As an added bonus, baby Charlie serves to bridge past and future, as he is named in memory of adult Charlie, and perhaps Penny's father, Charles Widmore.

One noteworthy couple on *Lost* neither dies tragically nor produces offspring during the course of the show. Rose and Bernard symbolize hope while at the same time modeling family dynamics for the other characters. Hope is symbolized by Rose kissing a wedding ring in the Pilot episode as she awaits the return of Bernard — yet another instance of absence making the plot grow thicker. Once reunited, they are an example of a couple who may experience disagreements yet remain committed. Rose and Bernard's marriage defies the literary trope that says love is a mystery of the universe and instead suggests that love is a learned and practiced behavior that can be modeled and passed down through the generations. Sartre's *Les Jeux Sont Faits* ends on this pedagogical note, beseeching older couples to pass the message on to the young that in spite of the odds against a couple's remaining together and in love for eternity, they should "try ... try it anyway" (186).

## *Eggtown*

Sun dies a romantic death, but surely there are fans who have a problem with the conclusion of her story. Before she dies, Sun's development is among the most significant in the series. From the passive, voiceless subject of a patriarchal culture, what theorist Gayatri Spivak would call a "subaltern woman," at the beginning of the series, she becomes the master of her father's empire in "There's No Place Like Home" (4.12). She achieves the ideal of Simone DeBeauvoir's "Independent Woman" and then throws it all away (along with the power and responsibility of motherhood) to search for Jin, and die submerged (679). Initially, Sun conceals her ability to speak English in Jin's presence, but when she loses her voice in the sixth season, Jin's presence restores it (6.13). What may be progress for these characters' marriage sends a backward message regarding a woman's dependence on a man to define her roles and abilities. Nevertheless, Jin's decision to stay with her at the end represents more than just a tear-jerking act of selflessness. Spivak, in *A Critique of Postcolonial Reason*, examines the phenomenon of "sati," the now-outlawed custom (which still rarely takes place) of a woman either voluntarily or by force immolating herself on her dead husband's funeral pyre. Such a practice is the epitome of subjugation, particularly since the act is perceived as voluntary on the part of the subaltern woman in question. Jin voluntarily stays with Sun, and in doing so performs his own act of "sati," a complete reversal of gender roles from his patriarchal ethos at the beginning of the series.

Finding a silver lining in the death of Juliet is more challenging. From her first off-island flashback in "Not in Portland" (3. 7), she appears to be in a position to both understand and harness a woman's power. Her character taps into the Foucauldian relationship between fertility, knowledge, and power, particularly during her "it worked" moments such as helping Sawyer retrieve a candy bar from a vending machine by unplugging and re-plugging it (6.17 and 6.18); fixing the island's fertility problems (in "LA X" (6.1), there are several children in the temple — in addition to Emma and Zach) by setting off the hydrogen bomb (5.17); and helping her sterile sister conceive after chemotherapy (3.7). When she injects her sister with an experimental drug, Juliet says, "I'm not doing it as your doctor. I'm doing it as your sister." Although she implies that she privileges sisterhood over the male power structure, she is blackmailed by her ex-husband into sharing her research. Later, Ben Linus also blackmails her, leveraging sisterly concern to co-opt Juliet into doing his bidding. Beneath her cool exterior, Juliet struggles with trust, and insecurity gets the best of her when she allows her fear of losing Sawyer's love prompt a fatal decision in "The Incident" (5.17). Even as she works with Kate and seems to be wielding the authority of decision making over the male characters, her death at the bottom of the Swan Station mineshaft comes as a result of her preferring oblivion to a broken heart. Her choice is a *sati* of the mind, and it becomes an act of thermonuclear suicide. Better to have never loved and *Lost*...?

The deaths of these and other female characters such as Shannon, Ana Lucia, Libby, Nikki, Danielle Rousseau, Alex, Charlotte, Nadia, Zoe, Naomi, Ilana, Jacob's birth mother, and Jacob's adoptive mother, along with the lengthy absence of Claire in the fifth season, create a disturbing trend on *Lost*. In the wake of these losses, perhaps one residual message is that women and children are particularly vulnerable in a violent society. On *Lost*, women's roles and skills seem easily reassigned: Ilana becomes the new Naomi ("I'm exotic and doomed") much as Charlotte becomes the new Shannon ("I'm multi-lingual") and Shannon becomes the new Nadia ("I'm Sayid's soulmate"). These transferences may create thematic continuity in the show's serpentine plot, yet they reinforce the idea that the women themselves are disposable. While "strong" female roles are defined by the possession of "male" skills such as tracking, shooting, and doctoring, a woman's power to nurture and sustain life becomes a lesser currency in the show's final accounting. When Jacob reveals that he crossed Kate's name off the list of eligible successors because she "became a mother," the audience also understands that the "Kwon" left on the list had not been Sun, as motherhood is a deal-breaker. Is motherhood a deal-breaker in objective interpretation of gender issues on *Lost*? The anachronistic quality of this motherhood-as-end-of-the-line message contradicts society's evolving notions of equality and women's roles, and even Kate looks confused by the idea that her empowering transformative experience should exclude her from leadership, as *Lost* yet again takes choices out of the hands of women. *Lost* shows women limited by traditional expectations, yet sensitive, long-haired (g)Hurley-men like Sawyer, Daniel, and Desmond do not seem hampered by the non-traditional aspects of their "evolved" personae.

Motherhood as limitation runs counter to the idea of fertility as power. Story arcs involving Kate, Sun, and Juliet and episodes such as "House of the Rising Sun" (1.6) appear to acknowledge this power. The symptoms of the island's fertility issues — that a man's sperm count increases, but pregnancy proves fatal — signal an inequity between its male and female natures, an impression reinforced throughout the series by repeated assertions that the island is a living entity with some agency in the overarching plot. Until the unfolding of Jacob's back story, viewers are led to believe that the island itself has brought the characters to it, and their job is to heal its imbalances even as they work through their own. Evidence for such an interpretation is everywhere. Consider such hints as yin/yang symbols in the Dharma logos found throughout the island, including the binary I Ching codes surrounding the graphic elements; the presence of electromagnetism, suggesting the attraction of opposites; the island's numerous holes, such as the well and the massive invagination left in the wake of the first "hatch" implosion (3.3); coupled with the yin/yangy idea that a simultaneous implosion and explosion could balance the island's energies. In this light, any plot points suggesting emergent female power take on added significance.

*Lost* reaches a high water mark of positive exploration of female power with Kate's role in Claire's jungle labor and delivery in seasons one and five, and the bonding between them in season six. Their bonding begins anew in "What Kate Does" (6.3) upon Kate's discovery of baby accessories in Claire's bag, including a black-and-white toy Orca (evoking Jin's elusive stuffed Panda in episode 4.7). The (final) act of helping Claire deliver Aaron triggers Kate's island memories, a noteworthy exception among the "awakenings" in the finale, which otherwise result directly from contact with a specific loved one. For the leading female character, participation in Aaron's labor and delivery is her life's most powerful moment. Kate's reaction to the birth of Aaron is as close as *Lost* comes to addressing the experience of motherhood. It is striking how little exploration of motherhood there is in the show. In *Birth as an American Rite of Passage*, author Robbie Davis-Floyd writes, "The birthing of a child constitutes one of the most profoundly transformative and uniquely *individual* experiences a woman will go through in her life" (60). A striking visual metaphor for the transformative nature of birth involves Desmond waking up naked near the huge hole in the jungle created by the implosion of the Swan Station (3.3), an event that precipitates Desmond's newfound clairvoyance. The show does create opportunities to explore the individual experiences of Claire and Sun, but having opened this door, the writers choose not to walk through it. Instead, viewers are privy to Sun's transformation as a wife and daughter, but not as a mother, and in the postpartum scenes with Claire, the focus quickly shifts to Charlie's stand-in fatherhood.

By emphasizing the rebirth experiences of male characters like Jack, Desmond, Locke, Boone, etc. and by focusing heavily on fatherhood and male perspectives of birth, the show's writers reduce birth from a genuinely transformative experience for real women to a metaphor of transformation for fictional men. Like the Others stealing children, the *Lost* writers misappropriate birth for their own purposes. *Lost* may be groundbreaking television in its depiction of so many pregnancies and births; unfortunately, this fact only highlights missed opportunities to leverage the potential of childbirth and fertility to make a statement on a tangible and profound source of women's power.

Birth and labor on *Lost*, regardless of setting and individual character arc, hew closely to the American technocratic model: labor and delivery in a supine position, attendants telling mothers when to push, babies being caught by attendants and presented as products to the mother. Particularly telling is the use of forceps on Penny — a strong, self-actualized woman — in the delivery of baby Charlie. As Davis-Floyd would put it, "All of these [patriarchal/technocratic] messages are reinforced if the baby is pulled out with forceps. The application of forceps shows the mother beyond all doubt that her machine is indeed defective" (130). In this light, the possibility that the writers use depictions of birth to attract a female audience seems a cynical calculation, an exercise in "How to get women, in a culture that purports to hold gender equality as an ideal, to accept a belief system that inherently denigrates them" (61).

The best developed statement on the balance of gendered power is the romance of Sun and Jin, but their love leaves a child orphaned. On *Lost*, women — and children — are loved, but they are also "othered," deprived of choice, and passed over in the succession of power. Any hope of an enlightened egalitarian resolution is crushed like the head of Jacob's mother in "Across the Sea" (6.15) with an act of woman-on-woman murder and baby stealing, followed by the emergence of a male-on-male rivalry that retroactively purports to explain some of the island's mysterious conflicts. Then there is the ending, about which there is very little to say other than: sometimes a phallus-like rock plugging a wet hole is just a phallus-like rock plugging a wet hole.

The oft-repeated theme on *Lost*, "letting go," may be an easy sell to contemporary audiences, as this theme is omnipresent in New Age literature in various incarnations, such as "purging," or "releasing toxic influences." While one might argue that the directive to "let go" could be interpreted as anathema to literary criticism or learning lessons from the past, the most conspicuous shortcoming of this mantra regards its application to parenthood. On *Lost*, "letting go" appears to be what most of the show's parents did with their own children. Much like the show's treatment of mothers, children are also left behind in the plot, eclipsed by the inner children of adults who are distracted by mortality and the need to let go of their own childhoods.

In the final analysis, *Lost*, like so many television shows, focuses its stories on human relationships and personal struggles; however, unlike other shows, issues of fertility and childbirth are instrumental in the exploration of its themes. *Lost* is not one of those series in which the occasional birth is only a sideshow to provide some "awww" factor and tug at the viewers' heartstrings. The deliberate, consistent emphasis on birth imagery may be unprecedented in scope; however, the statements are so divergent as to have resulted in a seminal work of birth-sploitation. In that sense, *Lost*, a work of quality if not equality, was itself like a birth that produced a "live" baby with enough episodes for syndication, but one whose development reflects the best laid birth plans of men.

## WORKS CITED

*Children of Men*. DVD Universal Pictures. Dir. Alfonso Cuarón. 2006.
Davis, Colin. "Sartre and the Return of the Living Dead." *Sartre Studies International* 11.1& 2 (2005): 222–233.
Davis-Floyd, Robbie E. *Birth as an American Rite of Passage*, 2nd Ed. Berkeley and Los Angeles: University of California Press, 2003.
De Beauvoir, Simone. *The Second Sex*. Trans. and ed. H.M. Parshley. New York: Vintage Books, 1989.
Head, Sydney W. "Content Analysis of Television Drama Programs." *The Quarterly of Film Radio and Television* 9.2 (Winter 1954): 175–194.
"Initiation: A Wisdom Archive on Initiation." *Global Oneness: Co Creating a Happy World*. Web. 27 June 2010.
Meyer, Michaela D.E., and Danielle M. Stern. "The Modern(?) Korean Woman in Prime-Time: Analyzing the Representation of Sun on the Television Series *Lost*." *Women's Studies* 36: 313–331.
"Regularly Spoken Phrases," *Lostpedia.wikia.com* Web. 25 June 2010.
Sartre, Jean-Paul. *The Chips Are Down (Les Jeux Sont Faits)*. Trans. Louise Varése. New York: Lear Publishers, 1948.
Spivak, Gayatri Chakravorty. *A Critique of Postcolonial Reason: Toward a History of the Vanishing Present*. Cambridge, MA: Harvard University Press, 1999.
Žižek, Slovoj. Comments on *Children of Men*. DVD Universal Pictures. Dir. Alfonso Cuarón, 2006.

*Part Four*

# Lost in the Twenty-First Century

# *Lost* in Capitalism: or, "Down Here Possession's Nine-Tenths"

*Elizabeth Lundberg*

Among the many genres *Lost* fits into, utopian/dystopian fiction is unquestionably one. At its core, setting aside the supernatural battle between good and evil and the science fiction properties of a time-jumping island, and even before we learn in the Swan orientation film about the Dharma Initiative's "utopian social" goals ("Orientation" 2.3), *Lost* is a show that asks how a given group of characters would function and organize itself if it were isolated from society. This basic premise situates the show in a tradition that includes *The Mysterious Island*, *Watership Down*, and *The Tempest*, among other texts to which *Lost* alludes. Indeed, as in the other texts mentioned, it is the characters' interactions and motivations, rather than the fantastic or science fiction elements of the story, that *Lost*'s producers have always insisted drive the show's popularity. While the writers and producers of *Lost* build a captivating world, then, it is the part of that world built by the characters themselves that really keeps us watching.

Knowing that *Lost* is utopian fiction, it makes perfect sense to examine the economic arguments underpinning the show. Georg Lukács defines his own "highly naïve and totally unfounded utopianism" as "the hope that a natural life worthy of man can spring from the disintegration of capitalism and the destruction, seen as identical with that disintegration, of the lifeless and life-denying social and economic categories" (20). As Fredric Jameson explains in *Postmodernism: or, the Cultural Logic of Late Capitalism*, at certain times (most notably the 1960s), "utopia" was "a code word that simply meant 'socialism'" (159). In his extensive study of utopian fiction, *Archaeologies of the Future: The Desire Called Utopia and Other Science Fictions*, Jameson further argues that "from Bellamy onwards," socialism and utopia have been conflated. "We have indicated, indeed, that More's initial utopian gesture — the abolition of money and property — runs through the Utopian tradition like a red thread, now aggressively affirmed on the surface, now tacitly presupposed in milder forms or disguises" (20). Jameson does discuss some more recent utopias that "enthusiastically affirm the jouissance of money making and the externalization of capitalism," but ultimately concludes "that it is still difficult to see how future Utopias could ever be imagined in any absolute dissociation from socialism in its larger sense of anti-capitalism" and that "no modern Utopia is plausible which does not address, along with its other inventions, the economic problems caused by industrial capitalism" (196–7). Present-day American utopias inevitably grapple with the problems of our present-day American economy in the process of creating new economies.

This utopian premise is played out over and over again on *Lost* by each new group of explorers, scientists, and castaways that arrives on the island. Will they replicate the world they left behind? Will they achieve something truly different? Will they even consciously think about this world building process? While multiple groups of people face the same situation on the island, the group that concerns us most as viewers is the one with which we are first asked to identify, the one that comes from our own time, society, and economy: the survivors of Oceanic flight 815. (Of course, the show's writers also come from our own historical-political setting, no matter which group they write about, so we could read any group on the island as reflective, in some sense, of our own historical moment.) Among the 815 survivors, a struggle between communal and individualistic — or socialist and capitalist — impulses develops almost immediately, and this tension continues throughout their time on the island. The conflict is often overt in the first two seasons, but even once the castaways settle into their new society and threats from outside that society increase, the effects of their economic decisions resonate through the show. By reading these effects, examining the show's depictions of the economic system the characters establish and the characters' resulting relationships with objects in that system, we can highlight *Lost*'s Marxist critique of late capitalism and its alienating effects. This critique is especially apparent in the characters' relationships with the objects that become commodities within their economic system, because that is one of the primary places alienation occurs (between people and the products of labor), and because *Lost* consistently places material objects in positions of prominence on the island.

Objects are especially important on *Lost* for a number of reasons. They are landmarks, mapping the island in both space and time (the *Black Rock*, the statue of Taweret, the well). They are devices meant to emphasize the characters' slow but inevitable adjustment to life on the island (Hurley's CD player, which loses battery power part way through the first season; Jin's watch, which is extremely valuable off the island but meaningless on it). Sometimes they are lightning rods of speculation whose only purpose seems to be to raise questions which may or may not be answered later (the glass eye, Kate's toy plane, Hurley's guitar case). When serving any of these functions, the objects on *Lost* carry heavy symbolic and fetishistic weight for both characters and viewers. One reason for this is simply that heavily significant objects refer back to the science fiction genre itself (think of the layers of meaning invested in most pieces of technology in science fiction) and to some of the literary texts referenced on the show. Food and drink in *Alice's Adventures in Wonderland*, shoes and a hot air balloon in *The Wonderful Wizard of Oz*, and glasses in *Lord of the Flies* all feature prominently, take on magical or near-magical properties, propel the plot, and signify more than those objects would outside the worlds of those texts. The same is true of objects on *Lost*, and especially on the island. (In fact, each of those particular objects is meaningful on *Lost* as well.) Elwyn Palmerton also points out, in his 2008 *PopMatters* article, "Dharma's Bent Reality: The Video Game Sensibility of *Lost*," that the "almost talismanic weight" given to objects and places in *Lost* is reminiscent of the way video games feel. "The graphical novelties of a new location (and its items)," he argues, "are [...] presented basically as a type of reward, but also, simultaneously, as the presentation of successive challenges." Palmerton points out that the hatch door is basically the door to the next level — a door which remains locked until the characters discover the item needed to open it, the dynamite, and whose opening heralds the beginning of the second season. This similarity with video games extends further: objects "that are initially sparse and valuable [...] become increasingly ubiquitous and mundane as your character progresses to new levels." So once the castaways learn how to obtain food and build shelters, they open the hatch to discover bunk beds, electricity, and a fully stocked pantry.

*Lost* consistently draws our attention to material objects in a number of ways, then, and at times raises them almost to the level of characters, all of which ultimately makes it easier for us to see the effects of capitalist alienation through the characters' interactions with those material objects. In his *Economic and Philosophic Manuscripts of 1844*, Marx describes the process by which the worker under capitalism becomes alienated from "his tools, from his product, from his productive activity, and from his species-being as such, or in other words his fellow workers" (quoted in Jameson, *Archaeologies* 152). In his exegesis of Lukács in *Marxism and Form: Twentieth-Century Dialectical Theories of Literature*, Jameson explains that when this alienation is reflected in art, we can see it in depictions of material objects: "the chairs and motorcycles, the food, houses, and revolvers which are no longer felt as the results of immediate human activity, which inhabit the work like so much dead furniture, tear through the human surface of the work like so much alien inorganic matter" (168). Jameson argues that because of this accumulation of so much alien matter in the world and in art, "modern literature has developed special techniques, elaborate methods of symbolism, in the express hope of giving meaning to such stubbornly resistant things" and, consequently, the presence of symbolic objects "in the work always stands as an indication that the immediate meaning of objects has disappeared: the process would not arise in the first place if objects had not already become problematical in their very nature" (168). Although "in their origin, all objects have a human meaning, [...] in modern industrial civilization this link is hard to find: objects appear to lead an independent life of their own, and it is precisely this illusion which is the source of the symbolic" (197). When we find such symbolic objects in fictional texts, seeming to lead lives of their own, we can read them as products of capitalist alienation and sometimes as indications of a critique of that alienation. In the world of *Lost*, our attention as viewers is frequently drawn to manmade objects — objects that indeed seem to have lives of their own and that carry heavy symbolic significance. These items more often than not, and increasingly as the show progresses, prove problematic, dangerous, or even deadly to characters, pushing Marx's, Lukács's, and Jameson's ideas about material objects to the extreme and showing the profoundly negative effects of living within a capitalist economy. We can trace the results of the characters' alienation from manmade objects through the course of the show by looking at the moments when a) objects acquire extreme symbolism and seem to take on lives of their own, and b) these objects on the loose threaten characters' safety.

The survivors of Oceanic 815 replicate certain features of capitalism during their time on the island. Despite Jack's belief that the castaways should "all be able to start over," they frequently seem doomed to recreate the society they came from ("Tabula Rasa" 1.3). And despite some characters' attempts toward communal living and Jack's constant warnings that they must live together or die alone, individualism prevails more often than community when it comes to possessions. When identity is the issue, however, individuality often takes a backseat to characters' roles in the island community and the skills they bring with them. Just as objects on *Lost* are raised to the status of characters unto themselves, characters are often simultaneously treated as objects. It becomes apparent very quickly in the first season that this particular group of people fulfills a variety of archetypes. Sawyer tells Jack in Part 2 of the Pilot, "You're the hero." Later he says to Sayid, "I'm the criminal. You're the terrorist. We can all play a part" and to Shannon, "Who you wanna be?" (1.2). This group of people was also either chosen by Jacob at least partially based on their skill sets or was extraordinarily lucky to find all their island needs met by the combination of people on their flight. On one level, then, we have the hero, the fugitive, the mother, and the trickster, but on another, more practical level we have the doctor, the hunter, and the fisherman. We have someone who can garden, someone who can build things, and someone who is good with electronics. These roles make many of the main characters vital to the community of survivors, but also in some sense strip away their humanity and reduce them to their functions, like objects. They also help establish a hierarchy among the characters in which some skills (medicine) are more important than others (teaching), and therefore the people who possess those skills also fall into hierarchical relationships — just ask Jack and Arzt.

In some momentary gestures toward communal living, the castaways are seen helping each other construct shelters and obtain food, but as Arzt points out, certain popular or powerful characters take or are given more or better things than others. Comparing the main characters of *Lost* to a high school clique, Arzt bitterly asks Hurley to explain to him "why Kate gets the best pieces of wreckage to build her shelter. And the Korean guy, does he catch fish for everybody on the island? No, he does not, he doesn't" ("Exodus, Part 2" 1.24 and 1.25). These questions are never answered (perhaps because Arzt blows up moments later), and since we continue to follow only the most popular and powerful characters, we hear very few complaints like this again, but it is clear from this conversation that at least some of the characters are concerned about the way material goods are distributed on the island.

Furthermore, Jack is reluctant to take on a leadership role, and other characters also sometimes bristle against the idea of anyone being in charge, but ultimately they all settle into a somewhat hierarchical society that seems to sway between representative government and dictatorship: the castaways elect Jack, Locke, Sawyer, or Hurley as their leader, but once each character occupies that role, they make decisions on behalf of the group without needing to achieve consensus or even a majority. Jack justifies this type of leadership when Kate complains that he has made a decision that he did not have the right to make: "Everybody wants me to be a leader until I make a decision that they don't like," he says. "You want to keep second guessing me, Kate? That's your call" ("Exodus, Part 2"). Other leaders also seem to operate this way, occasionally soliciting advice or opinions from the group but mostly ruling by fiat. One of the things each character who occupies any type of leadership role gets to decide is how to distribute or not distribute the group's belongings he controls. Hurley notably distributes the food from the Swan and the pallet drop evenly among the whole group ("Everybody Hates Hugo" 2.4, "Dave" 2.18) while Locke and Jack lock up the guns, ammunition, and medicine and try to limit access to and knowledge of the Swan entirely ("The Long Con" 2.13, "Everybody Hates Hugo"). Once again Arzt is a vocal protester. In "Exposé" (3.14), after learning that some of the survivors have kept a cache of weapons secret from most of the group, he compares the leaders' corruption to that of the socialist-turned-authoritarian leadership of *Animal Farm*, shouting, "You're all out of control. The pigs are walking!"

A system of trade and barter also develops among the survivors, with the scarcity of objects determining their value. Importantly, it is the items brought with the survivors on the Oceanic plane, the items from their prior lives, that first function in this kind of economy. Later, the items found in the Swan station and the food drop, as well as things initially from the outside world, also become part of this economy. After all, food, water, and building materials that naturally occur on the island are not scarce — as Sawyer points out to Kate, "Water has no value, Freckles. It's gonna rain sooner or later" ("White Rabbit" 1.5) — and the people who obtain these objects freely share and trade them, for the most part. Locke hunts boar for the whole camp, Jin is seen giving Hurley and Claire fish for nothing in return, Sun plants and tends a garden that will feed the whole group, and according to Hurley, Steve brings water from the caves to the beach every morning ("Walkabout" 1.4, "Pilot, Part 2," "Hearts and Minds" 1.13, "Left Behind" 3.15). It seems, given the relatively easy exchange of items native to the island, that the objects from the plane could be evenly distributed among the survivors, but they are hoarded and used for profit instead. The main agent of this economy is, of course, Sawyer.

Sawyer is the arch-capitalist: he operates by a code of finders-keepers, except when others find his stash. He has not made or purchased any of the items that he owns on the island; he is simply the first to exploit each situation that presents the group with new, potentially useful objects. He steals, scavenges, swindles, and gambles his way to material wealth, seeing the potential value in everything from food, guns, and medicine to sunscreen, deodorant, and reading material. He almost never gives away anything without getting something in return, whether he trades for other material objects or simply buys a more favorable opinion of himself, such as when he gives Claire a blanket in "Left Behind" after Hurley convinces him he needs to "make amends" with the group. He makes his economic philosophy explicit when he tells Jack, "I don't know what kind of Commie share-fest you're running over in Cavetown, but down here possession's nine-tenths" ("Confidence Man" 1.8). Objects to Sawyer truly are commodities. He acquires them to acquire power and he uses them to buy what he needs. He also sees clearly that it is only manmade objects that benefit him in this way. Sawyer nearly single-handedly creates and maintains an economic system reminiscent of the one the survivors come from.

Even apart from Sawyer's fledgling marketplace, the objects on *Lost* that originated off the island would still carry the alienation and symbolism of capitalism, because that is the world that produced the items and that shaped the characters' relationships to manmade objects. It makes sense given Lukács's and Jameson's arguments about objects and alienation in capitalist society that on *Lost*, the objects originating in that economic system continue to bear the effects of that system. Furthermore, these items are marked as significant by the show, often carrying heavy symbolic importance for characters and viewers, and some of these items seem to lead lives of their own, resonating with Jameson's description of objects in modern fiction. As the show progresses, these manmade objects cause more and more dissonance, violence, injury, and death, demonstrating how undesirable this kind of relationship to objects is. Objects from the island itself, on the other hand, are much more innocuous. They are useful and rarely cause any problems. In fact, they frequently fade into the background of the show — no individual log, mango, or rock carries for viewers or characters the same symbolic power as the wheelchair, the comic book, or the Dharma parka.

The process by which manmade objects become more symbolic and more dangerous begins with the castaways on the beach, creating this economic system and allowing it to cause strife among them. In the first two seasons, in addition to the numerous power struggles that occur over property, the handcuffs become agents of prejudice and misunderstanding, lifesaving medicine is traded for a case full of guns, and loyalties are bought and sold with sunscreen and insect repellant ("House of the Rising Sun" (1.6), "Whatever the Case May Be" 1.12, "Solitary" 1.9). Most of the conflict created by objects in these early days on the island is frustrating for the characters but not life-threatening. For example, Hurley's disordered relationship with food is beginning to become healthier as he eats only what is caught or gathered on the island. He tells Libby, "When we first crashed here, I thought, this isn't all bad. It's like the all mango diet." When the castaways discover the Swan station full of food, though, Hurley says he "tried giving it all away" but ultimately hoarded some of it and secretly binged. Hurley says, "I wish I could just get rid of it," and after he and Libby destroy his stash he says he feels "free." Moments later, however, the Dharma Initiative food pallet drops. This triggers a crisis for Hurley, and Libby observes that "it's like the island won't let [him] lose weight" ("Dave"). *Lost* consistently privileges objects native to the island over those that were brought from the outside world, but it also demonstrates the inescapability of the outside world. When packaged and branded food falls from the sky, we are reminded of the impossibility of starting over, the inevitable baggage we bring to utopia. We are also meant to see the clear difference between boar meat and Dharma macaroni and cheese: while both are food, only one is a product.

Some of the characters' encounters with objects from the outside world are more menacing than the Dharma food, though. When using the cradle made by Locke, Claire and Aaron are safe and happy, an experience that contrasts with Claire's nightmarish memories of the nursery in the Staff station. Significantly, of all the items present in the Dharma nursery, the only one left behind when the station is cleaned out is the knitted bootie Claire makes for Aaron. The paraphernalia of motherhood that is given to Claire separates her from the island by simulating a room in the outside world, full of mass produced objects, which form the backdrop for Claire's horrific flashbacks. The bootie Claire makes while in the Staff nursery, however, is benign. Claire's relationship to the bootie is not like her relationship to the plane mobile, the crib, or the other items in the nursery, because she made it herself. The bootie becomes a symbol of Claire's maternal love and is compatible with harmonious life on the island ("Maternity Leave" 2.15).

Finally and most dangerously in these early seasons of the show, guns are hoarded, hidden, distributed, and collected again and again. They bestow power on their owners and allow the survivors to feel protected at times, but they also allow characters to act rashly and carelessly. Charlie shoots Ethan out of rage and a desire for revenge before he can reveal any information about the Others; Michael shoots Libby and Ana Lucia out of desperation to save Walt ("Homecoming" 1.15, "Two For the Road" 2.20). Shannon is shot and killed accidentally, but when the air marshal is shot purposefully, it only adds to his suffering, as he still does not die right away ("Abandoned" 2.6, "Tabula Rasa" 1.3). We can read all these events simply as instances of characters making poor choices with guns, but it is important also to note that guns are prized commodities on the island. In "The Long Con," Sawyer manages to get all the guns for himself not because he needs or wants them at that moment, but because he rightly assesses that owning the guns makes him the "new sheriff in town." Like everything else in his stash, guns help Sawyer buy influence. Like no other objects in the first few seasons of *Lost*, guns possess talismanic power. It is hard to believe that any of the castaways realistically think Sawyer will use the guns for any purpose other than protecting the group, but the symbolic weight they carry still allows him to assert his authority over the group.

These strained and sometimes strange relationships to objects continue and escalate through the survivors' encounters with the Others in the second and third seasons and then with the scientists and the crew of the freighter in the fourth. The computer found in the Swan station definitely seems to lead a life of its own: it controls the characters rather than the other way around; it seems to initiate a lockdown and pallet drop of its own accord; it mysteriously facilitates communication between Michael and Walt, eventually leading to the murders of Libby and Ana Lucia and the capture of Jack, Kate, and Sawyer; and we learn that it was Desmond's failure to attend to this object that caused the crash of Oceanic 815 in the first place ("Lockdown" 2.17, "What Kate Did" 2.9, "Live Together, Die Alone, Part 2" 2.24). The second season dramatically ends with another failure to push the button. This time the Swan station implodes, first sending silverware, dumbbells, and appliances inside the Swan flying around as if possessed and then spewing manmade debris all over the island — we see the hatch door descend on the beach and almost kill Claire, Aaron, and Bernard ("Live Together, Die Alone, Part 2").

At the opening of the next season, when we first meet the Others in their own island society, seeing their houses full of material possessions is meant to be jarring and provide a contrast to the way the castaways live. The breakfast Ben provides for Kate on the beach is eerie partly because it points up this contrast: the Others have French presses, tablecloths, and dishes that clearly originated off the island ("A Tale of Two Cities" 3.1). This way of life is emblematic of the kind of economy the castaways seem doomed to recreate on the island. Palmerton points out that the sequence of "levels" on the show presents the castaways with a series of challenges. I would add that these challenges frequently take the form of exposure to manmade commodities which present a series of temptations to live the same way they did before the plane crash instead of creating a new utopian society. Of course, these objects also serve as reminders that the castaways can never completely escape the world they came from. Locke later points out that the island healed him but not Ben because Locke and the other castaways are living closer to the land and relying primarily on the products of their own work, while Ben has separated himself from the island and his own labor by relying on objects and an infrastructure that were imported to the island. Locke scolds Ben, saying, "You're cheating, you and your people. You communicate with the outside world whenever you want to, you come and go as you please, you use electricity and running water and guns, you're a hypocrite, a Pharisee. You don't deserve to be on this island" ("The Man from Tallahassee" 3.13). We also learn later that Ben has a substantial amount of money at his disposal ("The Economist" 4.3). But ultimately, especially under increasing threat from the freighter folk, the 815 survivors and the Others merge, with some of each group living on the beach and some in the barracks.

Manmade, branded objects become more and more ubiquitous as the third and fourth seasons progress and the castaways become more and more involved with the surviving Others and the scientists from the Kahana. The beginning of this transition, "the beginning of the end," is again facilitated by an imported, manmade object. Just as the Swan computer irreversibly changed life on the island and put the survivors in danger at the end of the second season, so too does the satellite phone Naomi brings to the island at the end of the third season ("Through the Looking Glass, Part 2" 3.23). As a result of the survivors using the satellite phone, bigger and more obviously destructive objects arrive on and near the island: the Kahana brings an influx of weaponry, including a bomb. The helicopter, like the freighter, seems at first like a useful piece of technology that will lead to the survivors' rescue, and this is partly true, but it also proves unreliable and fails the castaways, stranding the Oceanic Six on a raft in open water and leaving the rest of the survivors still stranded on the island ("There's No Place Like Home, Part 3" 4.13 and 4.14). Ultimately, objects are taken away from the survivors entirely as they begin jumping through time in the fifth season.

The remaining castaways' first clue as to what is happening after Ben turns the frozen wheel is the disappearance of their camp and all their belongings. It is as if they logged into the video game to find their inventories empty. Sawyer's impulse is to re-accumulate the things he has lost: when the survivors jump back in time and realize the Swan station has not been destroyed yet, he tells Daniel, "I ain't starting over [...] I ain't rubbing two sticks together to start a fire and I ain't hunting damn boar. There's Dharma food, beer, and clothing in there. And I'm getting Desmond to let me in one way or another" ("Because You Left" 5.1). This plan cannot work, however, both because of *Lost*'s laws of time travel and because every time the island jumps to a new time, the survivors lose most of the items around them. The only things that are "along for the ride," as Juliet puts it, are the things that were with them at the time of the first jump ("The Lie" 5.2). The characters must learn to relate to material objects in a completely different way, not relying on possessions they have accumulated but on what the island gives them at each time and place, and realizing that they don't individually "own" anything anymore. This process is painful, and the lesson is never completely learned.

It is during this time that we encounter one of the strangest manmade objects of the entire show: the compass that is handed back and forth between Locke and Richard in an infinite time loop. Finally in this case, a material object actually takes on semi-magical properties (since the compass paradoxically was never created and, despite its infinite travel, does not seem to decay) and exists in its own reality, carried by people but separate from them in its own subjective experience of time. The compass is a powerful symbol to Locke, Richard, and viewers, and while it is not directly dangerous to the characters, it is used by the Man in Black to further his deadly plans ("Because You Left," "Jughead" 5.3, "Follow the Leader" 5.15). When the time-travel stops, the survivors eventually find themselves in a previously established capitalist society, where they settle back into something like their pre-crash way of life for a time. The Dharma compound is full of items imported from the outside world, and although it seems to be simply a commune of "scientists and free-thinkers," it is financially backed by a corporation, The Hanso Foundation ("Orientation"). After spending several years living in this environment, the castaways face the climax of alienation, the ultimate examples of objects with lives of their own: a bomb that seems unwilling to help them and piles of metal objects that cannot be controlled. During the incident, metal tools, cars, and building materials seem to brutally attack a number of people, resulting in many deaths, most notably Juliet's. Jack, Sawyer, and Kate each later try to take responsibility for Juliet's death, but in the scene in question it appears to be the objects themselves that want her and others dead or injured. A tower collapses in such a way as to pin Pierre Chang's arm. A toolbox knocks Jack unconscious. Radzinsky's Jeep drives itself backward into the pit. Scaffolding traps Phil and a metal pole spears him through the chest. Finally, a chain wraps itself around Juliet's legs, dragging her into the pit ("The Incident, Part 2" 5.17). While we know these events were caused by electromagnetism, the objects all appear to move purposefully and of their own volition. We can read the incident as the culmination of alienation on the island. After this traumatic experience, the castaways are forced to shift to a nomadic, communal style of living, giving up on a stable supply of belongings. The remaining survivors on the island spend their time searching, running, hiding, and waiting at a variety of island locations such as the Temple, the beach, the Barracks, the Lighthouse, and Hydra Island, but they have no long-term home and only the possessions they carry with them. Their relationship to objects is no longer an important element of the show, because it is no longer problematic, and it is no longer problematic because it is no longer alienated.

The irony of this critique of capitalist alienation is that it takes place within a show that in other ways actively participates in and even contributes significant innovations to the commodity culture of contemporary American television. As Derek Johnson points out in "The Fictional Institutions of *Lost*: World Building, Reality and the Economic Possibilities of Narrative Divergence," despite the fact that *Lost* does not employ traditional product placement and was initially seen by advertisers as a dud (32–3), it does utilize some other kinds of advertising and commodification — namely, reverse product placement and world building. Adding to the strange juxtaposition of *Lost*'s diegetic and extra-diegetic realities, the concept of world building is oddly shared by socialist utopian projects and capitalist marketing plans — one is played out on the show itself and the other bridges the show and the real world. Johnson explains the concept of extra-diegetic world building using the Disneyland television series as an example: "Rather than draw the consumer into the Disney world, the Disney world was propelled outward into the real world of the consumer" (34). Just as Disneyland started as a television show and then became a real-world place, the Dharma Initiative started as a company that only appeared on *Lost* but later gained a real world presence. World building is "the construction of complex narrative universes that use the relative diegetic depth of episodic television to cultivate new forms of audience engagement in an increasingly fragmented and competitive media marketplace" (Johnson 34) and, in the case of *Lost*, includes web content and alternate reality games. Johnson also points out that "[t]he world-building project of *Lost* is very much an institution-building project," featuring "the institutional nexus of Oceanic, Dharma, Hanso, Mittelos, Widmore, Apollo, et al." (37).

Adding to the irony of these practices as utilized by *Lost*, many of the extra-diegetic world-building and money-making activities of Lost involve objects — sometimes the very objects that provide Marxist critique within the context of the show. Fictional corporations such as Oceanic, Ajira, Paik Automotive, and Widmore Industries are ever-present, sometimes overbearing forces in the lives of the castaways, reminding them and us that capitalist culture is detrimental and inescapable — but *Lost* fans are also encouraged to participate in the world of the show through these companies, which, Johnson points out, function as intermediaries between the fictional world of the characters and the real world of the viewers. At the 2008 *Lost* Comic-Con panel, the Dharma Initiative was introduced as a corporate sponsor of *Lost*, and Dharma representatives were on the scene to verify this development and launch the third alternate reality game, which consisted of recruitment and aptitude testing for careers within the DI. Along with *Lost* merchandise given away to fans who attended the panel, executive producers Damon Lindelof and Carlton Cuse handed out products from companies internal to the show, including an Oceanic brand bottle of water, an Apollo candy bar, a Hanso Foundation hat, a tub of Dharma ranch dressing, and a six-pack of Dharma beer. The presence of fictional corporations and sponsorship within the *Lost* universe can be seen as intertextual parody that appeals to viewers' awareness of themselves as always-marketed-to consumers. ABC (not coincidentally owned by Disney) and *Lost* then use this very parody to their advantage to sell things to *Lost* fans: in ABC's online store, along with the typical *Lost* fare, you can now buy a variety of products labeled with Dharma logos.

Because of the historical-economic context in which *Lost* appears, we can expect both the kinds of problematic relationships between humans and objects that appear within the diegetic reality of the show and the capitulation to and even celebration of capitalism that appears in the show's extra-diegetic world. As Lukács observes, art forms reflect the historical-political context from which they emerge. Furthermore, he argues, "All the fissures and rents which are inherent in the historical situation must be drawn into the form-giving process and cannot nor should be disguised by compositional means"

(60) — our current commodity culture should not and cannot be hidden in or by the television industry. It makes sense, then, that *Lost* reflects the economic reality of twenty-first century television in its branding and money-making moves, but that it also registers discontent with this system within the show itself. What is perhaps most interesting, finally, is that viewers of *Lost* so frequently fall into the same traps as the characters in their relationships to the objects of the show. Alienated from these objects, we assign them too much symbolic weight; we expect them to mean too much. While items from *Lost* are obviously not dangerous to fans (unless, perhaps, we eat the ranch dressing from Comic-Con), they are frequently disappointing, spawning questions and theories whose resolutions are inevitably anti-climactic. At the end of the day, outside the show itself, characters' stuff is simply characters' stuff. Despite fans desperately wanting Kate's toy plane to mean something, what could it mean that would be big enough to satisfy our desire for near-magical levels of symbolism? As Kate herself says, it's just a "stupid plane" ("Born to Run" 1.22).

## Works Cited

Jameson, Fredric. *Archaeologies of the Future: The Desire Called Utopia and Other Science Fictions.* London: Verso, 2007. Print.

———. *Marxism and Form: Twentieth-Century Dialectical Theories of Literature.* Princeton: Princeton University Press, 1971. Print.

———. *Postmodernism: Or, The Cultural Logic of Late Capitalism.* Durham: Duke University Press, 1991. Print.

Johnson, Derek. "The Fictional Institutions of Lost: World Building, Reality and the Economic Possibilities of Narrative Divergence." *Reading* Lost: *Perspectives on a Hit Television Show.* Ed. Roberta Pearson. London: I. B. Taurus, 2009. 27–49. Print.

Lukács, Georg. *The Theory of the Novel.* Trans. Anna Bostock. Cambridge: The MIT Press, 1971. Print.

Palmerton, Elwyn. "DHARMA's Bent Reality: The Video Game Sensibility of *Lost.*" *PopMatters.* PopMatters Magazine, 4 August 2008. Web. 26 February 2009.

# "Strangers in a Strange Land": Evading Environmental Apocalypse Through Human Choice

*Carlos A. Tarin and Stacey K. Sowards*

As the *Lost* series wrapped up its final episodes over the first half of 2010, themes related to the fundamental meanings of and questions about human nature, human relationships, religion, death, the afterlife, and even the idea of life itself became increasingly prominent (Vine). The series finale explored all of these themes and more, but left them open to audience interpretations as the main characters of the program reunited in a Los Angeles church in what was seemingly an afterlife or alternative timeline. For many of the 13.5 million viewers who watched the series finale on May 23, 2010, and the many more who watched and re-watched online, unlocking the island's mysteries and searching for explanations may have been a primary goal, but the finale was more about character involvement than answering questions (Fernandez 9). While audiences may have been caught up in the characters' stories and the numerous mysteries that unraveled throughout the six seasons of *Lost*, the broader meaning of the island's presence as a wild habitat and mysterious natural force was left unresolved in the series finale. Clearly, many of the characters of the show somehow navigated and survived the natural elements of the island, such as the preposterous and unexplained attack by a polar bear in season one ("Pilot, Part 2" 1.2).

Although the primary focus of *Lost* may be more about various characters and mysteries than about surviving on an isolated island, that survival element is a major and persistent feature of the series. As Japp and Meister explain, "The nature symbol is a powerful and popular visual as well as verbal construct that is consistently modified, manipulated, and redefined in popular culture [...] popular culture is a primary site of meaning construction, probably the major arena in which most understand, reinforce, and/or modify the circumstances of their lives" (2). In her analysis of films that present an agrarian mythology, Retzinger further observes that audiences learn about the characters in great detail, but not very much about the natural worlds they inhabit (57). Similarly, in *Lost*, viewers and characters do not consciously engage with the ideologies, meanings, and representations of nature, even though images of subsistence and interactions are ubiquitous throughout the series. The ubiquity and constant effect contribute to meaning formation about the natural world, as Dahstrom and Scheufele's study on cultivation effects for broader television viewing and environmental meaning making illustrates (55–56).

Audiences have searched for meaning about the philosophies and ethics that are themes throughout the series (*e.g.,* see Kaye), but the constructed meaning of the natural world in the series has been less explored by fans and academic scholars. In our essay, we argue that the *Lost* characters' survival and the island itself functions as an allegory for understanding environmental issues in the twenty-first century. First, we contend that although many of the *Lost* characters endure harsh conditions on the island, their survival is sanitized through the facility with which they interact with the island's natural elements. Audience interpretations of nature are often understood through paradigms of competition, resources, or paradise and the simplicity of survival in nature (Kaplan and Rogers 6; Retzinger 50–57). It is this portrayal of nature that leads us to our second argument, that *Lost* presents a dichotomous ecological consciousness, that the characters have an either/or choice to save or destroy the world, as evidenced through numerous difficult decisions that various characters must make. The sanitization of nature and the dichotomous decisions that confront *Lost* characters shape an understanding of environmental problems as apocalyptic (*e.g.,* see Cox; Foust and O'Shannon Murphy; Sowards, "Rhetoric"), requiring immediate action to prevent the imminent end of the world. Solutions to such issues are presented inherently as a form of human choice and agency, which allow us to control the future and nature. We begin our exposition with a brief discussion related to how humans have come to understand the natural world through paradigms of competition, resource, and paradise that function through a nature/culture dualism. We then engage in a close textual analysis of the *Lost* series to illustrate how these paradigmatic understandings are reinforced and ultimately serve as an allegory for broader environmental issues.

## *Nature/Culture Paradigms in Media*

Environmental scholars have long argued that the divide between nature and humans shapes our understanding of the natural world as "Other" (*e.g.,* Haila 156) rather than allowing humans to see themselves situated within nature or as part of what we think of as the natural world (Sowards, "Identification" 47). Val Plumwood contends that nature exists in juxtaposition to reason, and therefore, to humans: "Nature, as the excluded and devalued contrast of reason, includes the emotions, the body, the passions, animality, the primitive or uncivilized, the non-human world, matter, physicality and sense experience, as well as the sphere of irrationality, of faith and of madness" (19–20). She further explains rhetorical strategies that humans use to relate to nature that include processes such as objectification, separation, and homogenization. More broadly, Kaplan and Rogers contend that throughout history, humans have understood nature through competitive (nature as dangerous), pragmatic (nature as a resource), or romantic (nature as paradise) models that perpetuate the divide between nature and culture (6). They also offer a fourth model of dialectics, in which they recognize that "Nature and our relationship to it are complex [...] and human society develops out of the natural world" (6). In this model, humans come to respect but also see use-value for the natural world, but in a more symbiotic approach: "By recognizing that nature has its own laws and rules for survival, it is possible to live with nature and use it, but also to put something back and allow it to be maintained." (6)

Although Kaplan and Rogers suggest that we may be progressing towards this dialectic model given their historical account of how humans have understood nature, the nature/culture dualism persists, especially in mediated texts. Nils Elliot proposes that the nature/culture dualism is presented and represented in media texts, for example, as "extreme nature," such as in the popular television program *Crocodile Hunter*, or as "Edenic nature," such as in the sublime images used in advertising (2). These re/presentations, Elliot argues, exist in the nature of thirdness, or the "nature of signs, that is to say of words, images, thoughts and, more generally, all the media by means of which nature might be represented, and/or might be *made to present itself:* nature re/presented," which include the signs, representations, interpretations, and translations of nature (27, italics in original). Adding to Elliot's contention, Andy Opel notes that "Industrial, technological society then is said to shape both the nature we romanticize and the images of that nature we view though the mediations of our culture production industries" (35). Furthermore, it is not just the verbal mediated message, whether written or spoken, that is of importance in creating meaning, but also the visual element of the message. Anne Marie Todd, in her analysis of environmental rhetoric on the animated television show, *The Simpsons*, further clarifies the importance of understanding visual meaning, precisely because of the mediated aspect of re/presenting nature: "Television, particularly animation, misrepresents reality, masquerading as lived experience, in order to manipulate social contexts that provide meaning for personal experience, and guide individual action" (68–9). Clearly, televised programs can shape the way in which viewers understand and know nature in significant ways.

However, the television program *Lost* at first glance seemingly inverts the nature/culture dualism, by forcing the survivors of Oceanic 815 to integrate themselves into the natural world. As the plotline develops, audiences see Oceanic passengers, Dharma Initiative members, the Others, and various visitors surviving on an island that represents the broader natural world. Proceeding from Kaplan and Rogers's environmental framework, various characters and organizations throughout *Lost* exemplify qualities that are meant to demonstrate significantly different viewpoints about human-nature interactions. Although there are innumerable groups, factions, alliances, and organizations that rise to and fall from power throughout the progression of the series, we argue that three are vital for understanding the multi-dimensional perspectives about the environment evidenced on *Lost*: the Oceanic 815 survivors, the Dharma Initiative, and the Others. These groups each exhibit different levels of interaction with the natural world that uphold and reinforce Kaplan and Rogers's three dominant ontological perspectives about the role and function of the environment in daily human existence: nature as danger, nature as resource, and nature as paradise.

## *The Oceanic 815 Survivors — Nature as Danger*

For the Oceanic 815 survivors, nature represents a danger in terms of their very survival on the island. As Kaplan and Rogers explain, under this paradigm, "Nature is something to be feared and that fear is managed by attempting to assume control. It must be confronted and, as in the first words of the Bible, it is right and permissible to subjugate and control it. Humankind is the highest form of creation and hence, master of the earth" (6). As the series begins, viewers are introduced to a disturbingly chaotic scene juxtaposing a pristine ocean view with the disastrous wreckage of the Oceanic 815 aircraft ("Pilot, Part 1" 1.1). As the chaos subsides and the survivors begin to organize themselves while awaiting rescue, the concern quickly turns to addressing basic physical needs for food, shelter, and protection. Jack quickly assumes a leadership position, and begins to treat passengers from the flight to help them survive their injuries from the plane crash. In the initial scenes, the danger that the characters and audience members experience is the threat of survival that comes from being in an apparently deserted and extremely isolated island.

The stark contrast between the availability of commodities in modern societies versus the lack of availability on the island is made immediately clear by characters commenting on the unpleasantness of natural living. While trekking through the rain forest to reach the cockpit, for example, a powerful rainstorm begins to downpour on Jack, Kate, and Charlie. In response to this peculiarity, Charlie quips, "You guys, is this normal? This kind of day turning into night, you know, end of the world type weather? Is this ... Guys?" ("Pilot, Part 1"). In a later scene, as food supplies begin to run low, Jin offers Hurley a freshly caught and prepared sea urchin. Responding to the offer in disgust, Hurley replies, "Dude, I am starving, but I am nowhere near that hungry. No way, no" ("Pilot, Part 2"). These examples establish a tone for the survivors that is continuously echoed throughout the series as the natural world is something that must perpetually be fought against. Although these concerns are significant for the characters in the first episodes of the series, the ease of survival is, in many ways, simplified by a number of plot conventions that are never fully explained. An ax, for example, suddenly appears on the island and is used by the survivors in a variety of ways, yet it is never made clear where the tool came from. The availability of food, torches, and the simplicity of building campfires are also integrated into the story, but these conventions are a far cry from the realistic difficulties survivors on an island in the middle of the Pacific Ocean would likely face. While these oversights can be attributed to a necessitated dramatic need, their presences may condition audiences to understand nature less as a dangerous force and more as something that is easily surmountable. Indeed, it is clear that while many of the initial struggles endured by the survivors of Oceanic 815 deal primarily with the procurement and maintenance of basic resources and shelter for survival on the island, these issues are never given serious treatment to reflect the harsh realities of a tropical island setting. Nature is still dangerous, but becomes sanitized through the televised reality that the *Lost* characters encounter.

One character who seems to defy this attitude toward the environment is John Locke. Unlike many of the other survivors who view living in nature as a struggle or problem, Locke appears to wholeheartedly embrace such a lifestyle and, in some ways, seems to prefer it. Early in the series, Locke demonstrates a profound connection to the island and the natural habitat that is likely the result of the miraculous restoration of his mobility. Describing the walkabout that he was turned away from in Australia, he explains that the activity is a, "journey of spiritual renewal where one derives strength from the Earth and becomes inseparable from it" ("Walkabout" 1.4). His experiences on the island, therefore, can be understood as quite distinct from the other Oceanic survivors in that he is seeking to establish a deeper spiritual connection or communion with the environment. This disposition functions as Locke's impetus to constantly engage, question, and challenge the island and its inhabitants throughout the series.

The concerns for basic survival are, in many ways, alleviated once the Oceanic survivors discover and open the Dharma Swan station. Although the caves provide a bountiful source of food, fresh water, and shelter ("White Rabbit" 1.5), the Swan station improves living conditions by providing modern amenities that are simply unavailable in the natural environment. Electricity, running water, and a massive food supply are all taken advantage of by the Oceanic survivors and, consequently, their interaction with nature becomes extensively sanitized due to the perceived ease of living on the island with these resources. Even the possibility of rapidly extinguishing food supplies is eliminated as periodic food drops are provided to the Dharma stations (although the source of these drops is never revealed during the series) and continue to serve as a perpetual resource for the survivors ("Lockdown" 2.17). The newly afforded ease of living is significant insofar as representations of the environment become stripped of the potential for danger or struggle. On the contrary, the Oceanic 815 survivors come to view other forces on the island as far more treacherous. This sanitization carries significant implications for modern understandings of the nature-culture dualism because it minimizes the harsh realities of the natural world, thereby shaping viewer perceptions and attitudes about the island environment and the characters' interaction with it.

## *The Dharma Initiative—Nature as Resource*

The Dharma Initiative is one of the most mysterious, albeit significant, forces that occupy the island throughout the series. Although very little about the organization is disclosed, important information about the research and experimentation being conducted on the island provides evidence that the group saw the island as a resource that could potentially be harnessed for the betterment of humanity. Nature becomes a resource for the Dharma Initiative, as nature "offers us our subsistence and with some labor, it can be made to yield riches. These riches are boundless and exist for our sake. Indeed, so natural is this provisioning that it requires no thought or ethical consideration in proceeding with the agenda of exploitation. Or indeed, there is an ethics, in the sense of allowing any action that contributes to the self-preservation of an individual, group, or the human species" (Kaplan and Rogers 6).

The Swan Station orientation video, for instance, explains that "the Dharma Initiative was created in 1970 and is the brainchild of Gerald and Karen Degroot, two doctoral candidates at the University of Michigan [...] they imagine large scale communal compounds where research could be conducted into meteorology, psychology, parapsychology, zoology, electromagnetism" and other objectives ("Orientation" 2.3). With a research agenda clearly set on utilizing the unique characteristics of the island, the Dharma Initiative built several stations throughout the island to conduct their experiments. The Hydra station (or Hydra Island as it is often referred to throughout the series), for example, appears to be a site for experiments in zoology ("A Tale of Two Cities" 3.1), whereas the Orchid station conducts experiments in space and time ("There's No Place Like Home, Part 1" 4.12). Because it is understood that the island possesses unique physical characteristics, it is no surprise that the Dharma Initiative is attempting to harness the natural environment for its own means.

That the Dharma Initiative is utilizing the island as a resource is significant even though the Oceanic survivors and the Others also utilize the island for similar means in some way throughout the series. However, there is ample evidence to suggest that the Dharma Initiative's investment in the island is recklessly devoid of consideration of possible negative implications from the experiments that are being conducted. Pierre Chang, the lead scientist for the Initiative, acknowledges the risk of the experiments conducted near the electromagnetic pocket when he orders the workers to cease drilling because "if you drill even one centimeter further, you risk releasing that energy. If that were to happen, God help us all" ("The Variable" 5.14). Daniel Faraday, believing that the scientists are underestimating the severity of the danger, confronts Chang and requests a full evacuation of the island. This request is quickly dismissed (although later Chang does order an evacuation of all women and children from the island). The exchange between Chang and Faraday is significant because it highlights tensions that necessarily arise in understanding interactions between humans and nature. Despite clearly recognizable threats, operations and experiments on the island continue to take place and eventually results in the cataclysmic events that bring down Oceanic 815. The Dharma Initiative represents a form of environmental interaction that prioritizes the needs and desires of humans while recklessly ignoring potential implications. In viewing the environment as a resource which must be conquered, harnessed, and controlled, interaction between humans and nature becomes increasingly volatile, often resulting in damaging results.

## *The Others — Nature as Paradise*

Unlike the Oceanic survivors or the Dharma Initiative, who view the environment as something that must necessarily be worked against or used as a resource, the Others appear to advance a relationship with the natural world that is grounded in romantic notions of the island as paradise. In representing the island from the perspective of the Others, the island becomes a symbol for both nature and paradise. Kaplan and Rogers explain that the romantic model is nostalgic for pristine nature lost: "one can glimpse what humankind has lost and may never regain or may only recapture in part. Harmony reigns in nature and human society can only strive to imitate nature. Nature is perfect and needs no improvement or change" (6). Presumably, the Others have chosen to move to the island to have a different kind of life, one rooted in this romantic model of nature. After Benjamin Linus assisted the Others in eliminating the Dharma Initiative ("The Man Behind the Curtain" 3.20), the Others took control of the various Dharma stations in an attempt to close off contact with the outside world. The Looking Glass station, for instance, was utilized to jam radio communications with the mainland in order to prevent the island from being located by malicious forces ("Through the Looking Glass, Part 1" 3.22). Although the Others did maintain use of many of the original Dharma buildings such as the Barracks, the majority appear throughout the first half of the series as nomads, living in small camps in various parts of the island ("There's No Place Like Home, Part 2" 4.13 and 4.14). This close connection to the natural world and the extensive knowledge exhibited by the Others about the island are important indicators of the relationship that is being forged and maintained in a portrayal of that environment as paradise. What may be more striking about the Others is that, due to their apparently nomadic lifestyle, they can be interpreted as a group constantly and pervasively functioning on the periphery of the establishments on the island. As such, the Others are quite literally exemplifications of nature itself— constantly surrounding humans, yet simultaneously unrecognized.

Because the social norms and ideologies of the Others are cloaked in secrecy for the majority of the series, the depictions of their practices in the final season of *Lost* are extremely important. The revelation that the Others are actually deeply concerned with the preservation of the island is important in that the ambiguity about whether they are a force of good or evil is finally resolved. Preservation of nature and the island, therefore, becomes recognized as a moral and ethical imperative. While many of the events that transpire during the final season can be interpreted in a multitude of ways, we argue that the environmental undertones cannot be overlooked. Sayid being brought back to life in the temple waters, for example, speaks to the possible mystical effects of the island, but more importantly, provides evidence of the inherent power of nature ("LA X, Part 2" 6.2). Recognizing that traditional medicine and science can do little to heal Sayid's wounds, Jack allows for the possibility that the Others' alternative methods might be the only effective choice. This is not meant to imply that there is an inherent tribalism ascribed to nature, but rather, that the natural world can run contrary to traditional scientific norms or ideologies. Despite conflicts about motive or intention, the Others must necessarily be recognized as the faction most closely associated with preserving nature in its pristine form. The designation of Jacob as the arbiter of good, leader of the Others, and protector of the island effectually forces an ontology that preservation of the natural world is, perhaps, the only acceptable moral paradigm.

## *Confronting Conflict, Evading Apocalypse*

Given that the majority of the dramatic conflicts that occur throughout *Lost* are the consequence of disagreements about what constitutes the most acceptable course of action in a given (and usually urgent) situation, the varied ontological perspectives about human-nature relations must be necessarily considered with the context of human agency. Questions about faith or science, good or evil, action or inaction, constitute and govern the dramatic reality of the series by forcing characters to make decisions which carry irreversible and immediate consequences. As Daniel Faraday continuously reminds us, "Whatever happened, happened." The theoretical framework espoused by Kaplan and Rogers, then, serves as a method of understanding how nature/culture dichotomies are constructed based on confrontations between divergent ideological and ontological perspectives. Characters in *Lost* are forced to make significant decisions without fully realizing the potential implications of their actions and, thus, an emphasis on diverting apocalypse becomes the norm. Prioritizing nature as a dangerous force, resource, or pristine ideal creates an ecological consciousness wherein immediate action must be taken to prevent imminent disaster. Three elements in the series—the Hatch, the Incident, and the Source—specifically exemplify how these conflicting perspectives create significant implications for the characters and the island itself.

Perhaps the first major dilemma that dichotomizes decision making for the characters on the island deals with how the Hatch, and more specifically, the entering of the code into the computer station, should be handled. Throughout the second season of the series, the Swan station is explained as a site meant to control the unstable electromagnetic forces on the island, and the urgency of pushing the button every 108 minutes is justified as an act that prevents a literal apocalypse ("Orientation"). Much of the dramatic tension existing in the season revolves around various characters and their opinion about whether the computer actually serves a functional purpose. Jack, for instance, assumes his traditional role as the authoritative man of reason and argues that the station is nothing more than a psychological experiment. Locke, on the other hand, orients himself with a faith-based approach and believes that destiny has created a series of events that necessitate his presence to continue entering the code. Ultimately, however, Locke becomes disillusioned by the station and refuses to enter the code, creating a near disaster on the island ("Live Together, Die Alone" 3.23 and 3.24). This crisis is averted only when Desmond enters the crawlspace beneath the station and turns the key that triggers the failsafe. The competing perspectives toward the Swan station and the eventual outcome of the situation highlight the sort of tensions that arise when "environmental" concerns conflict with actions of humans. Despite previous knowledge about the implications of not pushing the button (the crash of Oceanic 815), a conscious decision is still made not to continue the process of entering the numbers into the computer. This disregard for consequence exemplifies the tension between preserving the natural world or taking actions that prioritize the social needs of humans. Moreover, this instance reifies the perception that disaster can easily be averted by mere intervention — saving the island and averting a potential apocalypse is, here, as simple as turning a key. The dichotomization of action and the reductionism of consequence become recurring themes throughout the series.

In our second example, the attempt to prevent Oceanic 815 from crashing, the survivors stuck in the 1977 timeline concoct a plan to detonate a hydrogen bomb in hopes that the electromagnetic energy released at the Swan site would effectively be neutralized by the explosion ("The Incident, Part 1" 5.16). This situation presents an obvious confrontation between the Dharma scientists, who seek to continue experimentation, and the Oceanic survivors, who recognize the dangerous implications of the situation and attempt to mitigate these consequences. Interestingly, however, very little attention is paid by the Oceanic survivors to the potential harms that could be caused by their plan to detonate the hydrogen bomb. Miles, questioning their strategy, asks, "Has it occurred to any of you that your buddy is actually going to cause the thing he says he's try to prevent? Perhaps that little nuke is The Incident, so maybe the best thing to do is nothing. I'm glad you all thought this through" ("The Incident, Part 2" 5.17). This direct confrontation to the decision made by the Oceanic survivors constitutes the type of complexity that is created by dichotomizing perspectives on proper courses of action. Considerations are never fully articulated about alternative consequences or courses of action and, thus, the characters pursue the directives that they believe carry the most significant implications for their personal betterment. Miles' concern is eventually proven true; the detonation of the hydrogen bomb did not prevent the crash of Oceanic 815 and, in all actuality, created consequences that could have been avoided — most obviously, the death of Juliet ("LA X, Part 1" 6.1). Other implications that have direct ties to the environment may also associatively follow from the detonation of the hydrogen bomb. For instance, the last known birth to take place on the island occurred in 1977 when Juliet helped to deliver Ethan Rom ("LaFleur" 5.8). Although it is never proven, it may be a logical assumption that the environmental fallout from the hydrogen bomb or the Incident created conditions that were exceptionally hostile to pregnant women and prevented future births on the island.

Perhaps a more obvious apocalyptic scenario unfolds in the final episode of the series when, quite literally, the fate of the island is at stake and depends upon the actions taken by the characters. The Source, which is referenced as a source of good and the heart of the island ("Across the Sea" 6.15), remains an enduring mystery at the conclusion of the series. While it is unknown exactly what role this site plays for the functionality of the island or the characters themselves, dramatic events unfold when actions are taken in the cave that create irrevocable consequences. As the newly appointed "protector" of the island, Jack allows Desmond to enter the Source and "unplug the cork" that the Man in Black believes will allow him to finally destroy and escape the island ("The End" 6.17 and 6.18). After the stone in the center of the water-filled chamber is removed, the light and electromagnetic energy in the cave recede and disastrous consequences begin to occur. This instance highlights the direct implications of human intervention and the ways that reckless abandonment of precaution can generate significant harm. As a result of Desmond's action, the island begins to fall apart, with large pieces of land tumbling into the sea. The implications of this scenario should not be overlooked. If Jacob, the Others, and finally, Jack are vested with the responsibility of protecting the goodness of the island, they are implicitly responsible for the protection of the natural world itself. The dichotomous decision presented here means that direct human intervention carries real consequences for the ways in which the island as a symbol representing the broader natural world is either preserved or destroyed. Inevitably, Jack is forced to sacrifice his own life to restore balance to the island, implying that the consequences of human actions can ultimately be reversed. By averting this apocalyptic scenario through a simple reversal of action, *Lost* presents a false ecological consciousness that ignores the reality of environmental catastrophe. The relationships between nature, culture, and human action are presented as false dichotomies that overlook the seriousness of consequences and effectually create reductionist understandings of the natural world.

These examples illustrate the tensions that are created by conflicting ontological perspectives about nature-human interactions. One problematic aspect is the repeating theme that it is possible to save or destroy the world by pushing a button, releasing a hydrogen bomb, or removing a rock in a certain location. Apocalyptic scenarios that necessitate human interaction to avert major crises may inadvertently create an assumption that intervention is always possible, simple, or easy, or that the consequences of actions are wholly shaped by human decisions. Unfortunately, this dichotomy of saving or destroying the world re/presents the nature-culture dualism in such a way that human interaction is entirely sanitized, far removed from reality, and most importantly, afforded unrealistic agential qualities. Foust and O'Shannon Murphy discuss the distinction between tragic and comic frames in understanding environmental apocalypse in global warming rhetoric. They argue that the tragic frame represents the cosmic universe, that the apocalypse is fated to happen, whereas the comic frame addresses the role of human agency in either causing or preventing apocalypse (151–2). An impending apocalypse can be a useful rhetorical device in environmental rhetoric (Cox 227–239) if human agency provides an out. *Lost*'s characters certainly have this agency, but they are often making decisions based on gut instinct with save/destroy the world consequences, which makes for great story telling, but improbable real world actions.

## *Conclusion*

Ultimately, *Lost* was one of the most interesting, most innovative, and greatest television shows in television history. Audiences watched with incredible intensity and response, watching and re-watching episodes, writing blogs and internet posts, and purchasing *Lost* merchandise. *Lost* provoked thought and discussion about each episode in ways that other television shows have not. Given that "nature" in the form of the island serves as the backdrop for this program, understanding audience response and interpretation is important, even though the very meaning of the island is open to multiple interpretations. For example, in post-finale interviews, the actor who played Richard Alpert (Nestor Carbonell) noted that "The island was ultimately redemption," while a *Lost* blogger said that "The island is an actual place that is guarding the gateway to hell and the light seems to be the evil that we have to guard against" (quoted in Fernandez 9). Although audiences may not immediately connect *Lost* with nature, the island's symbolic representation of nature is a constant throughout the series. As Dahlstrom and Scheufele indicate, messages that are ubiquitous and consistent can affect audiences' assessment of environmental risk (54). Clearly, this analysis does not attempt to measure audience effect, but the show's representation of nature has some impact on how audiences think about nature.

Our analysis of *Lost*'s depiction of nature through human/nature dualism paradigms and apocalyptic rhetoric serves to illustrate that *Lost* is a broader allegory for understanding potentially apocalyptic environmental problems such as climate change and oil spills as well as natural disasters such as earthquakes, tsunamis, and hurricanes. *Lost*'s enduring popularity suggests that audiences strongly desire stories in which there are clear representations of good and evil, heroes and villains, and the possibilities to save or destroy the world. In this sense, *Lost* represents how audiences also desire the maintenance of nature/culture dualisms as well as simple solutions to our (environmental) problems. Climate change serves as one example of how publics and governments desire quick technological fixes for a save-the-world solution that is unlikely to emerge. Smerecnik and Renegar argue that capitalistic agency, such as in the oil company BP's marketing campaigns (and much of the climate change debate), is rooted in incrementalism, consumerism, and technologicalism that constrains human capacity and agency for environmental solutions (152–64). This type of capitalistic rhetoric that encourages consumers to do "a little bit better," will ultimately have little impact on the environment, especially given the environmental catastrophe of near apocalyptic dimensions in the April 2010 BP oil spill in the Gulf of Mexico. The BP oil spill is another example of how the U.S. American public demands quick response and solution. Public dissatisfaction with BP and the U.S. government response, particularly from President Obama, demonstrate our desires for a more *Lost*-like story. Evading environmental apocalypse is not as simple or easy as *Lost* storylines might suggest. In the series finale, the alternate reality/afterlife may also indicate that no matter what happens, everything will end up being okay. Surely audiences do not translate the simplicity of these messages to broader, real world environmental or social problems, but the placement of the island as nature and as a backdrop to *Lost* storylines sanitizes and reduces nature to a simple representation that reinforces the nature/culture dualism that shapes how audiences come to understand the natural world.

## WORKS CITED

Cox, J. Robert. "The Die Is Cast: Topical and Ontological Dimensions of the Locus of the Irreparable." *Quarterly Journal of Speech* 68 (1982): 227–239. Print.
Dahlstrom, Michael F., and Dietram A. Scheufelle. "Diversity of Television Exposure and Its Association with the Cultivation of Concern for Environmental Risks." *Environmental Communication: A Journal of Nature and Culture* 4:1 (2010): 54–65. Print.
Elliot, Nils L. *Mediating Nature*. New York: Routledge, 2006. Print.
Fernandez, Maria Elena. "'Lost' Islands of Thought: Some Viewers Adore 'The End.' Others Don't Feel Closure. All Still Have Questions." *Los Angeles Times* 25 May 2010: D9. Web. 27 July 2010.
Foust, Christina R., and William O'Shannon Murphy. "Revealing and Reframing Apocalyptic Tragedy in Global Warming Discourse." *Environmental Communication: A Journal of Nature and Culture* 3:2 (2009): 151–167. Print.
Haila, Yrjö. "Beyond the Nature-Culture Dualism." *Biology and Philosophy* 15 (2000): 155–175. Print.

Hart, Philip Solomon, and Anthony A. Leiserowitz. "Finding the Teachable Moment: An Analysis of Information-Seeking Behavior on Global Warming Related Websites During the Release of *The Day After Tomorrow*." *Environmental Communication: A Journal of Nature and Culture* 3:3 (2009): 355–366. Print.

Japp, Phyllis M., and Mark Meister. "Introduction: A Rationale for Studying Environmental Rhetoric and Popular Culture." *Enviropop: Studies in Environmental Rhetoric and Popular Culture*. Eds. Mark Meister and Phyllis M. Japp. Westport, CT: Praeger Publishers, 2002. 1–12. Print.

Kaplan, G., and L. Rogers. "Our Human Fear and Indifference: The Plight of the Orangutan." *The Neglected Ape*. Eds. Ronald D. Nadler, Biruté F. M. Galdikas, Lori K. Sheeran and Norm Rosen. New York: Plenum Press, 1995. 3–12. Print.

Kaye, Sharon, ed. *Lost and Philosophy: The Island Has Its Reasons*. Hoboken, NJ: Wiley-Blackwell, 2007. Print.

Opel, Andy. "*Monopoly™ the National Parks Edition*: Reading Neo-Liberal Simulacra." *Enviropop: Studies in Environmental Rhetoric and Popular Culture*. Eds. Mark Meister and Phyllis M. Japp. Westport, CT: Praeger Publishers, 2002. 31–44. Print.

Plumwood, Val. *Feminism and the Mastery of Nature*. New York: Routledge, 1993. Print.

Retzinger, Jean P. "Cultivating the Agrarian Myth in Hollywood Films." *Enviropop: Studies in Environmental Rhetoric and Popular Culture*. Eds. Mark Meister and Phyllis M. Japp. Westport, CT: Praeger Publishers, 2002. 45–62. Print.

Smerecnik, Karl R., and Valerie R. Renegar. "Capitalistic Agency: The Rhetoric of BP's Helios Power Campaign." *Environmental Communication: A Journal of Nature and Culture* 4(2): 2010. 152–171.

Sowards, Stacey K. "Identification Through Orangutans as Cyborgs: Destabilizing the Nature/Culture Dualism." *Ethics and the Environment* 11(2): 2006. 45–61. Print.

_____. "Rhetoric of the Perpetual Potential: A Case Study of the Environmentalist Movement to Protect Orangutans." *The Environmental Communication Yearbook*. Ed. Stephen P. Depoe. Mahwah, NJ: Lawrence Erlbaum Associates, Publishers, 2006. 115–135. Print.

Todd, Anne Marie. "Prime-Time Subversion: The Environmental Rhetoric of the Simpsons." *Enviropop: Studies in Environmental Rhetoric and Popular Culture*. Eds. Mark Meister and Phyllis M. Japp. Westport, CT: Praeger Publishers, 2002. 63–80. Print.

Vine, Richard. "Lost Ending: The Final Episode Reviewed." *Guardian Unlimited* 24 May 2010. Web. 27 July 2010.

# Securitizing the Island: The Other Others' Defense of Environmental Management

*J. L. Schatz*

## A Pilot into Our World

There is no doubt that the hit show *Lost* changed our world when it premiered in 2004, and there is no doubt that it will continue to shape us now that the show has ended. Todd Leopold of CNN put it this way, "After Sunday's *Lost* finale, we'll all find ourselves in a new world." Put differently, if we fail to heed the warnings within the show, this new world may be plagued by smoke monsters of our own creation as we remained trapped on our island of Earth. Of course, all successful popular culture artifacts construct worldviews that influence observers.[1] However, *Lost* is much more than just another successful show. Certainly, "enjoying *Lost* means having a deep, existential experience, one that connects with the themes basic to our human existence. *Lost* produces this kind of experience in an especially clear and direct way [that] can [...] help us understand why [...] other puzzle-solving programs [...] continue to keep our interest" (Barris 262). No doubt, if *Lost* did not have influence over its viewers it would not have been able to hook "Julie Jordan[,] her husband [and] the 'zillion[s of] others'" week after week who felt "marooned" after the show's conclusion (Dickerson). Nor would it have been able to inspire millions in Britain to wake up at five in the morning to catch the season finale as it premiered in the United States (BBC News). As a result of this devotion, *Lost* will continue to effectively capture the world's imagination even though the finale has now aired. And, put simply, it is precisely the imaginations that *Lost* has inspired that we must attend to in order to more accurately understand the world we live in today.

By way of example, one needs to look no further than the Law of the Sea Treaty, popularly known by policymakers and reporters as LOST. The treaty attempts to define the rights of nations to use the world's oceans for business, military ventures, and the management of natural resources.² Like *Lost*, LOST leaves nations navigating bodies of unending water in order to survive in terms of biodiversity and monetary profits. Like the characters of *Lost*, the treaty strives to harness the light at the center of the island to protect our existence from those who threaten it. Also similarly to *Lost*, where characters are constantly moments away from discovering the truth, LOST always remains minutes away from ratification only to have new criticisms arise to derail its endorsement.³ While LOST was created by a United Nation's mandate more than a decade before the television program aired, the parallels should not be disregarded. Neither should the naming of programs like National Missile Defense, which received the name Star Wars by President Reagan.⁴ In both cases, the politics behind the entertainment and the legislation are based on co-constitutive ideologies that inspire the future of media representations and government action. Put plainly, the way *Lost* conceives of protecting the island against characters who seek to harm it for their own benefit closely connects with the desire of LOST to protect the ocean. Unfortunately, the way both the characters and national governments strive to manage and protect the environment ends up producing violent outcomes that subsequently create new problems to be solved.

Throughout the entirety of *Lost*, characters repeatedly act in the best interest of the island to protect it for various reasons. Oftentimes they are acting in the name of survival. But even when they are motivated by short-term considerations, their actions are based upon doing what is necessary to create a better world. Sadly, little attention has been paid to the subject of considering the island itself as an environment even though whole books have been published on the question of what inspires various character motivations.⁵ These discussions are by no means irrelevant. Yet their failure to look at how characters' choices are informed by views of the island as an ecological entity ignores a discourse of environmental managerialism that permeates the show. Political theorist Timothy Luke explains how concepts

> like "survival" or "sustainability" [...] empower these masterful conceptualizers to inscribe the biological/cultural/economic order of the Earth's many territories as [a] continuous enviro-discipline to guarantee ecological fitness. [...] This complex is what must survive; human life will continue if such survival-promoting services continue. [...] As an environmental engine, the planet's ecology requires eco-engineers [...] and systems of green governmentality [...] to monitor and manage the system of systems which produce all these robust services [146–147].

Such eco-managerial attempts can easily be seen in the actions of characters such as Jacob, Benjamin Linus, Charles Widmore, Jack, Locke, and many others as they struggle to protect the island. It can also be discerned even in the case of the smoke monster who wants to get off the island in order to return to an environment where he can have unlimited access to all the services the Earth can offer. Sadly, "inserting human bodies into the[se] machineries [...] generates systems of bio-power" that only further enslave the characters of *Lost* internally or lead to their external demise (Luke 142).[6]

Ultimately, because *Lost* reveals how managerial techniques operate in the real world beyond the television set, it is important to delve deeper into the ecology that guides each character's choice during the show. Even Maarten Hajer, Member of The Hague's Spatial Planning and Environment Committee, believes that there is no doubt that "today's environmental issues are discursively created. [...] Calamities only become a political issue if they are constituted as such in environmental discourse [and] if story-lines are created around them that indicate the significance of the physical events [...] The discursive construction of reality thus becomes an important realm of power" (20–21). To evaluate how these discourses operate, we must consider their impact within the show itself and how the show is read by those who watch it in the current political climate. In order to do so, the rest of this chapter looks at how the characters within *Lost* square up against each other as they adopt different views of how to relate to the island. By looking at how Jack and Locke first oppose one another for different reasons depending on the season, I argue that, regardless of whether their motivations are based in faith of the intrinsic value of the island or the scientific drive for knowledge, the ultimate outcome is the same. This reading can then be readily paralleled to the relationship between Benjamin Linus and Charles Widmore, and then lastly again to that between Jacob and his brother. In each of these instances, we find that *Lost* replicates the same struggles going on within the island of Earth, which we have thus far failed to adequately protect despite governmental managerial attempts. And, in each of these instances, we find the end result is often irreversibly disastrous.

## *Managing a Way Through the Jungle*

Both Jack and Locke have radically different ways of approaching their existence on the island from the moment *Lost* hit the screen. "While Locke is the 'man of faith,' Jack is the 'man of science' [and] only trusts the experience of his senses. [...] Thus, when Jack first encounters Locke's claim that the island brought them there for a purpose, he rejects it vehemently, even telling Kate in the first season finale that they have a 'Locke problem'" (Lee 63–64). During the first few seasons, Jack understands his role on the island to be merely that of a doctor to take care of the survivors of Oceanic Airlines flight

815. In season one episodes such as "White Rabbit" (1.5) and "House of the Rising Sun" (1.6), Jack takes on the quest of ensuring the survival of the group by establishing water filtration systems, safety, and medical assistance. In doing so, he readily participates in a managerial discourse that shepherds many of the Oceanic 815 survivors into the caves. Later that season, we see in "All the Best Cowboys Have Daddy Issues"(1.11) that Jack's desire to go above and beyond the call of duty to save others is inspired by his drive to make up for his father's past mistakes. Meanwhile for Locke, we see him in early episodes such as "Walkabout" (1.4) talk of his destiny to overcome the limitations placed upon him. Later, in "Deus Ex Machina" (1.19), we see that Locke is also trying to make up for past events that include his father. Unlike Jack, he infuses his memories with a sense of fate. While the destiny that reconnects Locke with his father results in the theft of his kidney, the episode ends with that same sense of destiny being validated as Locke begs for a sign at the hatch when a light turns on. Here as well we find Locke doing everything in his power to act as demanded by what he perceives to be the island's bidding. During season three, "Locke's faith in the mystic power of the island [...] leads him to try to destroy all possible means of escape from the island," even when it means using violence against his friends (Lee 69).

While Jack and Locke's interpretation of events differ between reason and faith, their motivations are not only based upon a history of failed connections with their fathers but also upon a desire to do what is needed at all costs. As a result, the outcome of both characters' actions appear one and the same. In the case of Jack, he quickly resorts to torture and violence in episodes like "Confidence Man" (1.8) when dealing with Sawyer to obtain medicine for the safety of others. As for Locke, he willingly sacrifices Boone's life in serving the island's bidding when he asks Boone to crawl into a crashed plane in "Deus Ex Machina." Even though both Locke and Jack feel sorry for their mistakes, they both maintain that they did what was necessary. In fact, at several points throughout the second season, Locke comes to question the choices that he has made. Most famously, in the second season's finale, "Live Together, Die Alone" (2.23 and 2.24), Locke refuses to push the very same button he has so much faith in earlier during the season. Desmond tells Locke, "I'm sorry for whatever happened that made you stop believing, but it's all real." After an explosion of electromagnetic energy really does happen when the numbers aren't inputted, Locke regains his faith in the island's grand design. Jack also goes through a similar internal questioning in later episodes that eventually persuades him to replace Jacob as protector of the island as an act of faith even though he does not fully understand. As Jack leaves behind reason in the sixth season to increasingly adopt faith and question his own actions, Locke, whose appearance is assumed by the smoke monster, becomes obsessed with finding answers and getting off the island. Ultimately, since the motivations of both characters are represented as being for the greater good of those around them, despite their doubts and flip-flopping of roles, these changes are but blips on their paths to a securitized perfection.[7]

Once again, the parallel between *Lost* and reality should not be overlooked. Timothy Luke, in his article titled "The (Un)Wise (Ab)Use of Nature," explains how "Newer ecological discourses [...] articulate [...] refined efforts to sustainably develop [...] bigger global processes [...] by accepting small correctives against particular [...] interests. [...] Environmental justice movements [...] are not [...] about attaining [...] justice as [much as] they are about moving injustices more freely around in the environment." Here we find that both governments and activists in their quest to protect the environment do so in order to make up for past ecological mistakes. After the Gulf Oil Disaster, a litany of articles questioned whether the event would be President Obama's Katrina, culminating in Obama's going so far as to call it a war in the Gulf.[8] Such media connections demonstrate how new environmental problems we face today, which are supposedly being met with new solutions, call upon characters in the real world to act in the same way as Jack and Locke do. Outside the show, as governments strive to protect the Earth's environment, they establish a "regime of ecologized bio-powers [that] operate [...] through ethical systems of identity as much as it does [...] policy [...] Environments are spaces under police supervision [and] technocratic control" (Luke 1997). Within the show, Jack and Locke continuously lead other characters through regimes of control that follow either the rationale of what is best for the survivors or what is fated by the island. In either case, these connections are what make *Lost* such a smash hit. Put plainly, the characters' failed attempts to manage their island enables us to better understand how we are lost in our own political climate that has produced successive failures even after supposedly correcting for past mistakes.[9]

Not so coincidentally, for those of you who believe, the token justification for the United States to ratify the Law of the Sea Treaty (LOST) is to make up for America's past scorecard of environmental mismanagement. Citizens for Global Solutions' vice-president for government relations Don Kraus explains, "According to the bipartisan Joint Ocean Commission Initiative, oceans and coasts are severely threatened. [...] The commission cited accession to the LOS convention as the key step the United States must take to improve its score [to] preserve the marine environment and conserve [...] living species." Kraus explains that absent U.S. leadership in LOST, the oceans will be lost since the treaty will lack adequate enforcement mechanisms to protect natural resources. He believes that ending America's exceptionalist stance towards resource management is essential to keeping the Earth safe. Whether this is the role of manifest destiny and fate or just reasoned scientific evidence concerning the ocean's collapse is inconsequential because the end result is the same. LOST must be ratified. The waters must be navigated. The island must be found. Meanwhile, Kraus and other advocates ignore Article 193 of LOST that preserves the "sovereign right of States to exploit their natural resources." This not only enables the oceans to be owned and commodified by the will of nations through determining commercial and military navigation routes, but also allows limitless use of the ocean ecology as individual nation-states see fit.[10] Of course, Widmore also gets others to ignore how he profits from his own interest in protecting the island throughout *Lost* as well. Despite these kinds of oversights, LOST remains able to elicit a high amount of grassroots support even though it remains primarily focused on naval coordination between militaries. Perhaps this is why the smoke monster is continually able to persuade the other characters of *Lost* to follow him once he takes the form of Locke throughout season six even though they all know the real Locke is already dead.

Before getting too caught up in the reality and losing the warnings *Lost* beckons us to find, it is worth looking beyond the character dynamics of Jack and Locke alone. Charles Widmore and Benjamin Linus also follow a very similar script as the international regulatory bodies that the show fatefully forewarns. Soon after Ben's plans to control and manipulate the survivors of Oceanic 815 begin to unravel, he shifts to coercing them to act out of their best interest even after he has been responsible for their torture and imprisonment. He begins to ask for the survivors' trust in his knowledge even though he rarely reveals what he knows. This begins as early as "Every Man for Himself" (3.4), in which Ben convinces Sawyer that he has a device implanted in his heart that will kill him if his heart rate gets too high. It further culminates in the season three finale, "Through the Looking Glass" (3.22 and 3.23), in which he begs Jack, Locke, and the rest of the survivors to believe him that the people coming to rescue them are their enemies. It also continues into seasons four and five, when Ben convinces the characters of *Lost* to trust him in order to save the island. Meanwhile, Widmore uses similar tactics in his dealings with the survivors in general and Desmond in particular during the sixth season. We watch Widmore and Sun share a mutual interest in killing Ben in "Because You Left" (5.1) only to have it subsequently revealed in "Dead Is Dead" (5.12) that Widmore had once been the leader of the same group as Ben before Ben banished Widmore from the island. Later, in "Happily Ever After" (6.11), Widmore convinces Desmond to make a sacrifice by helping him protect the island in order to save "everyone he has ever loved," even after being put into an electromagnetic device that threatened to kill Desmond. This pattern with Widmore continues in episodes such as "Recon" (6.8), in which Sawyer agrees to help him deal with the smoke monster. Again and again, we see characters convinced they are acting for the greater good even though other interests are at play.

This backdrop of Ben and Widmore reveals how "*Lost* invites us to examine the process of how ideology works, and how [...] people buy into an ideology that is socially constructed without thinking that it is socially constructed[, demonstrating] the multiple ways in which otherness operates [to] create [...] fear and [...] an 'us vs. them'" mentality (Gaffney 140). Hence, even though Ben and Widmore were enemies of those they eventually try to work with, they convince the characters of *Lost* to side with them against a greater threat. Ringing true with reality, Daniel Deudney, Hewlett Fellow at the Center for Energy and Environmental Studies at Princeton University, explains,

> Another motive for speaking of environmental degradation as a threat to natural security is rhetorical: to make people respond to environmental threats with a sense of urgency. [...] Yet the national security mentality engenders an enviable sense of urgency [along with] a corresponding willingness to accept great personal sacrifice ... linked to war and "us against them" thinking. [...] Taken to an [...] extreme [...] seeing environmental degradation in a neighboring country as a national security threat could trigger various types of intervention and imperialism.

This is why Kraus believes that for LOST, "timing is critical" and that the U.S. must act immediately to save the oceans. It is also why both Ben and Widmore act with a sense of urgency based upon threats to the island even when it means sacrificing their own children, as it does for Ben in "The Shape of Things to Come" (4.9). As a consequence, LOST, alongside both Ben and Widmore, continues to gain support despite its historical inadequacies. Sadly, people continue to believe that it can now be gotten right before it is too late.

The shift to coercing others to follow their desires out of their own good instead of literally forcing them to act in required ways allows both Ben and Widmore's control to be ever more present. This happens even as these threats become increasingly amorphous. After returning from the island in season four's episode "The Economist" (4.3), we learn that Sayid now works for Ben even though he swears to Locke on the island, "The day I start trusting him is the day I would have sold my soul." Sayid ends up convinced by Ben that Widmore's people "don't deserve your sympathies" because it is the only way he can save his friends who did not get off the island and avenge his lost love. What makes Sayid all the more conflicted is the fact that throughout the flashes during this episode, he finds himself killing people simply because their names are on his list, absent any deeper reasoning. Similarly, in season five's "The Life and Death of Jeremy Bentham" (5.7), Widmore convinces

Locke that he is there to help Locke return to the island. Widmore tells him that "there is a war coming, John. And if you're not back on the island when that happens, the wrong side is going to win." It is left to speculation what precisely that wrong side is, especially since the villains and heroes have flipped roles so many times by this point in the series.

This change in rationale from external means of control (the guns and cages of early seasons) to internal ones is not a neutral gesture. As eloquently put by Michel Foucault,

> There has been a parallel shift in the right of death [to] the right of the sovereign [to] the social body to ensure, maintain, or develop its life. [...] But this formidable power of death [...] now presents itself as the counterpart of a power that exerts a positive influence on life [by] subjecting it to precise controls and comprehensive regulations. Wars are no longer waged in the name of a sovereign who must be defended; they are waged on behalf of the existence of everyone; entire populations are mobilized for the purpose of wholesale slaughter in the name of life necessity: massacres have become vital. It is as managers of life and survival [...] that so many regimes have been able to wage so many wars, causing so many men [sic] to be killed. [...] The atomic situation is now at the end point of this process: the power to expose a whole population to death is the underside of the power to guarantee an individual's continued existence [136–137].

This is why Jack can be convinced to believe that exploding a hydrogen bomb is for the greater good in "The Variable" (5.14) and why Locke's life is sacrificed to bring the returning Oceanic survivors back to the island to protect it. It is also why former Secretary of State Lawrence Eagleburger and U.S. Ambassador John Norton believe that the true value of LOST is to "support [...] our military [...] and [...] national security [by providing] legal certainty for U.S. naval vessels navigating the world's oceans [...] into [...] the largest economic zone." What we must secure ourselves against however remains amorphous. Instead, the need to protect both the island and humanity mandates that people follow even without a clear answer in mind. The crucial point here is realizing how these motivations lead to atrocities like the mass graves Ben creates for the bodies of the Dharma Initiative employees in "The Man Behind the Curtain" (3.20). For Widmore, who engages in his own acts of violence, a little money and manipulation can clean up any mess he may create. For the U.S., there is nothing a new treaty cannot solve.

These themes are also readily apparent with respect to Jacob even though, as he reveals to Richard in "Ab Aeterno" (6.9), he doesn't want to intervene directly. In fact, Jacob's desire to go unseen and allow others to do his bidding for their own best interest is exactly the internal mechanism of control upon which Widmore and Ben rely. And that same amorphousness of the mission eventually drives Richard to want to kill himself in "Dr. Linus" (6.7). However, Richard's insanity is not really Jacob's fault. We learn in "Across the Sea" that Jacob was raised to believe that he needs to protect the island at all costs. These costs even include having to kill his own brother to prevent the Man in Black from leaving the island and leading other humans to harness the light's energy. In turn, even though Jacob has no proof that these people are bad aside from his faith in what other people have told him, he is still willing to do what is necessary for the good of the island. Unfortunately, it is his actions that result in the creation of a smoke monster; a mistake, as Jacob admits in "What They Died For" (6.16). As a result of this mistake, he must find a candidate to replace him as protector of the island. Just as before, even as Jacob has made grave errors in the past, he asks the remaining survivors of Oceanic 815 to believe him. While Jack jumps at the opportunity, Sawyer makes a crack about how it will only worsen Jack's God complex. No doubt, now it would give Jack the authority to act for the island's interests once and for all because he has been anointed to do so. The episode ends with Jack's eyes stabbing into the darkness, ready to kill the smoke monster by doing whatever is necessary. What Jack does not realize, and where Jacob goes wrong once again, is in forgetting to acknowledge that the nebulous nature of the smoke monster's threat to "everything" is socially constructed by the environment in which they find themselves. By failing to acknowledge this, they set up the same cycle which produced a self-fulfilling prophecy in previous seasons, which by faith or reason must end in violence.[11] In short, every Other has its Other and every Other has their reason for why the island must be dealt with in one way or an-other.

It is this linkage of the greater good with the island that is of particular interest since "in the environmental sphere 'We'— not 'They'— are the 'enemy'" (Deudney). This is why it is only when Jack questions himself in episodes like "Lighthouse" (6.5) and "Everybody Loves Hugo" (6.12), or when Ben submits himself to be judged by the smoke monster in "Dead Is Dead" (5.12), that these characters attempt to purge themselves from the enemy within and to constrain their actions for the betterment of the island. Even though this process happens internally, it is not without its external motivations. Certainly, there is a constant struggle to remain on the right side — despite how often that side keeps changing. Whether motivated by faith or by logic, the various characters of *Lost* struggle to either have the authority to know what is best (as in the instance of being a doctor or being anointed by Jacob) or the knowledge and know-how to save everyone or get them off the island (as in the instance of Widmore's wealth or Ben's vast connections). Thus, while both seasons five and six rely heavily on imagery that pits light against dark, it is important to remember that just because someone is dark does not mean that they are evil. Even the shabbily-clothed Others of seasons one and two, who once appeared as savages, had their noble intentions. No doubt, "in contrast to a number of movies and other television shows where good and evil are clearly [...] demarcated, *Lost* shows the ethical complexities of individuals and the situations in which they find themselves [just as in] life [where] things are rarely black and white" (Wrisley 49). This is why viewers waited anxiously for the final episode to air, seeking to discover who would save the island, who would survive, and who we should side with. But as this happened, viewers were reminded that no matter how the show ended, it was the course of the adventure of being lost that was integral to understanding how we arrived here in the first place. Therefore, now that the show is over, as we look outward to the ecology we so often strive to protect, we would be wise to remember how there can never be a single answer to our environmental problems. To try and create one will only result in the violent solutions that occur on *Lost* and what will be the almost inevitable outcome of LOST as militaries clash over the boundaries stipulated by the treaty and their right to resource sovereignty.

## *Refusing to Forget After the Finale*

What merits attention is more than simply the coincidence of the name of the television show and the acronym for this particular piece of environmental legislation. Certainly, any number of television shows could be compared to any number of governmental policies. What is significant is how the themes that media coverage of both *Lost* and LOST emphasize influence viewers who watch at home, follow online, and even participate as citizens. As the late professor of history and future studies at Binghamton University, Warren Wagar, once explained,

> What emerges from recent research into the history of science fiction is that writers of science fiction foresaw nearly every horror [...] decades before it materialized and that, as soon as it did materialize, every horror yielded a profusion of tales developing its implications, good or evil, for the future of humankind. Fiction anticipated truth and truth provoked more fiction. Nothing was too strange for either one.

No doubt, "as we see in *Lost*, the ethical situations that we may confront in life are terribly complex and difficult — even if we are not on an island" (Wrisley 55). Likewise, the ethical situations we see on the island remain influenced by the realities across the ocean that some characters chose to believe do not exist. As we look to *Lost* in this new era, we must be aware of how the gap that we transverse between the fictions we witness and the realities we imagine has the same power over our identity as how what takes place outside of the island influences what happens on it, and vice versa. Hence, we must seek to dispel readings that mandate which side one is on regardless of whether that side happens to represent good or evil, truth or fiction, reality or television. While some will claim that any resemblance *Lost* bears to current environmental policymaking is purely coincidence, others would say that it is destiny for the two to be aligned. Surely the producers of *Lost* keep up with current events at least as much as politicians watch television. Regardless, however we look at it, we must remember that as we are captivated by our fantasies, those very fantasies internally influence the managerialist tendencies within environmental planning.

In turn, while the island can shift around in time, our understanding of the present is shaped by past histories as well as future predictions of where we are heading, both fictional and otherwise. What *Lost* elucidates for us is the endeavor of being lost in our attempts to protect the island from prior mistakes and supposedly inevitable outcomes. While the characters of *Lost* defer to either reasoned appeals to authority or transcendental selection, this need not be the case.

> Despite the aspiration to the objective and neutral ideal of science, scientific expertise is [...] uncertain, contested and normative. [...] Science has in many issue areas taken on a post-normal character: facts are uncertain, values are in dispute, stakes are high and decisions are urgent [since hazards] cannot be adequately resolved by the traditional routines of "normal" science [...] There is a shift in emphasis from a unitary notion of science to an emphasis on different knowledge(s) [...] This implies questioning the borders between science and non-science, expert and lay knowledge, universal and local knowledge [as well as questioning] who is the legitimate expert [Baumlckstrand].

In life we must live those uncertainties and not rush to conclusions. This is why policies like the International Whaling Commission's 1988 ban on whaling continues to fail in the same way LOST neglects to fully address past failures.[12] As such, we must stop looking externally to determine our motivations for how to change the world or else our solutions are doomed to be quick fixes that raise more questions and similar problems. Instead, we should strive to escape the pressing need to secure our environments and discover the truth behind our universe. On *Lost*, Dogen warns Sayid in "Sundown" (6.6) that "If you allow him to speak it is already too late," echoing the Man in Black's words to Richard in "Ab Aeterno." Outside the show, the moment we try to grasp at environmental security, we will be doomed to step right back onto that island of self-created prophecies managed by our desires to conjure new amorphous smoke monsters from the society around us. Rather, we ought to embrace the unknown for what it is and not for how it can be instrumentalized to alter what we take for reality. From there, we can learn to act without the rigid borders upon which geopolitics and factionalized fictions of good and evil enact their dramas.

## Notes

1. Professor of Political Science at Arizona State University, Roxanne Doty, argues convincingly that popular constructions of reality influence U.S. policymakers and their constituents. She explains, "we [must] broaden our conception of [...] where foreign policy takes place [Foreign] policy making can also extend beyond the realm of official government institutions. The reception as meaningful of statements revolving around policy situations depends on how well they fit into the general system of representation in a given society. Even speeches and press conference statements produced for specific purposes [...] must make sense and fit with what the general public takes as 'reality.'" That conception of reality by the public is subsequently shaped by both the everyday news and the fictions that surround us since through both we discern concepts of morality, identity, and meaning.

2. See Wikipedia's entry on the United Nations Convention on the Law of the Sea for a general overview on the components of the treaty that the United Nations mandates in regards to maritime law.

3. While the treaty "has evolved over the last 50 years [...] almost every country on the planet has ratified the convention ... except the United States" (Porter). "In 1982, Ronald Reagan, concerned about the treaty's implications for our sovereignty and national security, formally rejected LOST[. However, in] 1994, William [...] Clinton [...] negotiated a parallel 'Agreement' that purported to address Mr. Reagan's concerns — and urged ratification. Since then, LOST has gathered dust in the bowels of the U.S. Senate Foreign Relations Committee [...] [but in 2007 it once again found itself] on a fast track to ratification" (North). However, despite Vice President Joe Biden being one of LOST's original supporters, the treaty still has not been ratified.

4. "Playing Secret Service agent Brass Bancroft, Ronald Reagan zapped an enemy plane with a beam weapon in his 1940 film 'Murder in the Air' [while as] president in 1983, he launched the Star Wars program. There is clearly a difference between the two events, but how much? Should the blame for the intercontinental ballistic missile, a descendant of rockets invented by Robert H. Goddard under the direct inspiration of H. G. Wells's *The War of the Worlds*, go to Goddard or Wells[?] Each has a way of moving and shaking the other" (Wagar).

5. I'm thinking here mainly of the prior collection of articles on *Lost* edited by Sharon M. Kaye that I quote throughout this chapter. They all neglect to deal with the show from an ecological perspective. Beyond Kaye's book, there is an endless list of articles, commentary, and fan reviews that look at *Lost* purely from a human perspective of freedom versus fate. The previous chapter in this book by Stacey K. Sowards and Carlos A. Tarin is one of the few that problematizes anthropocentric readings of the environment within the show.

6. For a more complete reading on how bio-power operates within *Lost* see Giancarlo Lombardi's chapter in this book on panopticism. For now, it will suffice to say that bio-power is a system of control that operates by motivating people to act in the name of their own well-being and not simply just for the good of another. Michel Foucault, in his groundbreaking books *The History of Sexuality* and *Discipline and Punish*, argues that it was at the point in history where the state began to articulate its needs as being in the best interest of the people that they were able to mobilize the masses to act however the sovereign saw fit. Perhaps this is why the smoke monster takes the form of Locke to gather followers to do his bidding out of their interests and not his alone.

7. See Francis Fukuyama's 1992 *New York Time's* best-selling book, *The End of History and the Last Man Standing*, to see the same tendency within political think tanks to represent past errors, whether it be Vietnam or the newest oil spill, as only minor mistakes on the road to America's liberal democratic perfection as the world's most trusted global police officer. Hence, in a similar fashion as both Jack and Locke, anything that America may feel sorry for still comes

from a desire to protect the greater good and can be forgiven once the answer of a perfect managerialism can be found.

8. After so much use of this phrase immediately after the BP oil spill even members of the White House staff began to deploy it. In the weeks that followed it was clear that "Obama officials [did] not want Deepwater Horizon to become their Hurricane Katrina" (Grier). Likewise, "The use of martial imagery throughout the President's June 15 Oval Office address was remarkable. He spoke of 'the battle we are waging against an oil spill that is assaulting our shores and our citizens.' He wished to inform us of 'what our battle plan is going forward'" (Kenny).

9. As *Washington Post* writer Hank Stuever put it, "America, it's so obvious: Millions of you loved 'Lost' because you feel lost. [...] 'Lost' leaves us [...] with a spooky idea of the 21st century thus far. It was the perfect show for our frustrated '00s era, in which no one had to answer for anything much — not for the real estate and Wall Street busts, the levee floods, the bad war intelligence. While we fought elusive enemies in distant lands; while we vanished down our personal, broadband rabbit holes; while we doubted our elected officials; while we spent ourselves into impossible debts, 'Lost' was along for the ride, with its unsolvable puzzles and its exhilarating but dorky extremes of fandom culture." See also William Spanos' groundbreaking book, *America's Shadow*, which covers how Vietnam has been ontologically figured as America's great mistake. He argues that since Vietnam the United States has strived to make amends through supposedly just interventions that have led to the routine invasions of Iraq, Afghanistan, and beyond.

10. As revealed in a *New York Times* article, "Under certain provisions of the Law of the Sea treaty, countries can extend claims to seabed resources beyond the standard 200 nautical mile limit if they can make a case that such features are a natural prolongation of the sloping edge of the shelf. In this case, the result could mean an eventual claim by the United States of thousands of extra square miles of undersea real estate" (Revkin).

11. Drawing the connection between fiction and foreign policy, professor of Cultural and Political Geography at Durham University, David Campbell explains, "As an imagined community, the identity of a state is the effect of ritualized performances [...] that operate in its name or in the service of its ideals. Discourses of danger and the multifarious ethical powers of segregation [...] establish a geography of evil that inscribes the boundaries of inside / outside. One would expect, in this context, that the boundaries of (the United States of) America would be written and reproduced within the parameters of this logic. [...] But what has been affirmed is a fictional representation of the past [where] the logic of identity has succumbed to the temptation of otherness [through] a fictive paragon [that] has been presented as a regulative ideal by which to make judgments" (130).

12. Independent news reporter Sandy Smith points out that while the International Whaling Commission (IWC) is suppose to impose a moratorium on all whaling since 1988, "Japanese whaling boats have caught more than 11,000 whales since that year. Japan has been able to do this because of another provision in the IWC protocol that allows member states to issue permits to themselves to kill whales for scientific research purposes." Also see Animal Planet's *Whale Wars* for a look at how both sides of the battle utilize the IWC to justify their actions either for or against the whales.

# Works Cited

Barris, Jeremy. "*Lost* and the Problem of Life After Birth." *Lost and Philosophy: The Island Has Its Reasons*. Ed. Sharon Kaye. Oxford: Blackwell Publishers, 2008. 253–262. Print.
Baumlckstrand, Karin. "Scientisation vs. Civic Expertise in Environmental Governance: Ecofeminist, Eco-modern and Post-modern Responses." *Environmental Politics* 13:4 (December 2004). 695–714. Print.
BBC News. "Sky to Screen *Lost* Finale as It Airs in the U.S." 21 May 2010. Web. 27 May 2010.
Deudney, Daniel. "Environment and Security: Muddled Thinking." *The Bulletin of the Atomic Sciences* 47:3 (April 1991). 23–28. Print.

Dickerson, Brad. "*Lost* fans feel marooned as show ends," *Highlands Today*. May 18, 2010. Web. 27 May 2010.
Doty, Roxanne. "Foreign Policy as Social Construction: A Post-Positivist Analysis of U.S. Counterinsurgency Policy in the Philippines." *International Studies Quarterly*. 1994. Print.
Eagleburger, Lawrence, and John Norton. "Taking Exceptions Opportunity on the Oceans America Wins with the Law of the Sea Treaty." *The Washington Post*. 30 July 2007. Web. 6 June 2010.
Foucault, Michel. *The History of Sexuality: An Introduction*. New York: Vintage Books, 1978. Print.
Fukuyama, Francis. *The End of History and the Last Man*. New York: Simon and Schuster, 1992. Print.
Gaffney, Karen. "'The Others Are Coming': Ideology and Otherness in *Lost*." *Lost and Philosophy: The Island Has Its Reasons*. Ed. Sharon Kaye. Oxford: Blackwell Publishers, 2008. 136–147. Print.
Grier, Peter. "Ken Salazar's Task: Make Sure BP Oil Spill Isn't Obama's Katrina," *The Christian Science Monitor*. 18 May 2010. Web. 27 May 2010.
Hajer, Maarten. *The Politics of Environmental Discourse: Ecological Modernization and the Policy Process*. Oxford: Oxford University Press, 1995. Print.
Kenny, Jack. "Obama's War on the BP Oil Spill." *The New American*. 20 June 2010. Web. 22 June 2010.
Kraus, Don. "Time to Ratify the Law of the Sea." *Foreign Policy in Focus*. 6 June 2007. Web. 6 June 2010.
Leopold, Todd. "Beyond the 'Lost' Horizon." *CNN*. 20 May 2010. Web. 27 May 2010.
Luke, Timothy. "Enivornmentality as Green Governmentality." *Discourses of the Environment*. Ed. Eric Darier. Oxford: Blackwell Publishers, 1999. 121–151. Print.
_____. "The (Un)Wise (Ab)Use of Nature: Environmentalism as Globalized Consumerism?" *International Studies Association*. 18–22 March 1997. Web. 27 Oct 2010.
North, Oliver. "Law of the Sea Treaty on Fast Track to Ratification." *Fox News*. 12 October 2007. Web. 27 May 2010.
Porter, Keither. "Law of the Sea Treaty: No More 'Wild West' on the 'High Seas,'" *About.com*. 4 September 2007. Web. 27 May 2010.
Revkin, Andrew. "Arctic Melt Yields Hints of Bigger U.S. Seabed Claim." *New York Times*. 12 February 2008. Web. 6 June 2010.
Smith, Sandy. "Japanese take advantage of loophole in whaling moratorium." *HULIQ*. 6 Jan 2010. Web. 27 May 2010.
Spanos, William. *America's Shadow: An Anatomy of Empire*. Minneapolis: University of Minnesota Press, 2000. Print.
Stuever, Hank. "'Lost' or not, we're still at loose ends." 21 May 2010. Web. 27 May 2010.
Wagar, Warren. "Truth and Fiction, Equally Strange: Writing About the Bomb." *American Literary History* 1:2 (Summer 1989). 448–457. Print.
Wrisley, George. "The Island of Ethical Subjectivism: Not the Paradise of *Lost*." *Lost and Philosophy: The Island Has Its Reasons*. Ed. Sharon Kaye. Oxford: Blackwell Publishers, 2008. 49–59. Print.

# We Have to Go Back: *Lost* After 9/11

*Jesse Kavadlo*

The television show *Lost* debuted in September 2001. It revolved around a group of strangers haphazardly thrown together with little more than the clothes on their backs. Despite individual differences, they needed to work together to escape from their unknown location — somewhere unspecified in the Pacific — to find their way back to America.

But wait, you're thinking: *Lost* debuted in 2004. And it was more much complicated, and far less clichéd, than my summary. Yet everything in the above paragraph is true, except perhaps for the first word, "the." The *Lost* I'm describing is not the *Lost*— it was a reality TV show with the same name, developed to compete against other early 2000s hits like *Survivor*. This forgotten *Lost* was cancelled just a month into its run, in part because of legal and logistical challenges following the attacks of September 11, 2001, but mostly because network executives believed that the "real-life terrorist attacks would lure viewers away from faux reality entertainment shows," including the now-forgotten *The Mole II* and *The Runner*, both also ill-fatedly introduced in September 2001 (Friedman and Goetzl).

Yet the similarities, beyond the name alone, between these two *Lost*s may be revealing in retrospect. For while the first, failed *Lost* may have seemed too topical in the immediate aftermath of 9/11— who wanted to see more threatened Americans or a show about people sneaking into the country?— the second *Lost*, the one that viewers came to know, love, and follow through six intense seasons, may have been more of its time than people have acknowledged.

When *Lost* premiered, its most distinctive features seemed to be its desert island genre mash-up — *Castaway* meets *Gilligan's Island* meets *Survivor*— now infused with the unusual particulars of life on *this* outlandish island. Yes, they faced the practical problems of food, shelter, medical care, and potential rescue, and the ethical issues of leadership and cooperation, but mostly they — and by extension, viewers — were fascinated by the metaphysical mysteries of healed paralysis, resurrections, polar bears, and, of course, the smoke monster.

And then there were, of course, the characters — their personalities, conflicts, development, redemptions, and in many cases, even their deaths. Their variety seemed as indebted to 2000s-era reality TV as the island premise, replacing *Survivor*'s influence for that of the *Real World*'s cast-to-clash archetypes: the straight man, the hothead, the druggie, and the bad girl, along with novel additions that even reality TV wouldn't have touched: a pregnant woman, a prepubescent boy, a paraplegic (as we would discover), a couple that speaks no English (or so we thought), an older (interracial) couple, semi-incestuous step-siblings, an ex–Republican Guard Iraqi torturer, an obese bilingual schizophrenic (although supernatural explanations would supersede psychological ones), and many more.

Yet now, beyond setting, characterization, and even story, two interconnected aspects of the show seem most striking in retrospect. First, the style: fractured and fragmented use of time and narrative, shifting perspective, and, seemingly straight from the theories of Jacque Derrida, a constant deferring of meaning through constantly differed storylines. Second, the philosophical and psychological implications that this style bears on America in the 2000s. Taken together, the changing narrative devices — flashback, flash-forward, time travel, and "flash-sideways," as Losties referred to the alternate storyline of season six — mirrored the ways in which *Lost* gauged and updated the fears — and, in Freudian reversal, desires and wish fulfillment — of a country reeling from its worst terrorist attack in history and the launch of two wars across the ocean, yet at the same time, the ways in which these plights were experienced, by most Americans, as television.

While most of the critical attention to *Lost* has focused on its inventive and compelling visual style, a few critics have also noted the relationship between its storytelling and its cultural relevance. As J. Wood, in *Living* Lost: *Why We're All Stuck on the Island*, explains, "*Lost* performs a very necessary function: It gives a narrative (and a safety-distant context) to a real-felt sense of trauma. By giving these abstract ideas a tangible narrative with a beginning and ending each week, that sense of terror is contained by the show, and this becomes something that might actually be manageable" (ix). Or, as Mikal Gilmore explains in a *Rolling Stone* piece barely longer than this quotation, *Lost*'s characters "are lost in their times — which is to say they are lost in our times, the uncertain reality of post–9/11. Planes hurtled from the sky that morning in 2001 and brought with them fear and irresolution; we now live with an unanticipated horror at our center. Like *Lost*'s survivors, we can't forecast the turns that horror will take, and we can't immediately fathom our own part in it." Finally, writing in *Slate*'s TV Club, Seth Stevenson echoes Gilmore:

When the show debuted in 2004, I think it was pretty clearly influenced by the post–9/11 context. An airplane no longer controlled by its pilots. A bewildering, catastrophic incident. Community forming in the wake of tragedy. Ben Linus, with his sinister methods and veiled motives, called to mind the paranoia of the anthrax-in-envelopes days.

Yet Stevenson, like me, seems reluctant to use the word "allegory," with its suggestion of a true meaning behind its emblems; unlike for Plato, *Lost*'s cave has meant many things, and sometimes a cave is just a cave. Despite — or perhaps, because of — its sheer length as a serial narrative and its concomitant intricacies, *Lost* has consistently been too elusive and ambiguous for such direct equivalencies. Rather than eschewing such equivalencies, however, Chadwick Matlin responds to Stevenson with further specifics, even using the word "allegory":

> Seth, if you want to talk about *Lost* as a reflection of its times, I'm more than eager. I can deliver a dissertation on how *Lost*'s time-travel season was written during a U.S. election that revisited the past as it looked into the future. I can wax philosophic on how this season's dual-timeline approach corresponds to an administration that has changed everything and nothing in Washington, and a viewing public that doesn't know which narrative to believe. And then there's Ben Linus, the best allegory for the Wall Street debacle television has provided. Ben built his power on a foundation of lies and deceit. It was followed by an inevitable crash and then (a potential) resurrection.

While Matlin does not quite deliver a dissertation, quickly shifting to the ways in which *Lost* has not changed and other topics, I want to emphasize his reading of *Lost* as an expression of our increasingly relativistic world, a common post–1960s lamentation but one that deserves reiteration after 9/11. Viewers, especially of a show steeped in the paranormal from the beginning, could be expected to accept continuously updated, retroactive explanations and continuously revised continuities; the same cannot be said of an invasion of Iraq based on erroneous intelligence, suspicious treatment of prisoners and detainees, and economic meltdowns that treat mortgages the way *Lost* treats storylines — constantly shifting, constantly differed and deferring. Again and again in the 2000s, viewers, and Americans in general, have been told that everything we thought we knew previously turned out to be mistaken, and that no one could have foreseen the current crisis. After 9/11, *Lost*— as well as reality TV and a number of other shows, films, and novels — allowed fans to find pleasure, rather than dismay, in narrative twists, surprises, reversals, and shifting justifications. The good storyteller, unlike the good leader, is entitled to be — *must* be — a good liar.

Even so, this emphasis on context, *Lost* as political parable, risks reducing the show to a cardboard morality play, and *Lost* is indisputably top-notch television. It is more than highbrow soap opera, the now-familiar tangled yarns of love triangles, betrayals, amnesia, coincidences, and returns from the dead, this time tricked out with philosophical name-dropping and postmodern bells and whistles. But as Wood and *Slate*'s writers suggest, context does matter, and certainly some of *Lost*'s success was due to its being the right show in the right place at the right time, a way for Americans to experience what felt like the escapist thrills of fantasy and science fiction but may also have provided a safe psychological and narrative outlet for the genuine trepidations gripping America. *Time* magazine concluded that the 2000s were the worst decade in American history (not even just recent history), vacillating between calling it "the Decade from Hell, or the Reckoning, or the Decade of Broken Dreams, or"—you guessed it—"the Lost Decade" (Serwer). If the name the Lost Generation had not already been coined by Gertrude Stein to describe the writers, artists, and expatriates unmoored by the pointless carnage of World War I, then that label would surely suit us now.

Indeed, as Gilmore and Stevenson suggest, *Lost*'s premise, imagery, sustained conflicts, and mysteries that bordered on conspiracies borrowed overtly from representations most frequently associated with 9/11: the premise of the plane crash itself, from the pilot through the concluding overhead image of "The End" (6.17 and 6.18), through the show's recurring conceits of Iraq, torture, air marshals, paranoia, the ways in which people from different backgrounds alternately mistrust each other and band together, the presence of infiltrators and Others in our midst, and the tensions between faith, reason, and coincidence. The airplane, for 9/11 and for *Lost*, came to symbolize the delicate, porous intersections between people the world over, perhaps a narrative convenience to bring disparate characters together, a contemporary version of John Ford's *Stagecoach* (1939)—or even Chaucer's pilgrimage in *The Canterbury Tales*.

The airplane—for 9/11, for *Lost*—also represents opposition and paradox: freedom vs. security; strength vs. vulnerability; destinations vs. liminal spaces; separation vs. connection; closeness vs. distance. And certainly 9/11 itself represents the greatest kinds of things lost—the lives lost, of course, but also the missing persons flyers that covered New York City after the attacks, even the moral direction and post–Cold War stability lost. *Lost* managed to embody each, but with the safe, requisite distance of a familiar, even corny, island conceit. If Manhattan was too obvious an island setting, if the first *Lost*'s reality TV was too close to home, then *Lost*'s unnamed, unclaimed island could provide the appropriate outlet for our post 9/11 fears, and our desire ultimately, not to be lost, but to be found—or, perhaps, to escape.

Yes, *Lost* is more than life-after-9/11's requisite components reshuffled, despite its preponderance of plane crashes, an island, torture, and a hiding, shape-shifting presence that kills people: the smoke monster is the ultimate force of terror on the island. Much of the show's resistance to allegory stems from its equal resistance to Manichean separations of good and evil: who on the island is unambiguously good—or evil? Otherwise, *Lost* would more closely resemble other TV shows of its time, *24* and *Heroes*. *24* explicitly addresses post–9/11 fears of terror, providing wish fulfillment in its straightforward solution: masculine muscle, the autonomous hero who single-handedly foils the unequivocal terrorists' plots. *Heroes*, despite its sci-fi trappings, squarely places the possibility of a manmade disaster in New York City at its center. Like *Lost*, both shows complicate chronology and narrative. In addition, like the movies *Crash* (2004) and *Babel* (2006), *24*, *Heroes*, and *Lost* all suggest significant links between seeming strangers, the ways in which the world after 9/11 seems smaller, more connected, and closer—for better and worse—as a result. But *Lost*'s moral complexity is greater; unlike *24*, the only bomb on *Lost* is detonated by our heroes, not ostensible terrorists. And the only plane to crash was the one metaphysically hijacked by our beloved Lostaways, who knew that their presence would cause the plane to crash on the island without knowing whether the other passengers would become collateral damage.

*Lost*'s treatment of 9/11 imagery, however, does more than play narrative games, or even just create fear and suspense. Instead, *Lost*'s distinctive narrative features, combined with its 9/11 tropes, create a kind of wish fulfillment that balances the show's mystery. The fantasy amidst the fear is crystallized in Jack's exhortation during the finale of season three that "We have to go back," a statement that, appropriately enough, applies retroactively to seasons one and two and foreshadows four, five, and six, as we will see.

Up until season three, *Lost* had alternated between a narrative present on the island with recurring flashes into an individual character's past. We *did* have to go back—to the characters' lives before the fated plane crash. *Lost*'s flashbacks, in its post–9/11 context, like the plane itself, supports the notion that the show's narrative structures were not separate from or incidental to its thematic tensions—rather, it epitomized them. Our characters, like we ourselves, could only understand the crisis of the present by delving into the past. Writing in *Newsweek* just a month after the 9/11 attacks, Fareed Zakaria asked, "Why Do They Hate Us?" without needing to provide a specific pronoun antecedent in his title for "they." Yet he also knew to preface his subsequent analysis this way:

> To the question "Why do the terrorists hate us?" Americans could be pardoned for answering, "Why should we care?" The immediate reaction to the murder of 5,000 innocents is anger, not analysis. Yet anger will not be enough to get us through what is sure to be a long struggle. For that we will need answers. The ones we have heard so far have been comforting but familiar.

*Lost*, in this sense, is completely unlike its desert island forebears. It was far less concerned with getting its castaways off the island than in understanding, epistemologically, how they wound up there in the first place. As the mysteries of the island unfolded, the flashbacks provided further and further evidence of furtive connections and coincidences between the characters. Several proved solvable and concrete, such as Jack and Claire's shared parentage. Others were explained much later, by introducing Jacob and his quest for candidates. Still others, like the meaning and import of the Numbers, were never resolved at all. Taken together, though, this accumulation of correlations, represented by the consistent juxtapositions between past and present, began to suggest an unlikely combination of concerns, concerns that again mirror *Lost*'s time: religion, paranoia, conspiracy, and quantum physics. For the believer, like John Locke and Mr. Eko; for the paranoiac, as Hugo, Desmond, Rousseau, and others have at times seemed; for the con man and the plotter, as Sawyer, Ben, and Charles Widmore have at times been; for the quantum physicist, like Marvin Candle, Eloise Hawking, and Daniel Faraday: everything happens for a reason, everything is significant, and everything is connected.

Of course, everything happens for a reason, everything is significant, and everything is connected for three other groups as well: gifted storytellers, their most avid fans, and die-hard conspiracy theorists. *Lost*'s flashbacks proved the best narrative device to merge plots of every kind: narrative plots, conspiracy plots, and funeral plots, as many major characters, beginning with Boone, began to die or disappear. This intersection between *Lost*'s form and content—flashback as editing and as metaphor—was striking even in the pilot, a title that for any other show would be the generic term for the test episode but here becomes a kind of dark, even ironic, allusion to the plane crash, an early introduction to death (the actual pilot in the pilot dies horrifically), or even to the key theme of *Lost* in general: who, metaphorically or literally, is flying this plane? (Thankfully Lapidus survived the submarine explosion, or no one would have gotten off the island at the series' end.) Put in other ways: who is the group's leader: Jack, Sawyer, or Locke? Who will Kate choose: Jack or Sawyer? Who are the Candidates—and who will inherit Jacob's role? Who is in control: Jacob, the Man in Black (or, as I like to call him, UnLocke), or Charles Widmore? Who truly understands the island: again, Jacob, MIB, Widmore—or Eloise Hawking, Daniel Faraday, or Desmond Hume? And finally: who will be found, who will remain, and who will die? The series progressed from the flashbacks necessary to develop connections towards the revelation that Jacob's hand, or touch, was behind those connections. Jacob's candidate-selection process mirrors the contestant-elimination structure of reality television. After nearly all the names have been crossed off the list, Jack seems to be the last — succeeded, finally, by Hugo. *Lost*'s initial premise may have been similar to its same-named, ill-fated reality-TV counterpart and *Survivor* knock-off, but so is its conclusion: who remains on the island? Who goes home? And what is the reward? *Survivor*'s goal, to remain last on the island, now seems even more applicable to *Lost*. And in the aftermath of 9/11, questions of power and control could be played for *Survivor*'s bathos or *Lost*'s pathos.

As flashbacks changed to a literal attempt to go back, and then to time travel and flashing sideways, each season's new alternate storylines, timelines, and constantly postponed but evolving discoveries, the cliffhangers and thrills that the show is famous for, continued to suggest our post–9/11 yearning to go back and remake, go back and fix, that which in life remains stubbornly in the past. In the end, both our suspense and our satisfaction comes from the characters' ability to keep going back — back narratively, psychologically, chronologically, and geographically — even as, or precisely because, in real life, as viewers, we cannot. Each season still maintained what might be thought of as its ongoing present, the saga of the survivors stranded on the island. But while the first seasons alternated between that narrative present and flashbacks that delved into the particular past and interior of one individual character per episode, the show switched gears and pulled a remarkable storytelling stunt for the finale of season three: that what viewers initially experienced as a flashback turned out to be a flash forward, the future after the castaways have been recovered. In this reversal, the show ushered in a powerful new narrative conceit, but also a powerful new post–9/11 metaphor.

The present-to-flashback structure was inventive, unusual for TV, and extensive, if still a reasonably common literary and film device. Jack's season three pronouncement, however, provided the satisfying confusion and excitement of a perfect twist. Having exhausted the flashback — and flashbacks within flashbacks, a televisual version of the pluperfect tense in grammar — it then shifted, and surprised the audience again, by flashing forward in time: that we were seeing something other than what we thought we were seeing, but we only know that in retrospect. Bearded, alcoholic Jack is trying to go back to the island from which he had spent the first two seasons trying to escape. And as the country's attitude toward 9/11 shifted, so did *Lost*'s metaphor: we had been desperate to heal, to recover, and come together, but also to declare war and exact vengeance on someone, anyone.

In the confusion overlapping *Lost*'s debut and continuation, perhaps America — ironically or appropriately, depending on one's political persuasion — became nostalgic for the immediate aftermath of the trauma. As TV political personality Glenn Beck describes in his "9-12" website, "The 9-12 Project is designed to bring us all back to the place we were on September 12,

2001. The day after America was attacked we were not obsessed with Red States, Blue States or political parties. We were united as Americans, standing together to protect the greatest nation ever created" ("The 9-12 Project"). (The website's recurring references to America's Founding Fathers suggest a desire to travel back in time even farther.) Beck, despite crocodile tears to nonpartisanship, takes this notion of having to go back to its reactionary extreme. As fiction, however, *Lost* is more subtle and supple: the plane crashes of 9/11, like the crash on the island, have become our postmodern primal scene, our national and narrative shock, and as a country, as a group of characters, we yearn to return to the site of the trauma in order to relive it, even as its repetition does not ease, and may even exacerbate, the pain.

Season three, post-island Jack is a textbook case of post-traumatic stress disorder, experiencing all of its key symptoms, from "feeling emotionally numb" and "difficulty maintaining close relationships" to "overwhelming guilt or shame" and "self-destructive behavior, such as drinking too much." The key symptom, however, ahead of each of these, is "flashbacks, or reliving the traumatic event for minutes or even days at a time" (Mayo Clinic).

The cinematic and psychological overlap of the word "flashback" is illuminating, and the return to the island makes the flashback palpable, but *Lost* did not truly exploit the chronological ambiguities and instabilities attendant to an age demarcated by a symbolic date (9/11, of course) until its characters began to travel though time in season five. By then, the show was very different from what it was when it had begun. The multiple timelines of flashing backwards and forwards were no longer narrative devices, but literal renderings of multiple and simultaneous timelines, the main storyline aware of the other. With this shift from metaphorical time travel-as-storytelling device to literal time travel-as-science fiction, the implication shifted as well. With the characters of *Lost*, the world in 2008 was no longer the post–9/11, post–Iraq invasion of *Lost*'s 2004 pilot. Instead, the characters, like the world, were wondering what exactly they had gotten themselves into, and the majority of Americans voted for change. Time travel, unlike mere flashback, allows not just for psychological reenactment of trauma, but of its wish fulfillment, an existential do-over, a way to rewrite and re-right the past in order to alter the present.

As viewers versed in time travel could have predicted, though, the return to the past proved no more lasting a solution than the return to the island: "we have to go back" creates the problem of infinite regress. There is always more "back," as *Lost* proved in the seasons that followed the pronouncement, going back to 1971, Richard Alpert's 1867, even Jacob's childhood about two thousand years ago. Going back — to the island, in flashback, and through time travel — answered little. Instead, it allowed *Lost* to continue to defer its questions, enlarge its histories, and deepen its mysteries. Viewers, in turn, saw less wish fulfillment and correction than further fragmentation and paradox. In keeping, season five ended with the final manifestation of multiple timelines. The attempt to detonate an atomic bomb — in historical homage to our pre–9/11 anxiety — to alter time, expunge the trauma, and go back not to 9/12, as Beck would have it, but something like earlier in the day on 9/11, did not erase the plane crash as much as it seemed to create an alternate timeline. In doing so, we seemed to leave the world of the flashback, flash-forward, and time travel, to enter that other mainstay of science fiction and comic books, the alternate time-stream, the What If? scenario. In keeping, the signals between worlds shifted from a fade to black to a fade to white, with an accompanying sound of white noise reminiscent of an airplane's ascent, a reminder of the way in which the castaways first found themselves lost and yet another link to 9/11, the day that airplanes equally represented the means by which Americans exercise the global freedoms of their borders but the vehicle by which the hijackers turned those symbols against the (equally symbolic) World Trade Center and Pentagon buildings.

Writing in 2006, David Hastings Dunn analyzes the ways in which *Lost* reflects 9/11, but he seems equally to anticipate the ways in which the series would escalate its fantastic elements:

> The series deliberately asks us to suspend disbelief, as if to ask whether the central scenario is any less plausible than the 9/11 attacks. After all, is the world that the 48 survivors inhabit any less weird and threatening than our own? For as is soon apparent this is not your usual story, in the same way that 9/11 changed the narrative of what we understood to be a normal hijacking, LOST has changed the narrative of the disaster epic. This is no ordinary plane crash, there is no rescue and they have been transported to an entirely different place. Nor is there any planned end point to the story or the experience. There is no rescue, no reckoning and there appears to be no understanding because the enlightenment project has run aground. Each revelation instead reveals more hidden layers of questions and weirdness [318].

What Dunn saw as "a different place" and "more hidden layers of questions and weirdness" had only just started, given that we had not yet traveled through time, into alternate universes as posthumous existential vestibules (or whatever fans ultimately decide season six consisted of), or discovered Jacob and MIB/UnLocke's relationship. Yet at the same time, season six seemed less ambiguous, and veered closer to a post–9/11 War on Terror Manicheanism of Good and Evil, that the show had previously avoided. The power struggles between the morally-intricate Jack and Locke, as well as with the even more morally compromised, and complex, Sawyer, Kate, or Sayid, seemed to move toward the straightforward duality of golden-boy Jacob and his black-clad, unnamed brother vying to control both the island and its inhabitants. The final movements toward resolving the show's mysteries in many ways also seemed to narrow its complexity. Even as *Lost*'s alternative timeline returned its characters to 2004, we were getting farther away from 2001; entering its terminal descent, *Lost* needed to jettison its existential baggage to prepare for "The End."

Nevertheless, this move toward philosophical simplification after seasons of moral complexity is understandable. For the finale, *Lost*'s writers almost seem to be taking a page from a classic of literary criticism, Frank Kermode's *The Sense of and Ending*, first published in 1966. Kermode sees narrative ends as inextricably linked to our sense of impending apocalypse: "fictions," Kermode says early on, "whose ends are consonant with origins satisfy our needs" (5). The conventions of story dictate a beginning and an ending; for every "once upon a time," a "happily ever after." He goes on to suggest that "one has to think of an ordered series of events which ends, not in a great New Year, but in a final Sabbath" (5). Kermode thus relates the endings of all stories to the endings of all things: narrative endings as death, but also death itself as a narrative ending. As he elaborates, "the End is a fact of life and a fact of the imagination. [...] As the theologians say, we 'live from the End,' even if the world should be endless" (58). *Lost*'s End provides the same sense finality, the same sense of an ending: the end of the series, presented specifically as an apocalypse, a Rapture, where all of the (main) characters have died and ascended to a new spiritual place.

The finale in retrospect again presents a title as straightforward as the pilot, but as well implies a dark ambiguity, since the episode, in keeping with Kermode, marked the parallel ends of the television series, the story, and each character's life. Faced with the final revelation of the flash-sideways world, Jack meets his father, back from the dead once again, to ask, of his friends, but also of presumably of himself, "They're all dead?" Christian Shephard, his overtly allegorical name never previously uttered aloud (here with sarcastic surprise, by Kate—"'Christian Shephard.' Seriously?"), responds, "Everyone dies sometime. Some of them before you, some of them long after you," telling Jack that their world "is a place that you all made together so you could find one another. The most important time of your life was when you were with these people. That's why you are all here. No one does it alone Jack. You needed all of them and they needed you. [...] To remember and to let go."

We, like Jack, come to learn that the final season's flash-forwards were less alternate reality in which the plane never crashed than a purgatory-like dream sequence, in which each character had amnesia and needed to relive a meaningful moment from the island in order to remember who they were. In this way it reverses—and not via time travel—season three's traumatic need to relive and reenact, positing the notion that the Lostaways—like all of us suffering from loss — should not necessarily move forward, or backward, or forget it entirely, but rather "remember and let go."

And yet this advice, in the end, seems less about 9/11 than it is Christian's advice to fans of *Lost*, about to lose their series and characters in a way that even resurrection and the afterlife cannot correct. The last season, then, was self-consciously and self-reflectively about television itself, away from the 9/11 allegory that began it. Indeed, the last scene of "The End" seems in keeping with the flash-sideways of season six, much of which was more self-referential than expository. The Side World, until its characters' self-consciousness, could have existed as its own television drama. But it was the intertextual references and reversals that made it resonate with fans: see Sawyer as a cop, in keeping with his LeFleur security persona rather than his grifter ways; see Ben conspire, but when the stakes are for leadership of a high school, not the Others; imagine Jack with a son, and Locke with a wife, Hugo with unambiguous good luck, and more. At the same time, as Seth Stevenson suggests in *Slate*, "What if each week's mainland storyline tackled a different film/television genre?," noting that Sawyer's episode was a buddy cop show, Locke's a *Married with Children*–like sit-com (thanks to Katey Sagal's casting), and Ben's "a demented Saved by the Bell"— to say nothing of as-yet unscreened horseback and flowing hair period romance (Richard) or swords and sandals epic (Jacob).

For nearly all of season six, the side world inspired further *Lost*-ian conjecture and mystery: it seemed to show what could have been, the alternate reality popular with so much science fiction, where the removal of the pivotal event — the plane crash, or in many other stories, America's victory over the Nazis — creates the famous butterfly effect. In other ways, the side world was more a parallel than alternate world, a place to reenact and reengineer the coincidences that originally connected the castaways. But even more than a way to emphasize the foils between island and sideways worlds, season six has been about television itself, a *Lost* version of past shows such as *Doctor Who*, *Quantum Leap*, *Voyagers*, and the more recent *Journeyman*. Perhaps this self-referentiality is in keeping with what J. Wood noted earlier about the series: "The *Lost* audience is following the narrative the same way we witnessed the events of 9/11 — on TV, with repeated viewings, and more in-depth analysis later in the press and on the Internet" (110). Perhaps, with its trademark close-up of the eye that opened the pilot and so many of the early episodes, *Lost* has always been about itself, and about television, just as 9/11 must be understood as the real, palpable, physical event that took over two-thousand lives, affected millions more, and brought down the World Trade Center. It is also the event as captured on camera, and rebroadcast, and reenacted, and analyzed, as television. Indeed, the vast majority of Americans, even New Yorkers, have only experienced the attacks, and the name — "9/11," "September 11" — as television. But even then, we would still have to go back, for the only way to understand it is through the kind of analysis and reflection that comes after — not "back."

Yet if "The End" were only about itself and about television, a ploy to stitch the cast reunion that followed on *Jimmy Kimmel Live* directly into the series itself, it also suggests that the survivors are not, and were not, able to change the past, and that remembering the past on the island, their time together, however terrible at times, is not something that they should want to forget. Perhaps in the end, and "The End," we are all lost after 9/11, all castaways struggling to find each other, and ourselves. Perhaps we should not wish to return to the past, or lament the inability to change our fate — the bomb that concluded season five, it seems, failed. Rather, we must remember, even celebrate, the time we have with those who matter most in life, since viewers, unlike the castaways, cannot know what will come afterward.

In retrospect, then, *Lost* has been a show about our post–9/11 fears and wishes, and about the ways in which narrative and television can best represent them. But perhaps it also was not so different from the question posed by that first, failed *Lost*'s foray into reality TV: who makes it home? In the end, Hurley, despite his bad luck, and Ben, despite his treachery, remain. Lapidus, Miles, Richard, Sawyer, Kate, and Claire managed to escape — for good, it seems, this time. But in the sideways timeline — which of course turned out not to be sideways as much as post — everyone, eventually, leaves their island, so to speak. Yes, we have to go back: return to the island, flash back, time travel — and now, posthumously, reunite in the End. But we can also go back anytime, to *Lost* and to 9/11, now that the series has concluded and the ten-year anniversary of the attacks is upon us, by watching and thinking about their mysteries again. As thoughtful viewers and close readers, we can be the kind of eyewitness open to reconsideration, rumination, and thought, even now that *Lost*'s eye has closed.

## Works Cited

Beck, Glenn. "Mission Statement." *The 9.12 Project*. 2009. Web. 6 June 2010.
Dunn, David Hastings. "LOST: (Adventures in the American Psyche After the 9/11 Fall)." *Defence Studies* 6.3 (September 2006): 318–321. *Academic Search Premier*. 10 June 2010.
Friedman, Wayne, and David Goetzl. "Few 'Survivors' as Reality Bites." *Advertising Age* 72.43 (22 October 2001): 61. *EBSCO*. 10 June 2010.
Gilmore, Mikal. "Get Lost." *Rolling Stone* 31 May 2007: 44–44. *Academic Search Premier*. 10 June 2010.
Kermode, Frank. *The Sense of an Ending*. 1966. New York, Oxford University Press, 2000. Print.
Matlin, Chadwick. "Sweet Mother of God." *Slate*. 17 March 2010. Web. 6 June 2010.
Mayo Clinic Staff. "Symptoms." *Post-traumatic Stress Disorder*. 10 April 2009. Web. 6 June 2010.

Serwer, Andy. "The '00s: Goodbye (at Last) to the Decade from Hell." *Time* 24 Nov. 2009. Web. 23 June 2010.

Stevenson, Seth. "More Literary References." *Slate.* 17 March 2010. Web. 6 June 2010.

Wood, J. *Living Lost: Why We're All Stuck on the Island.* New Orleans: Garret County Press, 2007. Print.

Zakaria, Fareed. "The Politics of Rage: Why Do They Hate Us?" *Newsweek* 15 October 2001. Web. 4 June 2010.

# About the Contributors

**Nancy L. Chick** is an associate professor of English at the University of Wisconsin–Barron County, where she teaches American literature, women's studies, and composition courses. She is also the co-director of the University of Wisconsin System's Wisconsin Teaching Fellows and Scholars Program. Her scholarly work has appeared in *Pedagogy*, *The International Journal of the Scholarship of Teaching and Learning*, *Feminist Teacher*, and *Teaching English in the Two-Year College*. She is also co-editor of the books *Exploring Signature Pedagogies: Approaches to Teaching Disciplinary Habits of Mind* and *Exploring More Signature Pedagogies: Approaches to Teaching Disciplinary Habits of Mind*.

**Deborah Davidson** is an independent scholar whose research interests include literature, language and rhetoric, philosophy, religion, psychology, gifted education, and popular culture. Her primary areas of expertise are the politics and practice of home birth. She is currently writing a memoir.

**Holly Hassel** is an associate professor of English at the University of Wisconsin–Marathon County and director of the University of Wisconsin Colleges Women's Studies program. She teaches composition, literature, and women's studies courses to first- and second-year students. Her scholarly work has appeared in *Pedagogy: Critical Approaches to Teaching Literature, Language, Composition, and Culture*; *Feminist Teacher*; and *Teaching English in the Two-Year College*. She is also co-author of the book *Critical Companion to J.K. Rowling*.

**Ryan Howe** is a Ph.D. student in the Theatre Arts Department at the University of Pittsburgh, where he has taught introductory courses in Shakespeare, dramatic literature, theatre, directing, and performance. He is currently working on his dissertation, which examines the American presidency on the theatrical stage during the Clinton and Bush years.

**Wayne Jebian** is a Ph.D. student at the Neag School of Education at the University of Connecticut. He holds an M.A. in English from UConn and a M.A.L.S. in American studies from Columbia University, where he co-founded the *Columbia Journal of American Studies*. He currently teaches English at Capital Community College in Hartford, Connecticut.

**Erika Johnson-Lewis** is an independent scholar who recently earned a Ph.D. in interdisciplinary humanities from Florida State University and is revising her dissertation, "Exceptional TV: Post-9/11 Serial Television and American Exceptionalism," for publication. She is also the author of articles on *Battlestar Galactica* and *The Wire* and the blog *Seriality*.

**Jesse Kavadlo** received a Ph.D. from Fordham University. He is an associate professor of English and humanities at Maryville University in St. Louis, where he teaches classes in writing, American literature, and special topics like monsters, superheroes, conspiracies, and rock 'n' roll. He is the author of the book *Don DeLillo: Balance at the Edge of Belief*, many essays in academic journals, and chapters in books about *Fight Club*, *The X-Men*, reality TV, pedagogy, and more.

**Randy Laist** received a Ph.D. from the University of Connecticut and is currently assistant professor of English at Goodwin College in East Hartford, Connecticut. He is the author of *Technology and Postmodern Subjectivity in Don DeLillo's Novels* and has published numerous articles on literature, television, film, new media, and pedagogy.

**Giancarlo Lombardi** is an associate professor of Italian and comparative literature at the College of Staten Island and at the CUNY Graduate Center. He has published extensively on Italian film and television. He is the co-editor of two forthcoming volumes on cultural representations of Italian terrorism and is working on a manuscript on the rhetoric of fear in post–9/11 transnational TV.

**Elizabeth Lundberg** is a doctoral student in the English department at the University of Iowa. Her research interests include twentieth and twenty-first century American literature, cultural studies, gender and sexuality studies, and science fiction.

**David Magill** is an assistant professor of English and women and gender studies at Longwood University, where he teaches courses in American literature and culture as well as masculinity studies. He has published several articles on race and masculinity, and is finishing one manuscript entitled *Modern Masculinities: Modernist Nostalgia and Jazz Age White Manhood* and beginning another on ethical manhood in contemporary American culture.

**Renee McGarry** is a doctoral candidate in the Ph.D. program in art history at the CUNY Graduate Center and is working on a dissertation titled "Exotic Contact: Flora and Fauna in Mexican (Aztec) Visual Culture."

**Aris Mousoutzanis** is a visiting lecturer in media and cultural studies at the Faculty of Arts and Social Sciences, Kingston University, London. He has researched and published on areas such as critical and cultural theory (especially psychoanalysis and trauma theory), technoculture and cyberculture, media and globalization, popular culture, science fiction, and the Gothic.

**Matthew Pangborn** received a Ph.D. in English from the State University of New York at Albany. He specializes in early American literature, Atlantic orientalism, literary theory, and early visual culture. He has published works on Edgar Allan Poe, Royall Tyler's *The Algerine Captive*, and Alfred Hitchcock and is writing a book on the oriental narratives of the early American republic.

**Jason M. Peck** is a visiting assistant professor in the Department of Modern Languages and Cultures at the University of Rochester. He has published articles on Kantian philosophy and the poetry of Paul Celan, and is co-editing a book on key terms in German aesthetics to be published by Harvard University Press.

**Michael Rennett** graduated from California State University Northridge with a B.A. in media theory and criticism and a minor in Jewish studies. He received his master's degree from Chapman University in the field of film studies and has contributed to *The Journal of Popular Culture*, *The International Journal of Baudrillard Studies*, and *The Journal of Religion and Film*.

**J. L. Schatz** is the director of debate at Binghamton University where he teaches courses in the English department on media and politics; literature and technology; and argumentative theory. His debate team has been ranked either first or second in the nation for the past five years. He received a Ph.D. in English and feminist evolutionary theory from Binghamton University.

**Stacey K. Sowards** is an associate professor in the Department of Communication and a research fellow in the Sam Donaldson Center for Communication at the University of Texas at El Paso.

**Carlos A. Tarin** is a graduate student at the University of Colorado at Boulder. He has completed a degree in communication studies at the University of Texas at El Paso, under the direction of Stacey K. Sowards, and is pursuing a master's degree in communication with an emphasis on rhetoric. In addition to television and pop culture criticism, his research interests include representations of the environment, HIV/AIDS rhetoric, and performance studies.

# Index

"Ab Aeterno" (episode 6.9) 31, 90, 103n, 223, 226
Abaddon, Matthew (character) 14
"Abandoned" (episode 2.6) 168, 196
Abrams, J.J. 106, 122, 171
Achara (character) 139
"Across the Sea" (episode 6.15) 23, 31, 55, 95, 155, 163, 184, 212, 224
Adam and Eve 91, 99–100
Adorno, Theodore 80
*Alias* 171
*Alice's Adventures in Wonderland* 1, 77, 82–86, 88n, 191
"All the Best Cowboys Have Daddy Issues" (episode 1.11) 20, 143–144, 160–161, 219
Alpert, Richard (character) 21, 31, 36, 37, 41, 90, 97, 101, 103n, 176, 177–178, 198, 213, 223–224, 226, 237, 240
"…And Found" (episode 2.5) 29, 175
Anderson, Benedict 54
*Animal Farm* 4, 194
Antonioni, Michelangelo 97–99
Aristotle 29
Arszt, Leslie (character) 193–194
Askwith, Ivan 15, 26, 28, 32
Austin, Kate (character): adventures 17, 31, 36–37, 40, 43, 86, 93, 95, 97, 99, 102, 147, 194, 196, 197, 206, 218, 239, 241; characterization 14, 29, 52, 87, 100–101, 103n, 140, 150–151, 169n, 170n, 182–183, 193, 201, 238; relationships 16, 32–33, 83–85, 138–139, 145, 164, 175, 180, 182, 191, 199, 235

*Babel* 234
*Bad Twin* 1, 12
Bakunin, Mikhail (character) 4, 54
Ball, Lucille 171
The Barracks (Dharmaville) 21–21, 43, 54, 130–132, 199, 209
Barthes, Roland 44
Bataille, Georges 110
Baudelaire, Charles 108
Baym, Nina 152n
"Because You Left" (episode 5.1) 33–34, 41, 50, 198, 221

Beck, Glenn 236–238
"The Beginning of the End" (episode 4.1) 32–33
Benjamin, Walter 80
Bentham, Jeremy (philosopher) 1, 75–77, 81, 92–95, 99
Bhabha, Homi K. 130
The Bible 59, 155, 178, 205
*The Black Rock* 20, 31, 53, 190
"Born to Run" (episode 1.22) 201
Bradbury, Ray 33
"The Brig" (episode 3.19) 36, 102, 154, 159, 163, 174, 177
Buddhism 43, 126–127
Burke, Edmond (philosopher) 4, 107
Burke, Juliet (character) 17, 20, 41, 54–55, 69, 93, 97–98, 100, 131, 138–139, 143, 146, 149, 151, 161, 167, 172–174, 180–183, 198, 199, 211, 212
Butler, Judith 56
*The Butterfly Effect* 50

"Cabin Fecer" (episode 4.11) 36, 176
*Candide* 111
*The Canterbury Tales* 233
Carlyle, Boone (character) 46, 48, 50, 138, 171, 175, 177, 184, 219, 235
Carlyle, Shannon (character) 46, 138, 140, 175, 182, 192, 196
Carlyle, Thomas 107
Carroll, Lewis 77, 82–86
Caruth, Cathy 46
Casares, Adolfo Bioy 77
*Cast Away* 46, 105
Castaneda, Carlos 77, 87
Cavell, Stanley 80
Chandler, Cindy (character) 38, 86
Chang, Pierre (character) 199, 208, 235
Chaucer, Gregory 233
*Children of Men* 173, 177
*A Christmas Carol* 180
Clark, Petula 173
Claudia (character) 15, 31, 48, 55, 155, 182, 184
Cline, Patsy 87
*A Clockwork Orange* 43, 81

Cold War 53–55, 233
"Confidence Man" (episode 1.8) 29, 30, 168, 194, 219
"The Constant" (episode 4.5) 15, 34
Cooper, Anthony (character) 142–144, 158–159, 160, 162–163
Cortez, Ana Lucia (character) 20, 40, 139, 145, 162, 166, 172, 182, 196
"The Cost of Living" (episode 3.5) 28, 56, 79
*Crash* (film) 234
*The Crocodile Hunter* 204
Cuse, Carlton 14, 25, 32, 40, 41, 77, 123, 129, 148, 200
*Cymbeline* 62

Dante 90
Dave (character) 78, 109, 115–117
"Dave" (episode 2.18) 30, 78, 109, 115–117, 193, 195
Dawson, Michael (character) 20, 31, 47–48, 52, 139, 140, 146, 149, 158, 164–168, 175, 196
"Dead Is Dead" (episode 5.12) 39, 124, 221, 224
DeBeauvoir, Simone 181
Deepwater Horizon oil spill 6, 214, 220
Defoe, Daniel 105–108
*Déjà vu* (film) 50
Deleuze, Gilles 80–85, 88, 154
DeLillo, Don 2
Derrida, Jacques 5, 44, 91–92, 95–99, 231
Descartes, René 112–114, 117, 118n
*Desert Island Discs* 105
"Deus Ex Machina" (episode 1.19) 14, 163, 219
Dharma hatches 2, 11, 93, 96, 145, 191, 198, 207, 210–211, 219
The Dharma Initiative 53–54, 56, 64, 81, 94, 121, 123, 126, 129, 130–132, 146, 162, 164, 167, 189, 195, 198–200, 205, 207–209, 223
Dharma van 30, 113, 117–118, 158, 169n
Dick, Philip K. 1, 75, 77, 87
Dickens, Charles 172, 180
*The Divine Comedy* 90, 94
"Do No Harm" (episode 1.20) 171, 176
"D.O.C." (episode 3.18) 167
"Dr. Linus" (episode 6.7) 39, 223
*Doctor Who* 15, 240
Dogen (character) 30, 226
Dorrit, Naomi (character) 53, 182, 197
Dostoevsky, Fyodor 77

Eco, Umberto 90
"The Economist" (episode 4.3) 53, 197, 222
"Eggtown" (episode 4.4) 87
Eko, Mr. (character) 7, 28–29, 67, 79, 177, 235
"The End" (episodes 6.17 and 6.18) 6, 23, 40, 70, 90, 102–103, 146, 182, 212, 233, 239–241
"Enter 77" (episode 3.11) 30, 47, 54
"Every Man for Himself" (episode 3.4) 31, 164, 221
"Everybody Hates Hugo" (episode 2.4) 38, 193
"Everybody Loves Hugo" (episode 6.12) 38, 224
"Exodus" (episodes 1.23, 1.24, and 1.25) 20, 31, 34, 55, 165–166, 193
"Exposé" (episode 3.14) 193

Faraday, Daniel (character) 20, 33–34, 37, 40, 50, 52, 131, 137, 178, 183, 198, 208, 210, 235
*Fear and Trembling* 77, 85–86
Fernandez, Nikki (character) 182
Film noir 27–28
"Fire + Water" (episode 2.12) 55
Flashbacks 3, 11, 13, 15–18, 27–32, 47, 49, 66, 85, 160, 231, 234–236
Flash-forwards 3, 6, 11, 13, 15, 16–18, 27, 32, 33, 47, 49–50, 66, 85, 92, 94, 231, 236
Flash-sideways 3, 11, 13, 18, 21, 23, 27, 37–40, 69, 84, 88n, 90, 102, 149, 161, 164, 175–176, 177, 179–180, 231, 238–240
"Flashes Before Your Eyes" (episode 3.8) 15, 34–35, 50
"Follow the Leader" (episode 5.15) 198
Ford, James (Sawyer) (character): adventures 1, 20, 29, 30–31, 37–38, 40, 41, 50, 100, 103n, 113, 156, 169, 192–194, 219, 221–222, 224, 240, 241; characterization 14, 52, 83–84, 93–94, 102, 137–151, 170n, 183, 196–199, 235, 238; relationships 6, 131, 158–160, 163–164, 166, 172, 180, 182
Ford, John 233
Foucault, Michel 5, 44, 91–95, 154, 182, 223
Freud, Sigmund 35–36, 44–45, 48–49, 92, 100, 231
Friendly, Tom (character) 152n, 179
*Friends* 19
"Further Instructions" (episode 3.3) 177, 183

*The Garden of Forking Paths* 1
Garner, Jennifer 171
Godard, Jean-Luc 80
Godwin, William 107

Goodspeed, Horace (character) 176
"The Greater Good" (episode 1.21) 51, 53, 170n
"Greatest Hits" (episode 3.21) 168
*Gulliver's Travels* 1

"Happily Ever After" (episode 6.11) 38, 221
Hawking, Eloise (character) 21, 34–35, 40, 50–51, 172, 178, 235
Hayles, N. Katherine 44
"Hearts and Minds" (episode 1.13) 177, 194
Heidegger, Martin 91
*Heroes* 44, 234
"He's Our You" (episode 5.10) 162
Hitchcock, Alfred 80
"Homecoming" (episode 1.15) 196
Homer 63, 66, 130
"House of the Rising Sun" (episode 1.6) 47, 99, 169n, 183, 195, 219
*How I Met Your Mother* 26
Hume, Charlie (character) 172, 180
Hume, David (philosopher) 75, 91, 107, 112
Hume, Desmond David (character) 1, 3, 4, 15, 20, 25–26, 34–35, 38, 49–52, 64, 75–76, 78, 87, 114, 138, 142, 147, 173, 180, 183–184, 197–198, 211–212, 219, 221, 235
"The Hunting Party" (episode 2.11) 54

*I Love Lucy* 171
"…In Translation" (episode 1.17) 152, 159
"The Incident" (episodes 5.16 and 5.17) 18, 23, 37, 39, 94, 103n, 155–157, 161, 163–164, 182, 199, 211, 238
*Indiana Jones* 63, 126
*The Invention of Morel* 77
*The Island of Dr. Moreau* 116

Jacob (character): adventures 15, 22, 23, 36, 55, 103n, 129, 146, 150–151, 182–183, 212, 235, 237, 238, 240; characterization 5, 6, 38–41, 56, 65, 79, 91, 92, 94–102, 123, 133n, 140–146, 155–164, 175–177, 192, 210, 217–219, 223–224
James, Henry 1
Jameson, Frederic 52, 80, 189–192, 195
Jarrah, Sayid (character) 14, 17, 29, 30–32, 36–37, 47–48, 52–53, 87, 95–96, 103n, 121, 137–140, 142, 144, 147, 149, 192, 209, 222, 226, 238
Jaseem, Nadia Abed (character) 30, 52, 182
*La Jetée* 36
*Les Jeux sont faits* 178–181
"Ji-Yeon" (episode 4.7) 17, 176, 183
*Jimmy Kimmel Live* 241
Johnson, Derek 12, 18, 199–200
*Journeyman* 240
"Jughead" (episode 5.3) 18, 36, 198

Kaye, Sharon M. 91, 203
Keamy, Martin (character) 39, 50, 164–165
Kermode, Frank 239
Kierkegaard, Søren 77, 85–87
King, Stephen 59
Kubrick, Stanley 43, 81
Kwon, Ji-Yeun (character) 167, 172, 180
Kwon, Jin (character) 14, 17, 29, 37, 52, 95, 98, 102, 113, 121, 138–139, 142–144, 147, 149, 158, 164, 166–167, 172, 175–176, 180–183, 198, 199, 211, 212
Kwon, Sun (character) 6, 14, 17, 29, 32, 37, 100, 102, 121, 138–140, 143–144, 147, 150–151, 166–167, 169n, 172–175, 179–184, 194, 221

Lacan, Jacques 5, 44, 91–92, 99–103
"LaFleur" (episode 5.8) 33, 56, 122, 212
Lapidus, Frank 64, 235, 241
Lawless, Lucy 171
"LA X" (episodes 6.1 and 6.2) 37=38, 85, 95–96, 99, 177, 182, 211
"Left Behind" (episode 3.15) 194
Lévi-Strauss, Claude 100
Lewis, C.S. 1
Lewis, Charlotte, Staples (character) 1, 20, 55, 131, 182
"The Lie" (episode 5.2) 198
"The Life and Death of Jeremy Bentham" (episode 5.7) 14, 76, 92, 222
"Lighthouse" (episode 6.5) 22, 39, 224
Lighthouse (structure) 22, 95, 129
Lindelof, Damon 14, 25, 32, 40, 41, 77, 106, 129, 143, 148, 200
Linus, Benjamin (character): adventures 1, 14, 20, 23, 31, 33, 41, 56, 87, 93–94, 96, 102, 103n, 120, 124–125, 129, 131, 169n, 172, 174, 182, 198, 209, 240, 241; characterization 22, 36–37, 39–40, 52, 54–55, 97, 100, 137–150, 175, 176, 178, 197, 217–218, 221–224, 232, 235; relationships 6, 156–167
"The Little Prince" (episode 5.4) 41, 85
Littleton, Aaron (character) 13, 17, 32, 55, 83, 101, 139, 144, 147, 150, 158, 168, 170n, 171–172, 175–177, 180, 83, 196, 197
Littleton, Claire (character) 31, 46, 48, 55, 97, 101–102, 138, 140, 147, 150–151, 157–158, 168, 170n, 171–172, 175, 177, 179, 182–184, 194, 196–197, 235, 241
"Live Together, Die Alone" (episodes 2.23 and 2.24) 34, 49, 78, 121, 166, 197, 211, 219
Lloyd, Walt (character) 13, 139, 146, 157–159, 165–166, 168, 172, 175–176, 180, 196
"Lockdown" (episode 2.17) 14, 197, 207
Locke, John (character): adventures 1, 7, 17,

22, 23, 34, 40–41, 48–50, 65, 67, 79, 87, 94, 124, 156–157, 169n, 172, 184, 193–194, 238, 240; characterization 4, 14, 31, 36, 55, 76–77, 85, 92, 96–100, 137–138, 140–152, 174–179, 197, 206, 210–211, 217–223, 235; relationships 6, 54, 102, 159–167, 196, 198
Locke, John (philosopher) 4, 75–77, 91, 98, 105, 107, 110, 112–114, 118n, 52, 156
"The Long Con" (episode 2.13) 29, 145–146, 193, 196
*Lord of the Flies* 1, 191
The Lost Experience (ARG) 12
*Lostpedia* 18, 121, 124, 126, 128–129
Lukács, Georg 189, 191–192, 195, 200–201

"The Man Behind the Curtain" (episode 3.20) 157, 162, 169n, 209, 223
"The Man from Tallahassee" (episode 3.13) 14, 163, 197
Man in Black (character): adventures 14, 22, 23, 26, 39, 41, 97, 143, 146–151, 198, 212, 224, 226, 235, 238; characterization 5, 31–32, 55, 65, 92, 96, 115, 117, 133n, 155, 161, 162–164; relationships 6, 15, 94, 98, 99–102, 140, 142, 144, 159, 175, 218
"Man of Science, Man of Faith" (episode 2.1) 173
Mandeville, Bernard 112
Martin, Karl (character) 43
Marx, Karl 191–192
"Maternity Leave" (episode 2.15) 31, 55, 196
"Meet Kevin Johnson" (episode 4.8) 31, 179
Minkowski, George (character) 3
Mittell, Jason 12, 15, 18, 25–27, 63, 66–67
*Mole II* (TV series) 230
"The Moth" (episode 1.7) 167–168
Mother (character) 143–144, 155, 159, 163, 169, 172, 175, 182, 184
*The Mysterious Island* 189

Nadler, Bernard (character) 178, 181, 197
Nadler, Rose (character) 37, 45, 46, 178, 181
"Namaste" (episode 5.9) 1
*The Name of the Rose* 94
Newbury, Michael 54, 138, 141, 143, 147
Newton, Isaac 107–108
Nicholson, Jack 98
*No Exit* 178
Norwood, Helen (character) 14, 31
"Not in Portland" (episode 3.7) 43, 81, 181–182
*Notes from the Underground* 77
The Numbers 48–49, 78, 109, 113–114, 118, 142, 146, 219, 235
"Numbers" (episode 1.18) 114–115

O'Brien, Flann 1, 77
*The Odyssey* 63, 180
*The Office* 26
"One of Them" (episode 2.14) 30
"One of Us" (episode 3.16) 168
"Orientation" (episode 2.3) 14, 31, 49, 67, 87, 103n, 189, 199, 207–208, 210
"The Other 48 Days" (episode 2.7) 16, 31, 47
"The Other Woman" (episode 4.6) 17
The Others 31, 36, 52, 54–56, 64, 76, 81, 93, 94, 97, 121, 123, 126, 130–132, 133n, 138, 140, 145–146, 166, 168, 171–172, 175, 184, 196–197, 205, 208–210, 212, 224–225
"Outlaws" (episode 1.16) 29, 46, 48, 158

Pace, Charlie (character) 11, 16, 31, 34–35, 38, 46, 52, 55, 67, 98, 113, 137–139, 142, 147, 158, 164, 167–169, 170n, 172, 176, 180, 184, 196, 206
"The Package" (episode 6.10) 37
Paglia, Camille, 141
Paik, Woo-Jung (character) 166–167
*The Parallax View* 81
*The Passenger* 97–99
*The Pawnbroker* 27–28
Pearson, Roberta 14
*Pericles of Athens* 62
Phil (character) 199
Phillips, Cassidy (character) 29, 138, 164, 172
"Pilot" (episodes 1.1 and 1.2) 16, 31, 48, 52, 192, 194, 202, 205, 206
Plato 97, 232
Porter, Brian (character) 157–158, 165
*The Prisoner* (TV series) 81
The Purge 54, 97, 102, 131, 164
Pynchon, Thomas 2

*Quantum Leap* 240

Radzinsky, Stuart (character) 199
"Raised by Another" (episode 1.10) 157, 168, 175, 179
*The Real World* (TV series) 231
"Recon" (episode 6.8) 31, 37, 221–222
*Repetition* 86–87
Reyes, David (character) 158
Reyes, Hugo (Hurley) (character): adventures 17, 20, 22, 31, 32–33, 36, 37–38, 40, 41, 46–47, 65, 85, 95–96, 148, 170n, 190, 191, 193, 194, 236, 241; characterization 5, 6, 29–30, 67, 78, 98, 108–118, 137, 142, 146, 159–150, 158, 178, 195, 206, 235, 240; relationships 52, 138, 144, 174

*Robinson Crusoe* 1, 5, 105–118
Rom, Ethan (character) 31, 46, 140, 168, 172, 173–174, 176–177, 196, 212
*Romeo and Juliet* 180
Rousseau, Alex (character) 30, 39, 40, 43, 55, 124–125, 162, 164–165, 172, 175–176, 182
Rousseau, Danielle (character) 4, 30, 48, 55, 75, 85, 97, 129, 164, 172, 175–176, 182, 235
Rousseau, Jean-Jacques 91, 105, 107
*The Runner* (TV series) 230

Sartre, Jean-Paul 178–181
Sedgwick, Eve 150
*Seinfeld* 171
*A Separate Reality* 77, 87
September 11, 2001 terrorist attacks 6, 7, 51–53, 61, 141–142, 145, 230–241
Shakespeare, William 4, 59–71, 178, 180, 189
"The Shape of Things to Come" (episode 4.9) 39, 50, 165, 222
Shephard, Christian (character) 5, 22, 39, 68, 70, 90, 92, 99, 101–103, 143–144, 149, 157, 160–162, 167, 172–173, 239–240
Shephard, David (character) 29, 161
Shephard, Jack (character): adventures 1, 22–23, 31, 34, 43, 48, 54–56, 65, 67–68, 77, 79, 90, 95, 110, 168, 171–173, 180, 192–194, 196, 199, 205–206, 209–211, 217–224, 234–240; characterization 7, 14–17, 36–41, 45–46, 83–87, 92–93, 98–103, 103n, 137–152, 176–178, 184; relationships 6, 70, 160–163
*The Simpsons* 204
Smith, Adam 112
Smith, Libby (character) 20, 30, 41, 55, 78, 177, 138, 139, 146, 166, 182, 195, 196
Smoke monster 13, 14, 55, 85, 97, 101, 124–125, 131, 137, 159, 218, 219, 221–222, 224, 226, 231, 233–234
"Solitary" (episode 1.9) 30, 195
"Some Like It Hoth" (episode 5.13) 178
"Something Nice Back Home" (episode 4.10) 83–85
The Source 6, 33, 65, 101, 212
"Special" (episode 1.14) 158, 165, 168
Spivak, Gayatri 181
*Stagecoach* 233
Stanhope, Goodwin (character) 31
*Star Wars* 84, 178, 217
Statue of Tawaret 20, 21, 121–124, 129, 132n, 190
Stein, Gertrude 233
"Stranger in a Strange Land" (episode 3.9) 139

Straume, Miles (character) 20, 55, 67, 172, 211, 241
"The Substitute" (episode 6.4) 87, 161
"Sundown" (episode 6.6) 97, 226
*Survivor* 13, 46, 230–231, 236

"Tabula Rasa" (episode 1.3) 16, 140, 155, 192, 196
"A Tale of Two Cities" (episode 3.1) 41, 47, 164, 173–174, 197, 208
*The Tempest* (play) 4, 59–71, 189
Temple 22, 85, 96–97, 124–128, 129, 147, 199
*The Terminator* 33, 35–36
"There's No Place Like Home" (episodes 4.12, 4.13, and 4.14) 33, 92, 181, 164, 198, 208, 209
*The Third Policeman* 1, 77
"This Place Is Death" (episode 5.5) 97
Thomas (character) 157–158
"Three Minutes" (episode 2.22) 166
"316" (episode 5.6) 31
"Through the Looking Glass" (episodes 3.22 and 3.23) 16, 32, 85, 198, 209, 221, 236
*Through the Looking Glass, and What Alice Found There* 84
*The Time Machine* 50
Time Travel 11, 13, 15, 27, 33–37, 43–44, 47, 50, 66, 85, 137, 198, 231, 237, 239
Trauma 3–4, 28, 44–56, 237, 239
"Tricia Tanaka Is Dead" (episode 3.10) 29, 109–110, 113–114, 158
*The Turn of the Screw* 1
*Twelve Monkeys* 50
*24* 234
"Two for the Road" (episode 2.20) 162, 196

*Valis* 1, 77
"The Variable" (5.14) 37, 178, 208, 223
Verdansky, Ilana (character) 182
Voltaire 111
*Voyagers* 240

"Walkabout" (episode 1.4) 14, 45, 53, 178, 194, 206, 219
*Watership Down* 189
Wells, H.G. 50, 116, 227n
"What Kate Did" (episode 2.9) 38, 79, 197
"What Kate Does" (episode 6.3) 30, 38, 179, 183, 209
"What They Died For" (episode 6.16) 40, 79, 97, 100–101, 103n, 142, 148, 150–151, 165, 177–178, 224
"Whatever Happened, Happened" (episode 5.11) 37, 97, 156, 164, 169n, 175

"Whatever the Case May Be" (episode 1.12) 195
"White Rabbit" (episode 1.5) 39, 40, 56, 65, 103n, 145, 160, 194, 207, 219
"The Whole Truth" (episode 2.16) 29, 166
Widmore, Penelope (character) 25–26, 34–35, 65, 138, 142, 172, 180, 184
*The Winter's Tale* 62
*The Wire* 19, 20

*The Wizard of Oz* 1, 191
Wood, J. 76, 231, 233, 240

*The X-Files* 55
*Xena: Warrior Princess* 171

Yemi (character) 28–29

Žižek, Slavoj 51, 80, 173, 180
Zoe (character) 131, 182

www.ingramcontent.com/pod-product-compliance
Ingram Content Group UK Ltd.
Pitfield, Milton Keynes, MK11 3LW, UK
UKHW041917140426
5217IPUK00013B/192